The U.S. Banking System

Felix I. Lessambo

The U.S. Banking System

Laws, Regulations, and Risk Management

palgrave
macmillan

Felix I. Lessambo
School of Business
Central Connecticut State University
New Britain, CT, USA

ISBN 978-3-030-34791-8 ISBN 978-3-030-34792-5 (eBook)
https://doi.org/10.1007/978-3-030-34792-5

This Palgrave Macmillan imprint is published by the registered company Springer Nature Switzerland AG
The registered company address is: Gewerbestrasse 11, 6330 Cham, Switzerland

Contents

Acronyms

AIRB	Advance Internal Rating-Based Approach
AMA	Advanced Measurement Approach
BCBS	Basel Committee on Banking Supervision
CCAR	Comprehensive Capital Analysis and Review
CCF	Credit Conversion Factors
CECL	Current Expected Credit Loss
CET1	Common Equity Tier 1
CFPB	Consumer Financial Protection Bureau
CFTC	Commodity and Futures Trading Commission
CLF	Central Liquidity Facility
CRA	Community Re-investment Act
CSBC	Conference of State Bank Supervisors
DFA	Dodd–Frank Act
DFAST	Dodd–Frank Act Stress Testing
EBA	European Bank Authority
ECL	Expected Credit Loss
EL	Expected Loss
ERBA	External Ratings-Based Approach
FDCPA	Fair Debt Collection Practices Act
FDIC	Federal Deposit Insurance Corporation
FED	Federal Reserve Bank
FFIEC	Federal Financial Institution Examinations Council
FinCEN	Financial Crimes Enforcement Network
FOMC	Federal Open Market Committee
FRBNY	Federal Reserve Bank of New York
FSOC	Financial Stability Oversight Council

GSIB	Global Systemically Important Banking Organization
IRBA	Internal Rating-Based Approach (for credit risk)
ISDA	International Swaps and Derivatives Association
LCR	Liquidity Coverage Ratio
LIBOR	London Inter-Bank Offered Rate
LGD	Loss Given Default
MBS	Money Services Business
NCU	National Credit Union
NCUSIF	National Credit Union Share Insurance Fund
OCC	Office of the Comptroller of the Currency
OFAC	Office of Foreign Assets Control
OTS	Office of Thrift Supervision
PD	Probability of Default
RW	Risk Weight
RWAs	Risk-Weighted Assets
SA	Standardized Approach
SAR	Suspicious Activity Reporting
SDR	Special Drawing Rights
SEC	Securities and Exchange Commission
SIPA	Securities Investment Protection Act
SMA	Standardized Measurement Approach
SOMA	System Open Market Account
TDF	Term Deposit Facility

List of Figures

List of Tables

List of Cited Cases

- CFTC v. McDonnell and CDM, EDNY (08/23/2018).
- Securities and Exchange Commission v. REcoin Group Foundation, et al., Civil Action No Securities and Exchange Commission v. Reginald, Case 1:19-CV-04625-CBA-RER.17-cv-05725 (E.D.N.Y., filed September 29, 2017).
- Securities and Exchange Commission v. Tambone, 550 F.3d 10 6 (1st Cir. 2008).
- Securities and Exchange Commission v. Reginald, Case 1:19-CV-04625-CBA-RER.
- Securities and Exchange Commission v. KIK Interactive Inc. Case 1:19-cv-05244.
- United States v. Nurgio, SDNY (September 19, 2016).
- United States v. Velastegui, 199 F.3d 590, 593 (2d Cir. 1999).

CHAPTER 1

Overview of the US Banking System

1.1 General

The US banking system is one of the oldest, largest, and most important sectors of our overall economy. There were no modern banks in colonial America nor American banks as late as 1781.[1] By the 1830s, to get away from the politicization and corruption involved in legislative chartering, a few states began to enact "free banking" laws. Without a central bank to provide oversight of banking and finance, the expanding banking system of the 1830s, 1840s, and 1850s suffered from some major problems, even as it supplied the country with ample loans to finance economic growth. One problem was financial instability. Banking crises occurred in 1837, 1839–1842, and 1857 years when many banks had to suspend convertibility of their banknotes and deposits into coin because their coin reserves were insufficient. A good number of these banks failed or became insolvent when borrowers defaulted on their loan payments. The banking crises led to business depressions with high unemployment.[2]

The passage of the Federal Reserve Act in 1913 was a watershed in US banking history. In 1913, after three-quarters of a century without

[1] Richard Sylla: The US Banking System: Origin, Development, and Regulation, the Gilder Lehrman Institute of American History (2009–2019).

[2] Richard Sylla: The US Banking System: Origin, Development, and Regulation, the Gilder Lehrman Institute of American History (2009–2019).

F. I. Lessambo, *The U.S. Banking System*,
https://doi.org/10.1007/978-3-030-34792-5_1

a central bank and a period punctuated by a number of banking crises, Congress created a new central bank, the Federal Reserve System.

In 1927, Congress passed the McFadden Act, which allowed national banks to become competitive with state banks by granting them jurisdiction to branch out within the state they were originally located to the extent that state law permitted. The banking architectural was strengthened with the Banking Act of June 1933 ("the Glass–Steagall Act") introduced federal deposit insurance, federal regulation of interest rates on deposits, and the separation of commercial banking from investment banking. Further, the Glass–Steagall Act strengthened the Federal Reserve's powers.

The American bank regulatory system is based upon the concept of dual oversight by federal and state agencies, and the primary regulators differ based upon a specific bank's charter. The structure and regulation of the US banking system differs from the rest of the world. The US system is made of big commercial and small banks coexisting, with more small banks holding the larger share in number. In contrast to the US system, other developed countries such as Japan, Germany, France, and Canada's banking systems tend to favor larger national institutions.[3] The US banking industry also is less highly concentrated than the banking industries in many other industrial countries. A study on "industry concentration ratio" by the Bank for International Settlements concluded that the five largest banks' US ratio was 26.6%, while the ratio for Canada was 77.1%, France stood at 70.2%, and Switzerland at 57.8%.

In 1999, Congress repealed the Glass–Steagall Act that had effectively separated commercial and investment banking. The business of banking, long stifled by regulation, suddenly became more exciting. Increasingly, banks were not limited in their lending by the size of their deposit bases. They could obtain more funding to make more loans and purchase new forms of securities by accessing the Wall Street and international money markets.

In the United States, banks have been classified as either commercial banks or investment banks. Commercial banks accept customer deposits and offer commercial loans; while investment banks underwrite and register new securities and market them to individual or institutional investors, provide brokerage services, advice on corporate financing and

[3]Federal Reserve Bank of San Francisco (2002): How Does the US Banking System Compare with Foreign Banking Systems?

proprietary trading, and assistance to merger and acquisitions. Banks are intermediaries between savers and borrowers. In its simplest form, the business model of commercial banks is to accept deposits from savers in order to make loans to borrowers; in other words, banks borrow from depositors and offer loans to individuals, business firms, nonprofits, and governments. The US banking system provides a secure way for consumers and businesses to store deposits. It is a primary conduit for capital markets activities and a source of credit for consumer mortgages, credit cards, auto loans, small business, and commercial lending.[4]

1.2 Size of the US Banks

According to The Banker's Top 1000 World Banks Ranking for 2018, total assets reached $124 trillion, worldwide,[5] when the total assets in the United States reached a peak of $17.5 trillion. The core banking functions held roughly 44% of total finance sector assets.[6] US banks handle trillions of dollars of daily transaction volume. Most Americans use depository financial institutions—such as commercial banks, savings and loan associations, and credit unions—to conduct their financial transactions.[7] Those who do not have access to depository financial institutions conduct their financial transactions using money services businesses ("MSBs") such as money transmitters, check cashers, currency exchangers, or businesses that sell money orders, prepaid access devices, and traveler's checks. While MSBs are subject to Bank Secrecy Act compliance requirements, some MSBs have failed to register with the proper authorities and thus are acting as unlicensed MSBs, used as vehicles by criminals in their illicit financial activities. In the context of globalization, banks often hold accounts with other banks in order to facilitate international business transactions in countries of the bank where the accounts

[4] US Department of the Treasury (2017): A Financial System That Creates Economic Opportunities: Banks and Credit Unions, p. 21.

[5] Danielle Myles, "Top 1000 World Banks 2018," The Banker, July 2, 2018.

[6] F.M Scherer (2014): The Banking Industry, Harvard Kennedy School, p. 8.

[7] Statement of Steven M. D'Antuono Section Chief Criminal Investigative Division Federal Bureau of Investigation Department of Justice Before the Committee on Banking, Housing, and Urban Affairs United States Senate For a Hearing Entitled "Combating Money Laundering and Other Forms of Illicit Finance: Regulator and Law Enforcement Perspectives on Reform" (November 29, 2018), pp. 2–3.

are held. There are over 5900 banks and 5800 credit unions operating in the United States. Regulated depositories reported total assets of $21.4 trillion as of December 31, 2016, or 115% of US GDP.[8] The US depository system is stratified by size and type of organization, with each playing a unique role serving its target client base. Key segments include the eight firms designated as US global systemically important banks (G-SIBs), regional banks, mid-sized banks, community banks, and credit unions.[9] The eight US G-SIBs currently have $10.7 trillion of assets, or approximately 50% of total US depository assets, while regional and mid-sized banks, which operate across multiple states, have in the aggregate $6.7 trillion of assets, or approximately 31% of total US depository assets. Community banks and credit unions have total assets of $2.7 trillion and $1.3 trillion, respectively.[10]

1.3 Banking Regulation

The banking industry is one of the most powerful in the United States. But the path from then to now has not been linear, rather it has been influenced by a variety of different factors and an ever-changing regulatory framework. Forces, such as the desire for greater financial stability, more economic freedom, or fear of the concentration of too much power in too few hands, are what keep the pendulum swinging back and forth.[11] Between 1782 and 1837, over 700 banks sprang up in the United States.[12]

Banking regulation can at best defined as the formulation and issuance by authorized agencies of specific rules or regulations, under governing law, for the conduct and structure of banking. US banking regulation addresses privacy, disclosure, fraud prevention, anti-money laundering,

[8] U.S. Department of the Treasury (2017): A Financial System That Creates Economic Opportunities—Banks and Credit Unions, p. 5.

[9] U.S. Department of the Treasury (2017): A Financial System That Creates Economic Opportunities—Banks and Credit Unions, p. 5.

[10] U.S. Department of the Treasury (2017): A Financial System That Creates Economic Opportunities—Banks and Credit Unions, p. 5.

U.S. Department of the Treasury (2017): A Financial System That Creates Economic Opportunities—Banks and Credit Unions, p. 5

[11] Matthew Johnston (June 25, 2019): History of the Banking Industry in the US.

[12] J. Van Fenstermaker (1965): The Development of American Commercial Banking.

anti-terrorism, anti-usury lending, and the promotion of lending to lower-income populations. In the United States, the banking industry is heavily regulated. Most banks obtain federal or/and state charters and are then subject to regular and continuous oversight and audits. Despite these oversights, the 2008 financial crisis revealed that the laws, regulations, and actions of federal banking oversight authorities were inefficient and the failure of regulatory agencies to apply existing mandates, left much to be desired. Since 2016, the new administration is engaged in the deregulation process ignoring the lessons of the 2008 financial crisis. While the pace of new regulations has decelerated under the current US administration, the role of the states may grow in prominence.

1.4 Bank Liquidation

Since 2010, strenuous efforts have been made by regulators to protect or at least mitigate the effects of bankruptcy proceeding in the banking industry. The Wall Street Reform and Consumer Protection Act of July 2011, for instance, requires financial institutions with assets exceeding (with some exceptions) $50 billion ("systematically important") to prepare living wills which identify how they intend to be reorganized in the event of a failure, inter alia, naming likely merger partners, and requiring increases in their stockholders' equity positions against possible adverse events.[13]

[13] F.M Scherer (2014): The Banking Industry, Harvard Kennedy School, p. 31.

PART I

The Legal Background

CHAPTER 2

Banking Laws

2.1 General

Banking laws are laws that govern how banks and other financial institutions conduct business. Federal banking regulations often supersede state and local regulations. In total, there are thousands of regulations, large and small, that banks need to understand and comply with.

2.2 The National Bank Act (1863)

The National Banking Acts of 1863 and 1864 were two US federal banking acts that established a system of national banks and created the US National Banking System. The Act shaped today's national banking system and its support of a uniform US banking policy. The National Banking Acts of 1863 and 1864 gave the federal government the power to:

- charter banks;
- require that banks hold an adequate amount of gold and silver reserves;
- issue a national currency.

F. I. Lessambo, *The U.S. Banking System*,
https://doi.org/10.1007/978-3-030-34792-5_2

2.3 The Federal Reserve Act (1914)

The Federal Reserve Act is an Act of Congress that created the Federal Reserve System, and which created the authority to issue Federal Reserve Notes (commonly known as the US Dollar) as legal.[1] The Federal Reserve Act aimed to provide the nation with a safer, more flexible, and more stable monetary and financial system. The need for a central bank, in the United States of America, became painfully evident during the financial panic of 1907, when the stock market collapsed, banks failed, and credit evaporated.[2] As the federal government lacked the tools to respond, it had to depend on private bankers, such as J.P. Morgan, to provide an infusion of capital to sustain the banking system. To correct the problem of an "inelastic currency," Congress created a National Monetary Commission, chaired by Rhode Island Republican Senator Nelson Aldrich. Aldrich proposed a system that would be run by private bankers who would act as federal agents.

Aldrich's proposal was vehemently opposed by liberals who mischaracterize it as a surrender to the "Money Trust" and blocked it. It was not until 1912, when Democrats won the White House and majorities in both houses of Congress that President-elect Woodrow Wilson began encouraging congressional leaders to enact banking and currency reform. In March 1913, the Democratic Senate created its first Banking and Currency Committee, chaired by Oklahoma senator Robert D. Owen. In June of 1913, President Wilson formally proposed the creation of a government-run Federal Reserve System. The House took up the issue first and passed a bill in September, after which the Senate Banking Committee began holding hearings. By December 1913, the US Senate was debating and voting on its version of the bill. When all of the Senate Republicans voted for a substitute measure, Senate Democrats opted to make the banking and currency bill a "party question." The Senate therefore passed the Federal Reserve Act by an almost party-line vote. The bill then went to a conference Committee, which forged the necessary compromises and reported it back on December 22, when it was

[1] The Federal Reserve was created on December 23, 1913, when President Woodrow Wilson signed the Federal Reserve Act into law.

[2] www.senate.gov.

accepted by the House. Today, the Federal Reserve's responsibilities fall into four general areas[3]:

- Conducting the nation's monetary policy by influencing money and credit conditions in the economy in pursuit of full employment and stable prices.
- Supervising and regulating banks and other important financial institutions to ensure the safety and soundness of the nation's banking and financial system and to protect the credit rights of consumers.
- Maintaining the stability of the financial system and containing systemic risk that may arise in financial markets.
- Providing certain financial services to the US government, US financial institutions, and foreign official institutions and playing a major role in operating and overseeing the nation's payment systems.

2.4 The McFadden Act (1927)

The McFadden Act was passed by Congress in 1927. It was modified in 1994 by the Riegle-Neal Interstate Banking and Branching Efficiency Act, which allowed banks to open limited service bank branches across state lines by merging with other banks.

From 1863 through 1927, banks operating under corporate charters granted by the federal government (known as national banks) had to operate within a single building. Banks operating under corporate charters granted by state governments (called state banks) could, in some states, operate out of multiple locations, called branches. However, laws concerning branching varied from state to state.

The McFadden Act allowed a national bank, to the extent permitted by state governments, to operate branches. Conversely, in a state that prohibited branch banking, national banks could not open branches. More, in a state that allowed state-chartered banks to operate branches in the same city as their headquarters, a national bank could operate branches in the same city as their headquarters. Like the Federal Reserve Act, the McFadden Act's branch banking provisions were also

[3] www.federalreserve.gov.

controversial. Populist opponents of branch banking complained that the law gave too much power to big-city bankers and hurt local communities. Financial reformers claimed that the law did not go far enough and prevented banks from adopting safe, efficient, modern practices. The controversy continued for decades, until reforms in the 1980s and 1990s allowed financial institutions to operate branches throughout the United States.

The McFadden Act also revised a wide range of outdated banking laws, legalized new practices requested in order to level of playing field among several banks. For instance, the McFadden Act allowed member banks to own and operate subsidiary corporations for the explicit purpose of limiting the member banks' exposure to risk. Previous legislation neither authorized nor prohibited this practice, but regulators were skeptical and restricted its use. The McFadden Act expanded the size and types of loans that member banks could make. These expansions included the ability to invest more in real estate and to loan larger sums to single corporations. It can be said that the McFadden Act changed the structure of the commercial banks regulated by the Federal Reserve. Before the act, a FED member bank was a single corporation operating out of a single building in a narrow range of activities. After the Act, a FED member could be a complex corporation with multiple legal layers operating from multiple locations; these organizations became larger and more complex as decades passed.

2.5 The Banking Act of 1933

The Glass–Steagall Act, also known as the Banking Act of 1933 (48 Stat. 162), was passed by Congress in 1933 and prohibits commercial banks from engaging in the investment business. It was enacted as an emergency response to the failure of nearly 5000 banks during the Great Depression. The Glass–Steagall Act effectively separated commercial banking from investment banking and created the Federal Deposit Insurance Corporation (FDIC), among other things. It was one of the most widely debated legislative initiatives before being signed into law by President Franklin D. Roosevelt in June 1933. The Senate passed a version of the Glass bill that would have required commercial banks to eliminate their securities affiliates. The final Glass–Steagall provisions contained in the 1933 Banking Act reduced from five years to one year the period in which commercial banks were required to eliminate such affiliations. In 1999, Congress passed the Gramm–Leach–Bliley Act, also known as the Financial Services Modernization Act of 1999, to repeal them. Eight days later, President Bill Clinton signed it into law.

2.6 The Federal Deposit Insurance Act (1950)

The Federal Deposit Insurance Act of 1950[4] is a statute that governs the FDIC. The FDIC was originally created by the Banking Act of 1933, which amended the Federal Reserve Act of 1913. The FDI Act has set up the FDIC with the responsibility to insure bank deposits in eligible banks against loss in the event of a bank failure and to regulate certain banking activities. The standard deposit insurance coverage limit is $250,000 per depositor, per FDIC-insured bank, per ownership category. Deposits held in different ownership categories are separately insured, up to at least $250,000, even if held at the same bank.

Not all deposit products are insured by the FDIC. FDIC insurance protects only the following deposit products:

- checking and savings accounts;
- time deposits, like CDs;
- official payments issued by covered banks, including cashier's checks and money orders;
- money market accounts.

FDIC insurance does not cover:

- securities such as stocks and bonds;
- mutual funds, including money market mutual funds;
- life insurance products, including annuities;
- the contents of safe deposit boxes.

[4] Pub. L. 81–797, 64 Stat. 873, enacted September 21, 1950.

2.7 The Bank Holding Company Act (1956)

The Bank Holding Company Act of 1956 regulates the actions of bank holding companies. The law was implemented, in part, to regulate and control banks that had formed bank holding companies to own both banking and non-banking businesses. The 1956 Act redefined a bank holding company as any company that held a stake in 25% or more of the shares of two or more banks.

A company has control over a bank or over any company if:

- the company directly or indirectly or acting through one or more other persons owns, controls, or has power to vote 25 per centum or more of any class of voting securities of the bank or company;
- the company controls in any manner the election of a majority of the directors or trustees of the bank or company; or
- the Board determines, after notice and opportunity for hearing, that the company directly or indirectly exercises a controlling influence over the management or policies of the bank or company.

Stake holding included outright ownership as well as control of or the ability to vote on shares. For the purposes of the law, a bank was defined as any institution that takes deposits and makes loans. The law generally prohibited a bank holding company from engaging in most non-banking activities or acquiring voting securities of certain companies that are not banks.

The interstate restrictions of the Bank Holding Company Act were repealed by the Riegle-Neal Interstate Banking and Branching Efficiency Act of 1994 (IBBEA). The IBBEA allowed interstate mergers between adequately capitalized and managed banks, subject to concentration limits, state laws, and Community Reinvestment Act (CRA) evaluations.

2.8 The International Banking Act (1978)

The International Banking Act of 1978[5] is the first comprehensive legislation that brings foreign-owned banking operations in the United States under federal regulations comparable to those faced by domestic financial institutions. Its major objectives are to promote competitive

[5] International Banking Act of 1978, Pub. L. 369, 95th Cong., 2nd Sess.

equality between foreign and domestic banks, to improve federal control over monetary policy, and to provide a federal presence in the regulation and supervision of foreign bank activities in the United States.[6] Under the Act, the deposits of foreign-owned bank branches operating outside of their home state are limited to the international finance related credit balances allowed by the agencies. Thus, while such branches may make loans, they are restricted in their ability to compete with local domestic banks for wholesale or retail deposits. The Act allows foreign banks to obtain federal licenses for branches and agencies and a Federally chartered national bank under liberalized regulations. This ensures that in states where foreign banks are welcome they will have a state/federal option which is similar to that of domestic banks. More, the US non-banking activities of foreign banks operating in the United States are placed under the same restrictions as their domestic counterparts, and FDIC insurance is made available to foreign branches desiring such coverage. Pressure for legislation to deal with American branches of foreign banks intensified over the course of the 1970s as the number and size of foreign banks operating in the United States increased significantly. In 1973, 60 foreign banks with assets of $37bn were operating in the United States; by April 1978, this had grown to 122 banks with $90bn in assets. By that stage, they also held $26bn worth of loans in the United States.[7] Those American branches of foreign banks, for the most part, escaped the US banking regulations. Concerned that foreign banks had advantages over domestic banks in attracting deposits through their multistate operations, the Federal Reserve Bank and US Treasury Department decided to level the playing ground. The International Banking Act of 1978 put all American branches and agencies of foreign banks under the control of US banking regulators. It allowed FDIC insurance to be provided to these branches. It also required them to conform to US banking regulations related to issues such as reserves and accounting and regulatory requirements, so that all banks operating domestically are treated equally from a regulatory perspective.

[6]John P. Segala (1979): A Summary of the International Banking Act of 1978, Economic Review, January/February 1979, pp. 20–21.

[7]John P. Segala (1979): A Summary of the International Banking Act of 1978, Economic Review, January/February 1979, p. 16.

2.9 The Gram–Leach–Bliley Act (1999)

The Gramm–Leach–Bliley Act requires financial institutions—companies that offer consumers financial products or services like loans, financial or investment advice, or insurance—to fully explain their information-sharing practices to their customers and to safeguard sensitive data.[8] Financial institutions must allow their customers the option to "opt-out" if they do not want their sensitive information shared. The *Gramm–Leach–Bliley Act* of 1999 (GLBA) was a bi-partisan regulation under President Bill Clinton, passed by Congress on November 12, 1999. GLBA was passed on the heels of commercial bank Citicorp's merger with the insurance firm Travelers Group. This led to the formation of the conglomerate Citigroup, which offered not only commercial banking and insurance services, but also lines of business related to securities. Its brands at this stage included Citibank, Smith Barney, Primerica, and Travelers. Citicorp's merger was a violation of the then-existing Glass–Steagall Act, as well as the *Bank Holding Company Act* of 1956.[9] To allow the merger to take place, the US Federal Reserve gave Citigroup a temporary waiver in September 1998—a precursor to Congress's passage of *GLBA*.

Put differently, the GLBA consists of three rules:

- The Financial Privacy Rule, which regulates the collection and disclosure of private financial information;
- The Safeguards Rule, which stipulates that financial institutions must implement security programs to protect such information;
- The Pretexting provisions, which prohibit the practice of pretexting (accessing private information using false pretenses).

In so doing, the Gram–Leach–Bliley Act repealed the Glass–Steagall Act of 1933 and open doors for financial institutions to merge and create conglomerate financial firm.

[8] www.ftc.gov.

[9] www.investopedia.com.

2.10 The Dodd–Frank Act (2010)

The Dodd–Frank Act, also known as "the Dodd-Frank Wall Street Reform and Consumer Protection Act," was enacted in July 2010 in response to the financial crisis that hit the United States in 2007–2009. Banks were permitted to use hidden fees and lend to unqualified consumers. The Dodd–Frank Act put regulations on the financial industry and created programs to stop mortgage companies and lenders from taking advantage of consumers. In fact, it's considered the most comprehensive financial reform since the Glass–Steagall Act, which was put in place after the 1929 stock market crash.

The Dodd–Frank Act places strict regulations on lenders and banks in an effort to protect consumers and prevent another all-out economic recession. Dodd–Frank also created several new agencies to oversee the regulatory process and implement certain changes. The new law introduces several key provisions, including:

- Banks are required to come up with plans for a quick shutdown if they approach bankruptcy or run out of money.
- Every bank with more than $50 billion of assets must take an annual "stress test," given by the Federal Reserve, which can help determine if the institution could survive a financial crisis.
- Forbids banks from making certain investments with their own accounts. For example, banks cannot invest, own, or sponsor any proprietary trading operations or hedge funds for their own profit, with some exceptions.

Further, the Dodd–Frank Act created two new bodies: the Financial Stability Oversight Council (FSOC) and the Consumer Financial Protection Bureau (CFPB)

i. The Financial Stability Oversight Council identifies risks that affect the financial industry and keeps large banks in check.
ii. The Consumer Financial Protection Bureau protects consumers from the corrupt business practices of banks. The agency works with bank regulators to stop risky lending and other practices that could hurt American consumers. It also oversees credit and debit agencies as well as certain payday and consumer loans.

2.11 Bank Secrecy Act (BSA) of 2018

The Bank Secrecy Act (BSA) establishes program, recordkeeping, and reporting requirements for national banks, federal savings associations, federal branches, and agencies of foreign banks. As of April 1, 2013, financial institutions must use the Bank Secrecy Act BSA E-Filing System in order to submit Suspicious Activity Reports. Under the Bank Secrecy Act (BSA) and related anti-money laundering laws, banks must:

- establish effective BSA compliance programs;
- establish effective customer due diligence systems and monitoring programs;
- screen against Office of Foreign Assets Control (OFAC) and other government lists;
- establish an effective suspicious activity monitoring and reporting process;
- develop risk-based anti-money laundering program.

A financial institution is required to file a suspicious activity report no later than 30 calendar days after the date of initial detection of facts that may constitute a basis for filing a suspicious activity report. If no suspect was identified on the date of detection of the incident requiring the filing, a financial institution may delay filing a suspicious activity report for an additional 30 calendar days to identify a suspect. In no case, shall reporting be delayed more than 60 calendar days after the date of initial detection of a reportable transaction.

Under the Bank Secrecy Act (BSA), financial institutions are required to assist US government agencies in detecting and preventing money laundering, such as:

- keep records of cash purchases of negotiable instruments;
- file reports of cash transactions exceeding $10,000 (daily aggregate amount); and
- report suspicious activity that might signal criminal activity.

The BSA was amended to incorporate the provisions of the US Patriot Act, which requires every bank to adopt a customer identification program as part of its BSA compliance program. BSA reporting also allows the United States to take a macro-view of financial crime. That is, enforcement agencies can map out significant criminal networks and identify trends and patterns of criminal and terrorist activity, which they can then share with the financial community to strengthen their ability to identify and report priority illicit activity as well as assess risk.[10] BSA reporting also implements strict controls governing access to such information to ensure it is not misused and remains confidential.[11] Under the BSA regulatory regime, each bank's BSA/AML compliance program must be designed to (1) identify and verify on a risk-basis the identity of each of its customers; (2) conduct appropriate risk-focused due diligence on those customers; and (3) identify, monitor, and report suspicious activity.

BSA information helps FinCEN further the core national security priority of protecting the financial system from exploitation by illicit actors or financial institutions with complicit insiders and broken controls. FinCEN does this in a number of ways, including through the use of Section 311 of the US Patriot Act. This authority allows us to identify jurisdictions and financial institutions to be of primary money laundering concern and impose a range of special measures to safeguard the US financial system. This powerful tool can lead to impactful systemic change.[12]

- BSA Obligations of Money Services Business

The BSA and its implementing regulations require MSBs to develop, implement, and maintain an effective written anti-money laundering program ("AML program") that is reasonably designed to prevent the MSB

[10]Testimony for the Record Kenneth A. Blanco Director, Financial Crimes Enforcement Network U.S. Department of the Treasury Committee on Banking, Housing and Urban Affairs United States Senate (November 29, 2018).

[11]Information from Suspicious Activity Reports ("SARs"), Currency Transaction Reports ("CTRs"), Form 8300, Reports of International Transportation of Currency or Monetary Instruments ("CMIRs") and other reports are used on both a proactive and reactive basis to investigate specific individuals and entities and to identify leads, connect the dots, and otherwise advance investigations.

[12]Testimony for the Record Kenneth A. Blanco Director, Financial Crimes Enforcement Network U.S. Department of the Treasury Committee on Banking, Housing and Urban Affairs United States Senate (November 29, 2018).

from being used to facilitate money laundering and the financing of terrorist activities. To that end, the AML program must, at a minimum[13]:

a. incorporate policies, procedures, and internal controls reasonably designed to assure ongoing compliance (including verifying customer identification, filing reports, creating and retaining records, and responding to law enforcement requests);
b. designate an individual responsible to assure day-to-day compliance with the program and BSA requirements;
c. provide training for appropriate personnel, including training in the detection of suspicious transactions; and
d. provide for independent review to monitor and maintain an adequate program.

[13] FIN-2019-G001 (May 9, 2019): Application of FinCEN's Regulations to Certain Business Models Involving Convertible Virtual Currencies, p. 10.

CHAPTER 3

The Crypto-currency Regulations

3.1 General

The development of crypto-assets and distributed ledger technology is evolving rapidly, as is the amount of information surrounding it. Such a trend is forcing central banks, regulators and financial institutions to recognize a growing knowledge gap between the legislators, policymakers, economists and the technology.[1] A crypto-currency is a digital asset designed to work as a medium of exchange that uses strong cryptography to secure financial transactions, control the creation of additional units, and verify the transfer of assets.[2] It is a digital currency created and stored electronically in blockchain, which is described as a distributed ledger, or a database of records shared by all clients that have access to the software protocol. Crypto-currency is a disruptive concept that is an alternative to fiat currency used in the present monetary system. The Financial Action Task Force (FATF) has defined "virtual currency" as "a digital representation of value" that "does not have legal tender status ... in any jurisdiction," and serves one or more of three functions: (1) "a medium of exchange"; (2) a "unit of account"; or (3) "a store of value".[3] It uses encryption techniques to control the creation of

[1] Ana Berman (2019): MF and World Bank Launch Quasi-Crypto-currency in Exploration of Blockchain Tech, https://cointelegraph.com.

[2] https://en.wikipedia.org/wiki/Cryptocurrency.

[3] FATF 2015 Guidance, *supra* note 2, at 26.

F. I. Lessambo, *The U.S. Banking System*,
https://doi.org/10.1007/978-3-030-34792-5_3

monetary units and to verify the transfer of funds. Crypto-currencies are being employed in several different applications including virtual money, identity authentication, security issuance, voting, and gambling, among others.[4] According to one estimate, the global market capitalization of crypto-currencies exceeded US$602 billion in the fourth quarter of 2017, before falling below US$300 billion in 2018.[5] The overall crypto-currency market is projected to reach US$1.40 trillion by 2024, at a CAGR of 6.18% during the forecast period. The market for crypto-currency is segmented into software and hardware.[6] A recently published A.T. Kearney report finds that:

> By the end of 2019, Bitcoin will reclaim nearly two-thirds of the crypto-market capitalization as altcoins lose their luster because of growing risk aversion among crypto-currency investors.

The online ecosystem surrounding crypto-currency opens new cyber and insider threat vulnerabilities, while the iterative nature of the DLT underlying crypto-currencies prevents reversibility when a fraudulent or unlawful transaction has occurred. Finally, the absence of in-built geographic limitations makes it difficult to resolve which jurisdiction, or jurisdictions, may potentially regulate each underlying activity.

3.2 Crypto-currency Benefits, Risks and Challenges

Digital currencies have developed and grown over the last 24 years as part of the continuing integration of information technology (IT) into the financial system. Virtual currencies, perhaps most notably Bitcoin, have captured the imagination of its bakers, struck concerns among regulators, which for long have relied on financial intermediaries to help them detect, prevent, and investigate illegal transactions.

[4]Scott D. Hughes (2017): Crypto-currency Regulations and Enforcement in the US, *Western State Law Review*, 45 W. St. L. Rev. 1, p. 4.

[5]Jay Clayton (2017): Statement on Crypto-currencies and Initial Coin Offerings, https://www.sec.gov/news/public-statement/statement-clayton-2017-12-11.

[6]https://www.transparencymarketresearch.com.

- Benefits/Advantages

Proponents of crypto-currency credit it with some virtues. They often allege that digital currencies can prove valuable to those in developing countries without access to stable financial systems, while others believe it could prove to be a next generation payment system for retailers both online and in the real world.[7] Some assert that digital currency introduces advancements in electronic payments and money transfers, potentially materially lowering costs for businesses around the world, decreasing fraud risk for consumers and merchants, increasing consumer privacy, and expanding the market for consumer financial products on a worldwide basis.[8] Most importantly, proponents of crypto-currency praise its anonymity. Such anonymity covers the extent to which identity and transactions are, or can be, disclosed to transaction parties, third parties, and the government. Such anonymity is credited with numerous benefits: (i) It is a way to avoid customer profiling—commercial use of personal information, and (ii) it limits exposure to hacking.[9]

- Risks/Disadvantages

Opponents of the crypto-currency, on the other hand, argue that virtual currencies can be an effective tool for those looking to launder money, for those looking to traffic illegal drugs, for those looking to exploit children around the world.[10] Others claim that the anonymity of the marketplace and near anonymity of the currency made it nearly impossible for law enforcement to track and, therefore, made it an attractive place for criminal activity.[11] That "An illicit actor may choose to use virtual currency because it enables the user to remain relatively anonymous, is easy to navigate, may have low fees, is accessible across the globe with a simple

[7] Committee on Homeland Security and Governmental Affairs (2013): Beyond Silk Road: Potential Risks, Threats, and Promises of Virtual Currencies, p. 1.

[8] Committee on Homeland Security and Governmental Affairs (2013): Beyond Silk Road: Potential Risks, Threats, and Promises of Virtual Currencies, p. 31.

[9] IMF (2018): Casting Light on Central Bank Digital Currency, p. 10.

[10] Committee on Homeland Security and Governmental Affairs (2013): Beyond Silk Road: Potential Risks, Threats, and Promises of Virtual Currencies, p. 2.

[11] Committee on Homeland Security and Governmental Affairs (2013): Beyond Silk Road: Potential Risks, Threats, and Promises of Virtual Currencies, p. 3.

Internet connection, can be used to both store and make international transfers of value, does not typically have transaction limits, is generally secure, features irrevocable transactions, and depending on the system may have been created with the intent to facilitate money laundering; and, finally provides a loophole from AML/CFT regulatory safeguards in most countries around the world."[12] In the same vain, others have alleged that criminals are drawn to virtual currencies for two main reasons: (i) their perception that virtual currencies offer greater anonymity than traditional financial services, and (ii) the irreversibility of many virtual currency transactions.[13] More, crypto-currency undermines public policy goals: financial integrity, financial stability, and monetary policy effectiveness. Financial integrity covers, among other things, anti–money laundering and combating the financing of terrorism (AML/CFT) rules, including customer due diligence measures and additional measures aimed at fighting corruption and fostering good governance.[14] More, crypto-currencies are not the liability of any institution and are not backed by assets. Thus, their value is usually volatile, because most have rigid issuance rules.[15]

- Challenges

Very often, when new financial technologies are introduced, regulators are confronted with a similar set of key challenges: how to best protect consumers while fostering innovation, promoting competition, enforcing legacy regulations and resisting the urge to over-regulate. As opposed to fiat currency, which is centralized, crypto-currency is completely decentralized and out of the control of central banks. A central bank control over fiat currencies is key to regulation in many ways. However, with crypto-currencies, central banks are no longer the one dictating rules. That is, a government cannot, for example, determine how much of a currency to print in response to external and internal pressures. Rather, the generation of new coins or tokens would be dependent upon independent mining operations.

[12] Committee on Homeland Security and Governmental Affairs (2013): Beyond Silk Road: Potential Risks, Threats, and Promises of Virtual Currencies, p. 5.

[13] Committee on Homeland Security and Governmental Affairs (2013): Beyond Silk Road: Potential Risks, Threats, and Promises of Virtual Currencies, p. 7.

[14] IMF (2018): Casting Light on Central Bank Digital Currency, p. 11.

[15] IMF (2018): Casting Light on Central Bank Digital Currency, p. 13.

3.3 Crypto-currency and Public Policy Goals

The advent of crypto-currency undermines key international finance public policy goals, such as financial integrity, financial stability, and monetary policy effectiveness.

3.3.1 Crypto-currency and Financial Integrity

The establishment and maintenance of a currency has traditionally been regarded as a core prerogative of the government or the central bank. However, crypto-currencies, which rely on decentralized networks to facilitate transactions in a particular unit of account, have no central administrator in the way that a government issues and backs fiat currencies.[16] Crypto-currencies can be used to conceal or disguise the illicit origin or sanctioned destination of funds, thus facilitating money laundering, terrorist financing, the evasion of sanctions, fraud, and cybercrime.

3.3.2 Crypto-currency and Financial Stability

Financial stability is a state in which the financial system is resistant to economic shocks and eager and able to fulfill its basic functions: the intermediation of financial funds, management of risks and the arrangement of payments. Financial stability is significant as it reflects a sound financial system, which in turn is important as it reinforces trust in the system and prevents phenomena such as a run on banks, which can destabilize an economy. The crypto-currency ecosystem does not provide such. The Digital Ledger Technology that underlies crypto-assets facilitates the trading of crypto-assets on decentralized trading platforms, with potential implications for financial stability. In the event of a liquidity crisis on the exchange, there may be no official institution to supply emergency liquidity, with important financial stability implications if such exchanges grow to become systemically important.[17] Individual crypto-currency holders and users may be exposed to significant risks as the

[16] US Department of the Treasury (2017): Public–Private Exchange—Risks and Vulnerabilities of Virtual Currency, p. 18.

[17] IMF (2019): FinTech: The Experience so Far, p. 38.

crypto-currency ecosystem is susceptible to disruptions, including security breaches, bankruptcy, financial fraud, and payment-like system risk such as operational risk, credit risk, liquidity risk, and legal risk. Large-scale use of crypto-currencies and greater interconnectedness with other parts of the financial sector could generate systemic financial risks.

3.3.3 Crypto-currency and Monetary Policy

Economic science teaches us that money performs three fundamental functions: (i) a unit of account, (ii) a means of payment, and (iii) a store of value. As a unit of account, money serves as a measuring stick ideally linked to the same basket of goods over time. As a means of payment, it facilitates transactions. As a secure store of value, it provides refuge from various sources of risk.[18] Crypto-currencies' viability to perform the three traditional functions of money is highly questionable. More, Crypto-currencies lacks critical features that stable monetary regimes would typically provide to guard against three key monetary stability risks.[19]

3.4 Crypto-currencies: The US Current Legal and Regulatory Framework

Under BSA/AML virtual currency exchanges qualify as money transmitters (MTs), a subcategory of money service businesses (MSBs).[20] As such, they are required to register with FinCEN and create a sound AML compliance program.[21] Banks involved in crypto-currency transactions must consider the following factors into consideration when

[18] IMF (2018): Casting Light on Central Bank Digital Currency, p. 9.

[19] The risk of structural "deflation"; flexibility to respond to temporary shocks to money demand and thus smooth the business cycle; and the capacity to function as a lender-of-last-resort.

[20] 31 U.S.C. § 5312(a)(2), https://www.gpo.gov/fdsys/pkg/USCODE-2011-title31/pdf/USCODE-2011-title31-subtitleIV-chap53-subchapII-sec5312.pdf.

[21] US Department of the Treasury-Financial Crimes Enforcement Network (2013): Guidance on the Application of FinCEN's Regulations to Persons Administering, Exchanging, or Using Virtual Currencies, https://www.fincen.gov/sites/default/files/shared/FIN-2013-G001.pdf.

risk-weighting their MSB customers and allocate resources in proportion to the level of risk associated with an account[22]:

- Purpose of the account.
- Anticipated account activity.
- Types of products and services offered by the MSB.
- Locations and markets served by the MSB.

For FinCEN,[23] the key elements of Customer Due Diligence include: (i) identifying and verifying the identity of customers; (ii) identifying and verifying the identity of beneficial owners of legal entity customers (i.e., the natural persons who own or control legal entities); (iii) understanding the nature and purpose of customer relationships; and (iv) conducting ongoing monitoring. Collectively, these elements comprise the minimum standard of CDD, which FinCEN believes is fundamental to an effective AML program. FinCEN does not distinguish between banks and other financial institutions dealing with crypto-currencies. Both money transmitters, crypto-currency exchangers, and administrators can perform within the legal boundaries as long as they (i) Register with FinCEN,[24] (ii) put in place AML protections, controls in place to harden to the likelihood that bad actors will take advantage of their system, and (iii) maintain records and provide certain reports to FinCEN, including suspicious activity reports. Thus, FinCEN requires that Bitcoin operators implement Bank Secrecy Act provisions. However, those laws and regulations would not adequately capture the crypto-currency business as Bitcoin is not a company with an easily identifiable executive, but instead it is an open-source project and a community.[25]

[22] FFIEC Bank Secrecy Act Anti-Money Laundering Examination Manual, https://www.ffiec.gov/bsa_aml_infobase/pages_manual/manual_online.htm.

[23] US Department of the Treasury—FinCEN Rule (2016): Customer Due Diligence Requirements for Financial Institutions, https://www.gpo.gov/fdsys/pkg/FR-2016-05-11/pdf/2016-10567.pdf.

[24] It is an online form, and it is free.

[25] Committee on Homeland Security and Governmental Affairs (2013): Beyond Silk Road: Potential Risks, Threats, and Promises of Virtual Currencies, p. 35.

3.5 The Overlapping Regulatory Authority

While several regulators have each consider regulating crypto-currency, they seem not to agree as to the holistic approach, as each looks solely from the lenses of its mission. That is, various US regulatory agencies have different stances toward crypto-currency. The Financial Crime Enforcement Network, the Securities and Exchange Commission, the Commodity Futures Trading Commission, the Internal Revenue Service may have concurrent or overlapping jurisdiction over crypto-currency.

- FinCEN

Under FinCEN (2013) guidance, persons administering, exchanging, or using virtual currencies qualify as money services businesses and thus should be regulated under the Bank Secrecy Act.[26] FinCEN distinguishes between users[27] and exchangers, and administrators of virtual currency. In subsequent administrative rulings, FinCEN has clarified that its definition of MBS does not include companies, which buy and sell crypto-currencies for their own use or software developers that do not operate exchanges.[28] "MSBs play an important role in a transparent financial system, particularly because they often provide financial services to people less likely to use traditional banking services and because of their prominent role in providing remittance services, both domestically and abroad."[29] The Murgio case[30] illustrates FinCEN effort to combat Unlicensed Money Transmitting Business.

[26]FIN-2013-G001 Application of FinCEN's Regulations to Persons Administering, Exchanging, or Using Virtual Currencies (March 18, 2013), https://www.fincen.gov/sites/default/files/shared/FIN-2013-G001.pdf [hereinafter FinCEN Guidance].

[27]Those who merely use virtual currency to purchase goods or services.

[28]Application of Money Services Business Regulations to the Rental of Computer Systems for Mining Virtual Currency, FIN-2014-R007 (April 29, 2014); Application of FinCEN's Regulations to Virtual Currency Software Development; and Certain Investment Activity, FIN-2014-R002 (January 30, 2014).

[29]Jamal El-Hindi (May 26, 2017): Conference of State Bank Supervisors (CSBS) Federal Supervisory Forum.

[30]In US v. Nurgio, SDNY (September 19, 2016).

- Section 1960, the statute prohibiting the operation of an unlicensed money transmitting business was enacted in order to combat the growing use of money transmitting businesses to transfer large amounts of the monetary proceeds of unlawful enterprises.[31]
- Murgio's unlicensed money transmitting business facilitated both traditional crimes (narcotics and other contraband trafficking) and new frontiers of criminal conduct (ransomware schemes) by offering criminals a financial platform beyond the view and scrutiny of banks and regulators.
- In or about March 2013, Murgio began operating Coin.mx, an online Bitcoin exchange that allowed users to purchase Bitcoins over the internet using several different payment methods, including cash deposit, credit card, and ACH.
- Coin.mx was headquartered in Florida, where Murgio was located, but also had operations overseas, most notably in Russia.
- Despite being aware of federal and state registration requirements for money transmitters like Coin.mx, Murgio purposely failed to register Coin.mx with FinCEN or obtain a license in Florida. Instead, Murgio tried to set up Coin.mx as a purported "Private Membership Association" in an attempt to skirt the anti-money laundering regulations and avoid scrutiny of Coin.mx.
- Murgio used phony front companies, such as "Collectables Club," "Currency Enthusiasts," and "Collecting Club," to open bank accounts for Coin.mx because Murgio understood that banks would not knowingly conduct business with a Bitcoin exchange.
- Murgio also created phony websites, such as collectpma.com for Collectables Club, and supplied false Merchant Category Codes ("MCCs"), which were used to open and maintain bank and payment processing accounts.
- In furtherance of Coin.mx's operations and further to conceal its illegal nature, Murgio and his co-conspirators used various foreign bank accounts to move funds used to support Coin.mx's operations.
- Murgio and his co-conspirators also used overseas payment processing companies, including processors in Baku, Azerbaijan, to process Coin.mx credit card transactions. Typically, such transactions were disguised as relating to children's toys or wedding fashion in order to conceal their true Bitcoin nature.

[31] *United States v. Velastegui*, 199 F.3d 590, 593 (2d Cir. 1999).

- Approximately 30–40% of customers of Coin.mx were using Bitcoin to make illicit purchases on Darknet market websites that sold drugs, guns, and fake identities, among other contraband.
- Murgio and his co-conspirators bribed the head of HOPE FCU to take control of and operate that federal credit union, including to process tens of millions of dollars of risky ACH transactions.
- In their defense, defendants asserted that: (i) Bitcoin does not qualify as "funds"; (ii) exchanging Bitcoin does not involve "transferring" customers' funds to other persons or places; and (iii) operating a Bitcoin exchange in the state of Florida, where Coin.mx operated, does not require a license.
- The SDNY brushed away the three arguments by establishing that: (i) the term "funds" encompasses any pecuniary resources that can be used as a medium of exchange, and that Bitcoin meets that description; (ii) whether the defendants acted merely as a seller of Bitcoin and not as a "transmitter" of funds is debatable. The Government file indicated that Coin.mx not only sold customers Bitcoin for currency but also transferred their Bitcoin for them to third parties; and (iii) the licensed would have been required.

The Murgio decision reflects a growing judicial consensus around the application of state and federal money transmitting laws to Bitcoin exchangers.

- The Securities and Exchange Commission

Securities regulators have increasingly become involved given the similarities of some types of crypto-assets with securities.[32] The SEC has issued guidelines identifying crypto-assets that would be regulated as securities. For those assets, the SEC has warned that persons or entities dealing in, providing trading services and offering the assets publicly should comply with securities regulation and would need to consider whether they may require a license.

[32] IMF (2019): FinTech: The Experience so Far, p. 23, http://www.imf.org/external/pp/ppindex.aspx.

- In SEVC v. Recoin Group[33]
  - The SEC sued crypto-currency issuer (an offering of digital securities) under the antifraud and registration provisions of the federal securities laws.
  - The SEC alleges that Maksim Zaslavskiy and his companies have been selling unregistered securities, and the digital tokens or coins being peddled don't really exist.
  - Maksim Zaslavskiy allegedly touted REcoin as "The First Ever Cryptocurrency Backed by Real Estate." Zaslavskiy and REcoin allegedly misrepresented they had raised between $2 million and $4 million from investors when the actual amount is approximately $300,000.
- In SEC v. Reginald[34]
  - The Securities and Exchange Commission brought fraud charges against a Brooklyn individual and two entities under his control who allegedly engaged in a fraudulent scheme to sell digital securities to investors and to manipulate the market for those securities.
  - Middleton and Veritaseum with violating the registration and antifraud provisions of the US federal securities laws, and Middleton with additionally violating the antifraud provisions on the basis of his manipulative trading.
  - On August 12, 2019, the court entered an emergency freeze to preserve at least $8 million of the $14.8 million the defendants raised in 2017 and 2018 in an offering of digital securities.
- In SEC v. Kik Interactive Inc.[35]
  - The Securities and Exchange Commission today sued Kik Interactive Inc. for conducting an illegal $100 million securities offering of digital tokens in violation of the registration

[33] *Securities and Exchange Commission v. REcoin Group Foundation*, et al., Civil Action No Securities and Exchange Commission v. Reginald, Case 1:19-CV-04625-CBA-RER.17-cv-05725 (E.D.N.Y., filed September 29, 2017).

[34] Securities and Exchange Commission v. Reginald, Case 1:19-CV-04625-CBA-RER.

[35] Securities and Exchange Commission v. KIK Interactive Inc. Case 1:19-cv-05244.

requirements of Section 5 of the Securities Act of 1933. The SEC charges that Kik sold the tokens to US investors without registering their offer and sale as required by the US securities laws.

- In early 2017, the company sought to pivot to a new type of business, which it financed through the sale of one trillion digital tokens. Kik sold its "Kin" tokens to the public, and at a discounted price to wealthy purchasers, raising more than $55 million from US investors.
- By selling $100 million in securities without registering the offers or sales, we allege that Kik deprived investors of information to which they were legally entitled.

• The FFTC

The CFTC needs to extend its knowledge in order to be able to perform independent market analysis using data from various sources including decentralized blockchains and networks instead of relying on self-regulatory organizations and market intermediaries. In 2014, the CFTC observed that crypto-currencies may constitute commodities under the Commodity Exchange Act ("CEA"), such that the CFTC has broad jurisdiction over derivatives that reference crypto-currencies and market participants that transact in such contracts. In addition, under its enforcement authority, the CFTC has asserted authority to pursue suspected fraud or manipulation with respect to the crypto-currency itself, an authority recently affirmed in federal court. Persons that act as futures commission merchants ("FCM") or introducing brokers ("IBs") for crypto-currency derivatives under the CEA are also covered by BSA AML requirements.

• In CFTC v. McDonnell and CDM[36]

- The Commodity Futures Trading Commission—Division of Enforcement Virtual Currency Task Force—brought a lawsuit alleging fraud in connection with virtual currencies, including Bitcoin and Litecoin.
- McDonnell and CDM engaged in a deceptive and fraudulent virtual currency scheme to induce customers to send money and virtual currencies to CDM, purportedly in exchange for real-time

[36] CFTC v. McDonnell and CDM, EDNY (August 23, 2018).

expert virtual currency trading advice and for virtual currency purchasing and trading on behalf of the customers under McDonnell's direction.
- McDonnell and CDM used their fraudulent solicitations to obtain and then keep customers' funds— McDonnell "ruthlessly misled customers and misappropriated their funds."
- To conceal their fraudulent scheme, soon after obtaining customer funds, McDonnell and CDM removed the website and social media materials from the Internet and ceased communicating with CDM Customers, who lost most if not all of their invested funds due to Defendants' fraud and misappropriation.
- Neither McDonnell nor CDM has ever been registered with the CFTC in any capacity.
- In an accompanying 139-page Memorandum (Decision) entered on August 23, 2018, following a four-day bench trial, Judge Jack B. Weinstein of the US District Court for the Eastern District of New York found that McDonnell and CDM were engaged in a deceptive and fraudulent virtual currency scheme.

- The IRS

For US federal tax purposes, convertible virtual currencies are treated as "property" and are subject to existing tax principles for property transactions. Individuals that mine Bitcoins are responsible for legally claiming the fair market value as gross income at that point in time, regardless of when the funds held in a virtual wallet are converted into fiat money. Depending on whether or not the property is a capital asset, the gain or loss in value will be determined at the point in time when the property held in the virtual wallet is converted fiat money.[37]

3.6 The US Approach

Drafting holistic regulations to provide a stable regulatory framework for digital assets without hurting their innovativeness is a difficult task and no agency or regulator alone can deliver on. A one-size fit all approach would be irrelevant as crypto-currency assets are not a homogeneous

[37] IRS Publication 2014-21, https://www.irs.gov/pub/irs-drop/n-14-21.pdf.

asset class—they may feature characteristics of securities, commodities, currency units, or a combination thereof. US regulators, in a concerted manner, are doing their bests to circumvent the crypto industry with safe- and sound- regulations. Rather than rushing, the US regulatory agencies are drafting and releasing guidelines over the development and use of the crypto-technology to develop organically rather than establishing premature oversight which could inadvertently stifle a technology that is still in its infancy. To date, FinCEN—the organization that enforces AML regulations—had provided much clearer guidance the regulatory framework that exist in the European Union, Switzerland or else. The US leading and not left behind as some have argued.

3.7 The EU 5th Directive

The Crypto-currency's market cap is over \$200 billion. Criminals quickly sensed that Bitcoin has distinctive properties that serve their interest in evading law enforcement. The EU has adopted the 5th AML, each of the EU's 28 member states now have 18 months to "transpose" the 5th AML Directive and make it law in their respective countries. EU-wide adoption should therefore be achieved by the end of 2019. The new legislation covers two types of crypto-currency business:

1. "providers engaged in exchange services between virtual currencies and fiat currencies", and
2. "custodian wallet providers" i.e. crypto-currency wallet services (where the service holds its users' private keys).

These businesses are obligated to implement measures to counter money laundering and terrorist fundraising, such as customer due diligence (including KYC) and transaction monitoring. They will also be required to maintain comprehensive records and report suspicious transactions.

3.8 The Central Bank Digital Currency Experiments

Central banks in some developed, developing, and emerging economies are exploring the issuance of CBDC. In some advanced economies, the falling use of cash is cited as the motivating factor behind the study of CBDC as an alternative, robust, and convenient payment method, as well as the potential to have negative interest rates. The CBDC could also facilitate contestability of the payment market and reduce the chances of a few large providers dominating the system, as it is the case in some developed countries. In developing countries, the focus is more on improving operational and cost efficiency. For countries with underdeveloped financial systems and many unbanked citizens, the CBDC is seen as means to improve financial inclusion and support digitalization.[38] Other reasons for considering CBDC include enhancing financial integrity. Overall, central banks that consider the CBDC favor a non-anonymous CBDC approach that allows the relevant authorities to trace transactions, and facilitate the monitoring of transactions. From a central bank perspective, the case for CBDC is likely to differ from country to country and on the effectiveness of regulation.[39] A cooperation between regulators and firms with new financial technologies is also explored in many jurisdictions.

3.9 The Sandbag Regulation Approach

A regulatory sandbox is a framework set up by a financial sector regulator to allow small scale, live testing of innovations by private firms in a controlled environment under the regulator's supervision.[40] The term "regulatory sandbox" was coined by the UK Financial Conduct Authority in 2015. The concept aims to foster and encourage rapid technological innovation in financial markets and preserving its integrity and soundness at the same time. A regulatory sandbox introduces a formal and open dialogue between the regulator and financial services providers. It enables the regulator to revise and shape the regulatory and supervisory framework in a timely fashion. The first sandbox-like framework was set up by the US Consumer Financial Protection Bureau (CFPB) in 2012 under the name Project Catalyst (CFPB 2016).[41] There are several regulatory sandbag approaches with a common objective of promoting competition and efficiencies through innovation.[42] Regulatory sandbag is more appropriate to products or services, whose innovative nature deserves a special treatment. Assuming that a product or service is deemed innovative, a sandbox firm may be allowed to continue

[38] IMF (2019): FinTech: The Experience so Far, p. 30.

[39] IMF (2019): FinTech: The Experience so Far, p. 30.

[40] Ivo Jenik and Kate Lauer (2017): Regulatory Sandboxes and Financial Inclusion, p. 1.

[41] Ivo Jenik and Kate Lauer (2017): Regulatory Sandboxes and Financial Inclusion, p. 1.

[42] Ivo Jenik and Kate Lauer (2017): Regulatory Sandboxes and Financial Inclusion, p. 3.

its operations outside the regulatory framework, while the regulator is conducting the testing. If testing fails, the sandbox firm is required to cease running its innovation.[43] It is of paramount significance that all regulators share timely the information concerning new product / service, and the consumers' interests well assessed.

[43] Ivo Jenik and Kate Lauer (2017): Regulatory Sandboxes and Financial Inclusion, p. 4.

CHAPTER 4

Anti-Money Laundering Laws

4.1 General

Banks and most financial institutions, and many non-financial institutions, are required to identify and report transactions of a suspicious nature to the financial intelligence unit in the respective country. Money laundering consists of masking the source of criminally derived proceeds so that the proceeds appear legitimate, or masquerading the source of monies used to promote illegal conduct. Money laundering generally involves three steps: placing illicit proceeds into the financial system; layering, or the separation of the criminal proceeds from their origin; and integration, or the use of apparently legitimate transactions to disguise the illicit proceeds.[1] Money laundering can take several forms, although most methods can be categorized into one of a few types. These include bank methods, smurfing, currency exchanges, and double invoicing.

In its mission to safeguard the financial system from the abuses of financial crime, including terrorist financing, money laundering, and other illicit activity, the Financial Crimes Enforcement Network acts as

[1] Statement of Steven M. D'Antuono Section Chief Criminal Investigative Division Federal Bureau of Investigation Department of Justice Before the Committee on Banking, Housing, and Urban Affairs United States Senate For a Hearing Entitled "Combating Money Laundering and Other Forms of Illicit Finance: Regulator and Law Enforcement Perspectives on Reform" (November 29, 2018).

F. I. Lessambo, *The U.S. Banking System*,
https://doi.org/10.1007/978-3-030-34792-5_4

the designated administrator of the Bank Secrecy Act (BSA). The BSA was established in 1970 and has become one of the most important tools in the fight against money laundering. Since then, numerous other laws have enhanced and amended the BSA to provide law enforcement and regulatory agencies with the most effective tools to combat money laundering. An index of anti-money laundering laws since 1970 with their respective requirements and goals is listed below in chronological order.

4.2 Bank Secrecy Act (1970)

Established requirements for recordkeeping and reporting by private individuals, banks, and other financial institutions. It is designed to help identify the source, volume, and movement of currency and other monetary instruments transported or transmitted into or out of the United States or deposited in financial institutions. It required banks to (1) report cash transactions over $10,000 using the Currency Transaction Report; (2) properly identify persons conducting transactions; and (3) maintain a paper trail by keeping appropriate records of financial transactions

- The Bank Secrecy Act (aka the Financial Recordkeeping of Currency and Foreign Transactions Act of 1970)

The Bank Secrecy Act (BSA), initially adopted in 1970, establishes the basic framework for AML obligations imposed on financial institutions. Among other things, it authorizes the Secretary of the Treasury (Treasury) to issue regulations requiring financial institutions (including broker–dealers) to keep records and file reports on financial transactions that may be useful in investigating and prosecuting money laundering and other financial crimes. The Financial Crimes Enforcement Network (FinCEN), a bureau within Treasury, has regulatory responsibilities for administering the BSA.

4.3 Money Laundering Control Act (1986)

The Money Laundering Control Act of 1986[2] passed in 1986 is the first federal law that criminalized money laundering. The Money Laundering Control Act of 1986 was enacted as Title I of the Anti-Drug Abuse Act.

[2] Public Law 99-570.

It also amended the Bank Secrecy Act, the Change in Bank Control Act, and the Right to Financial Privacy Act.

Section 1956 prohibits individuals from engaging in a financial transaction with proceeds that were generated from certain specific crimes, known as "specified unlawful activities" (SUAs). Additionally, the law requires that an individual specifically intends in making the transaction to conceal the source, ownership, or control of the funds. There is no minimum threshold of money, nor is there the requirement that the transaction succeeds in actually disguising the money. Moreover, a "financial transaction" has been broadly defined and need not involve a financial institution, or even a business. Merely passing money from one person to another, so long as it is done with the intent to disguise the source, ownership, location, or control of the money, has been deemed a financial transaction under the law. Section 1957 prohibits spending in excess of $10,000 derived from an SUA, regardless of whether the individual wishes to disguise it. This carries a lesser penalty than money laundering and, unlike the money laundering statute, requires that the money passes through a financial institution.

4.4 Anti-Drug Abuse Act (1988)

Enacted as part of the federal government war on drugs, the Anti-Drug Abuse Act of 1988 sought to increase penalties for those who were involved in the sale and use of illegal narcotics. Through this Act, Congress expressly intended to punish and deter anyone who intentionally kills or counsels, commands, induces, procures, or causes an intentional killing of: (A) any person while (1) engaging in or (2) working in furtherance of any continuing criminal enterprise, or (3) while engaging in a major Federal drug felony; or (B) any law enforcement officer during or in relation to a Federal drug felony. The Anti-Drug Abuse Act of 1988 contained a myriad of changes, enhancements, penalties, and funding for the war on drugs. It focused on both the seller and the user of illegal narcotics. It was the government's answer to battling the drug epidemic by providing changes to the law, making for harsher sentences for those involved in the drug trade.

4.5 Annunzio-Wylie Anti-Money Laundering Act (1992)

Outlined the procedure to subpoena bank records. The Act amended federal law relating to international monetary instrument transaction reporting requirements to prohibit: (1) failure to file the requisite reports; (2) filing material omissions or misstatements of facts in such reports; and (3) participation in structuring any importation or exportation of monetary instruments. The Act makes the penalty for conspiracy to commit a money laundering offense the same as the penalty for the substantive offense itself. More, it amended the Right to Financial Privacy Act of 1978 to prohibit certain personnel connected with a financial institution from disclosing the existence of a grand jury subpoena to a person named in such subpoena for bank records related to money laundering and controlled substance investigations. Also, it requires the Attorney General, the Secretary of the Treasury, and the head of any other Federal agency or instrumentality to disclose to the appropriate Federal banking agency any information raising significant concerns regarding the safety and soundness of any depository institution doing business in the United States.

4.6 Money Laundering Suppression Act (1994)

Money Laundering Suppression Act of 1994 Amends Federal law to prescribe guidelines for both mandatory and discretionary exemptions from monetary transaction reporting requirements for depository institutions. The following sections are of paramount significance:

- Section 402

Section 402 of the Act directs the Secretary of the Treasury to:

- submit an annual status report to the Congress on the consequent reduction in the overall number of currency transaction reports;
- streamline currency transaction reports to eliminate the information of little value for law enforcement purposes;
- assign a single designee to receive reports of suspicious transactions; and
- submit annual reports to the Congress on the number of suspicious transactions reported.

- Sec. 404

Section 404 requires each appropriate Federal banking agency to review and enhance:

- training and examination procedures to improve the identification of money laundering schemes involving depository institutions and
- procedures for referring cases to appropriate law enforcement agencies.

Further, it requires the Secretary and each appropriate law enforcement agency to provide information regularly to each appropriate federal banking agency regarding money laundering schemes and activities involving depository institutions in order to enhance agency ability to examine for and identify money laundering activity. It also requires the Financial Institutions Examination Council to report to the Congress on the usefulness of the reporting of criminal schemes by law enforcement agencies.

- Sec. 405

Section 405 includes negotiable instruments drawn on foreign banks within the purview of monetary transactions subject to Federal recordkeeping and reporting requirements.

- Sec. 406

Section 406 requires the Secretary to delegate to Federal banking agencies any authority to assess civil money penalties.

- Sec. 407

Section 407 expresses the sense of the Congress that the States should:

- establish uniform laws for licensing and regulating non-depository institution businesses which engage in currency transactions;
- provide sufficient resources for regulatory enforcement; and
- develop a model statute to implement the regulatory scheme.

It also directs the Secretary to study and report to the Congress: (i) on the States' progress toward such a model statute and (ii) on possible Federal funding sources to cover costs incurred by the States in implementing a licensing and enforcement scheme.

- Sec. 408

Section 408 sets forth federal registration requirements for money transmitting businesses, directs the Secretary to prescribe regulations establishing a threshold point for treating an agent of a money transmitting business as a money transmitting business, and establishes civil and criminal penalties for violation of such requirements.

- Sec. 409

Section 409 amends federal law regarding monetary instruments transactions to include within the definition of "financial institution" a casino, gambling casino, or gaming establishment with specified annual gaming revenues which is either State-licensed, or a certain class of Indian gaming operation (thus subjecting Indian casinos to the more comprehensive currency reporting and recordkeeping requirements of the Bank Secrecy Act).

- Sec. 411

Section 411 sets forth criminal penalties for structuring domestic and international transactions to evade Federal reporting requirements (currently such violations must be willful in order to be penalized).

- Sec. 412

Section 412 requires the Comptroller General to study and report to the Congress on: (i) the vulnerability of cashiers' checks to money laundering schemes and (ii) the need for additional recordkeeping requirements for such checks.

4.7 Money Laundering and Financial Crimes Strategy Act (1998)

Money Laundering and Financial Crimes Strategy Act of 1998 amends Federal law governing monetary transactions to redefine money laundering and related financial crimes as either: (1) the movement of illicit cash or cash equivalent proceeds into, out of, or through the United States or through certain US financial institutions or (2) the meaning given under State and local criminal statutes pertaining to the movement of illicit cash or cash equivalent proceeds.

Section 2 of this Act directs the President (acting through the Secretary of the Treasury and in consultation with the Attorney General) to develop and submit to the Congress a national strategy, with five annual updates, for combating money laundering and related financial crimes. Such a strategy shall include:

1. research-based goals, objectives, and priorities;
2. prevention measures coordinated with other agencies;
3. detection and prosecution initiatives (including seizure and forfeiture of proceeds and instrumentalities derived from such crimes);
4. an enhanced partnership between the private financial sector and law enforcement agencies to target crime detection and prevention;
5. enhanced intergovernmental cooperation between Federal, State, and local officials; and
6. a description of geographical areas designated as high-risk money laundering and related financial crime areas.

Section 2 also instructs the Secretary to submit to the Congress contemporaneously with such strategy an evaluation of the effectiveness of policies to combat money laundering and related financial crimes. More, it requires:

1. an element of the national strategy to be the designation of certain geographic areas, industries, sectors, or institutions as areas in which money laundering and related financial crimes are extensive or present a substantial risk; and
2. the Secretary to take specified factors into consideration when identifying such areas.

It also authorizes certain Federal, State, and local officials and prosecutors to submit a written request for: (i) the designation of a high-risk money laundering and related financial crimes area or (ii) funding for a specific prevention or enforcement initiative, or to determine the extent of financial criminal activity in an area.

It directs the Secretary to: (1) establish a grant program to support local law enforcement efforts in a money laundering detection, prevention, and suppression program and (2) report to specified congressional Committees on the effectiveness and need for the designation of high-risk money laundering and related financial crime areas. Finally, it sets forth grant eligibility criteria and authorizes the Secretary, one year after the national strategy is submitted to the Congress, to review, select, and award grants for State or local law enforcement agencies and prosecutors to provide funding necessary to investigate and prosecute money laundering and related financial crimes in high-risk areas.

4.8 Uniting and Strengthening America by Providing Appropriate Tools Required to Intercept and Obstruct Terrorism Act of 2001 (USA PATRIOT Act)

The purpose of the USA PATRIOT Act is to deter and punish terrorist acts in the United States and around the world, to enhance law enforcement investigatory tools, and other purposes, some of which include:

- to strengthen US measures to prevent, detect, and prosecute international money laundering and financing of terrorism;
- to subject to special scrutiny foreign jurisdictions, foreign financial institutions, and classes of international transactions or types of accounts that are susceptible to criminal abuse;
- to require all appropriate elements of the financial services industry to report potential money laundering;
- to strengthen measures to prevent use of the US financial system for personal gain by corrupt foreign officials and facilitate the repatriation of stolen assets to the citizens of countries to whom such assets belong.

Below is a brief, non-comprehensive overview of the sections of the USA PATRIOT Act that may affect financial institutions.

Section 311: Special Measures for Jurisdictions, Financial Institutions, or International Transactions of Primary Money Laundering Concern

This section allows for identifying customers using correspondent accounts, including obtaining information comparable to information obtained on domestic customers and prohibiting or imposing conditions on the opening or maintaining in the United States of correspondent or payable-through accounts for a foreign banking institution.

4.9 Intelligence Reform & Terrorism Prevention Act (2004)

Subtitle G of the Act aims to combat terrorist financing by requiring better coordination and building on international coalitions. It states the Sense of Congress that the Secretary of the Treasury should continue to promote the dissemination of international anti-money laundering and combating the financing of terrorism standards. It expands reporting requirements for the Secretary of Treasury to include assessments of progress made in these areas. It also requires the Secretary of Treasury to convene an inter-agency council to develop policies to be pursued by the United States regarding the development of common international anti-money laundering and combating the financing of terrorism standards.

4.10 The USA Patriot Improvement and Reauthorization Act of 2005

The USA PATRIOT Act was enacted by Congress in 2001 in response to the September 11, 2001, terrorist attacks. Among other things, the USA PATRIOT Act amended and strengthened the BSA. It imposed a number of AML obligations directly on broker–dealers, including:

AML compliance programs;

- customer identification programs;
- monitoring, detecting, and filing reports of suspicious activity;
- due diligence on foreign correspondent accounts, including prohibitions on transactions with foreign shell banks;
- due diligence on private banking accounts;

- mandatory information sharing (in response to requests by federal law enforcement); and
- compliance with special measures imposed by the Secretary of the Treasury to address particular AML concerns.

4.10.1 The AML Programs

Section 352 of the USA PATRIOT ACT amended the BSA to require financial institutions, including broker–dealers, to establish AML programs. Broker–dealers can satisfy this requirement by implementing and maintaining an AML program that complies with SRO rule requirements. In September 2009, the SEC approved FINRA's new AML compliance rule, FINRA Rule 3310. FINRA's new rule adopts NASD Rule 3011 and most of NASD IM-3011-1 and deletes NYSE Rule 445 as duplicative. As with NASD Rule 3011 and NYSE Rule 445, FINRA Rule 3310 requires member organizations to establish risk-based AML compliance programs. Please note, however, that FINRA Rule 3310 does not contain the exception in NASD IM-3011-1 to the independent testing requirement. FINRA Rule 3310 became effective on January 1, 2010.

An AML program must be in writing and include, at a minimum:

- policies, procedures, and internal controls reasonably designed to achieve compliance with the BSA and its implementing rules;
- policies and procedures that can be reasonably expected to detect and cause the reporting of transactions under 31 U.S.C. 5318(g) and the implementing regulations thereunder;
- the designation of an AML compliance officer (AML Officer), including notification to the SROs;
- ongoing AML employee training; and
- an independent test of the firm's AML program, annually for most firms.

4.10.2 The Customer Identification Program

Section 326 of the USA PATRIOT Act amended the BSA to require financial institutions, including broker–dealers, to establish written customer identification programs (CIP). Treasury's implementing rule requires a broker–dealer's CIP to include, at a minimum, procedures for:

- obtaining customer identifying information from each customer prior to account opening;
- verifying the identity of each customer, to the extent reasonable and practicable, within a reasonable time before or after account opening;
- making and maintaining a record of information obtained relating to identity verification;
- determining within a reasonable time after account opening or earlier whether a customer appears on any list of known or suspected terrorist organizations designated by Treasury; and
- providing each customer with adequate notice, prior to opening an account, that information is being requested to verify the customer's identity.

The CIP rule provides that, under certain defined circumstances, broker–dealers may rely on the performance of another financial institution to fulfill some or all of the requirements of the broker–dealer's CIP. For example, in order for a broker–dealer to rely on the other financial institution the reliance must be reasonable. The other financial institution also must be subject to an AML compliance program rule and be regulated by a federal functional regulator. The broker–dealer and other financial institutions must enter into a contract and the other financial institution must certify annually to the broker–dealer that it has implemented an AML program. The other financial institution must also certify to the broker–dealer that the financial institution will perform the specified requirements of the broker–dealer's CIP.

4.10.3 The Correspondent Account

Sections 312, 313, and 319 of the USA PATRIOT Act, which amended the BSA, are interrelated provisions involving accounts called "correspondent accounts." These interrelated provisions include prohibitions on certain types of correspondent accounts (those maintained for foreign "shell" banks) as well as requirements for risk-based due diligence of foreign correspondent accounts more generally.

In addition, Treasury has clarified that, for a broker–dealer, a "correspondent account" includes:

- accounts to purchase, sell, lend, or otherwise hold securities, including securities repurchase arrangements;
- prime brokerage accounts that clear and settle securities transactions for clients;
- accounts for trading foreign currency;
- custody accounts for holding securities or other assets in connection with securities transactions as collateral; and
- over-the-counter derivatives contracts.

A broker–dealer is prohibited from establishing, maintaining, administering, or managing "correspondent accounts" in the United States for, or on behalf of, foreign "shell" banks. Broker–dealers also must take steps to ensure that they are not indirectly providing correspondent banking services to foreign shell banks through foreign banks with which they maintain correspondent relationships. In order to assist institutions in complying with the prohibitions on providing correspondent accounts to foreign shell banks, Treasury has provided a model certification that can be used to obtain information from foreign bank correspondents. In addition, Under Sections 313 and 319 of the USA Patriot Act, broker–dealers must obtain records in the United States of foreign bank owners and agents for service of process.

Due Diligence Regarding Foreign Correspondent Accounts: A broker–dealer is required to establish a risk-based due diligence program for any "correspondent accounts" maintained for foreign financial institutions. The due diligence program, which is required to be a part of the broker–dealer's overall AML program, must include appropriate, specific, risk-based policies, procedures, and controls reasonably designed to enable the broker–dealer to detect and report, on an ongoing basis, any known or suspected money laundering conducted through or involving any foreign correspondent account.[3] Treasury has finalized a related rule that states when enhanced due diligence on foreign financial institutions is required.

4.10.4 Due Diligence Programs for Private Banking Accounts

Section 312 of the USA PATRIOT Act amended the BSA to, among other things, impose special due diligence requirements on financial

[3] Section 312 of the Patriot Act.

institutions, including broker–dealers, that establish, maintain, administer, or manage a private banking account or a "correspondent account" in the United States for a "non-United States person." Treasury's regulations provide that a "covered financial institution" is required to maintain a due diligence program that includes policies, procedures, and controls that are reasonably designed to detect and report any known or suspected money laundering or suspicious activity conducted through or involving a "private banking account" that is established, maintained, administered, or managed in the United States by the financial institution. In addition, the regulations set forth certain minimum requirements for the required due diligence program with respect to private banking accounts and require enhanced scrutiny to any such accounts where the nominal or beneficial owner is a "senior foreign political figure." The regulations define a "private banking account" as an account that: (a) requires a minimum deposit of assets of at least $1,000,000; (b) is established or maintained on behalf of one or more non-US persons who are direct or beneficial owners of the account; and (c) has an employee assigned to the account who is a liaison between the broker–dealer and the non-US person.

The definition of "senior foreign political figure" extends to any member of the political figure's immediate family, and any person widely and publicly known to be a close associate of the foreign political figure as well as any entities formed for the benefit of such persons (such persons are commonly referred to as PEPs, or Politically Exposed Persons). Broker–dealers providing private banking accounts must take reasonable steps to:

- determine the identity of all nominal and beneficial owners of the private banking accounts;
- determine whether any such owner is a "senior foreign political figure" and therefore subject to enhanced scrutiny that is reasonably designed to detect transactions that may involve the proceeds of foreign corruption;
- determine the source of funds deposited into the private banking account and the purpose and use of such account;
- review the activity of the account as needed to guard against money laundering; and
- report any suspicious activity, including transactions involving senior foreign political figures that may involve proceeds of foreign corruption.

4.10.5 *Suspicious Activity Monitoring and Reporting*

Section 356 of the USA Patriot Act amended the BSA to require broker–dealers to monitor for, and report, suspicious activity (so-called SAR reporting). Broker–dealers must report the suspicious activity using a form Treasury has issued for the securities and futures industry, the SAR-SF (also referred to as FinCEN Form 101). The form, which is confidential, includes instructions. Broker–dealers must maintain a copy of any SAR-SF filed and supporting documentation for a period of five years from the date of filing the SAR-SF. In situations that require immediate attention, such as terrorist financing or ongoing money laundering schemes, broker–dealers should immediately notify law enforcement in addition to filing a SAR-SF. In addition, if a firm wishes to report suspicious transactions that may relate to terrorist activity, in addition to filing a SAR-SF.

4.11 Global Organizations

4.11.1 *The Financial Action Task Force on Money Laundering (FATF)*

Formed in 1989 by the G7 countries, the Financial Action Task Force on Money Laundering (FATF) is an intergovernmental body whose purpose is to develop and promote an international response to combat money laundering. The FATF Secretariat is housed at the headquarters of the OECD in Paris. In October 2001, FATF expanded its mission to include combating the financing of terrorism. FATF is a policy-making body that brings together legal, financial, and law enforcement experts to achieve national legislation and regulatory AML and CFT reforms. As of 2019, its membership consists of 36 countries and territories and two regional organizations. FATF works in collaboration with a number of international bodies and organizations. These entities have observer status with FATF, which does not entitle them to vote, but permits them full participation in plenary sessions and working groups. FATF has developed 40 recommendations on money laundering and nine special recommendations regarding terrorist financing. FATF assesses each member country against these recommendations in published reports. Countries seen as not being sufficiently compliant with such recommendations are subject to financial sanctions.

FATF's three primary functions with regard to money laundering are:

1. monitoring members' progress in implementing anti-money laundering measures;
2. reviewing and reporting on laundering trends, techniques, and countermeasures; and
3. promoting the adoption and implementation of FATF anti-money laundering standards globally.

The FATF currently comprises 34 members' jurisdictions and two regional organizations, representing most major financial centers in all parts of the globe.

4.11.2 The Five Eyes Law Enforcement Group's Money Laundering Working Group ("FELEG MLWG")

The mission of the group is to collaborate, inspire, and innovate to prevent, disrupt, and dismantle the money laundering activities and capabilities of international crime groups and networks impacting adversely on FELEG jurisdictions. The FELEG MLWG is comprised of members from the Australian Federal Police, Australian Criminal Intelligence Commission, New Zealand Police, the Royal Canadian Mounted Police, the United Kingdom's National Crime Agency, the DEA, the IRS, HSI, and the FBI.

4.11.3 The International Money Laundering Information Network (IMoLIN)

The International Money Laundering Information Network (IMoLIN) is an Internet-based network assisting governments, organizations, and individuals in the fight against money laundering. IMoLIN has been developed with the cooperation of the world's leading anti-money laundering organizations. Included herein is a database on legislation and regulation throughout the world (AMLID), an electronic library, and a calendar of events in the anti-money laundering field. Please be advised that certain aspects of IMoLIN are secured and therefore not available for public use. This multifaceted Web site serves the global anti-money laundering community by providing information about national money laundering and financing of terrorism laws and regulations and contacts for inter-country assistance. Inter alia, it identifies areas for improvement in domestic laws, countermeasures, and international cooperation. Policy practitioners, lawyers, and law enforcement officers all regularly use IMoLIN as a key reference point in their daily work. The information on IMoLIN is freely available to all Internet users, with the exception of AMLID, which is a secure database. The key features of the IMoLIN system are: the Anti-Money Laundering International Database (AMLID), a compendium of analyses of anti-money laundering laws and regulations, including two general classes of money laundering control measures (domestic laws and international cooperation) as well as information about national contacts and authorities. AMLID is a secure, multi-lingual database and is an important reference tool for law enforcement officers involved in cross-jurisdictional work. The AMLID questionnaire was updated to reflect new money laundering trends and standards and takes into account provisions related to terrorist financing and other current standards, such as the revised FATF 40+9 Recommendations. In addition, the revised AMLID questionnaire now includes a Conventions Framework section. This new section gives an overview of the status of a country or territory to the international conventions applicable to anti-money laundering/countering the financing of terrorism (AML/CFT) as well as the status of a country or territory to bilateral/multilateral treaties or agreements on mutual legal assistance in criminal matters and extradition; the reference section that contains details of the UN's latest research, abstracts of the best new research from governments and international organizations and a bibliography; a click-on map that takes users to regional lists of national legislation. Eventually, this section will contain the full text or links to the full text of all national anti-money laundering/countering the financing of terrorism (AML/CFT) legislation and regulations throughout the world. The database now contains legislation from some 163 jurisdictions, and since January 2005, more than 250 new/amended AML/CFT legislation and regulations were collected to be included in the database; International Norms and Standards: model laws for common law and civil law systems, standards, conventions, and legal instruments; a worldwide calendar of events that lists current training events and conferences at national, regional, and international level; and a links section that includes links to the Web sites of related regional organizations active in the field of AML/CFT and financial intelligence units (FIUs).

4.11.4 The New EU Anti-Money Laundering Legislation

1. The Fifth Money Laundering Directive

On April 19, 2018, the European Parliament has adopted the Fifth Anti-Money Laundering Directive. The final text was published on June 19, 2018. EU members have 18 months to transpose the Fifth Directive into national law. That is, EU member states must give effect to the provisions of 5AMLD under local law by January 10, 2020. However, some countries have already done so. The fifth Anti-Money Laundering Directive improves the powers of FIUs, increases the transparency around beneficial ownership information, and regulates virtual currencies and prepaid cards to better prevent terrorist financing. The Fifth Directive is more of a series of amendments to the structure of the Fourth Directive, adding various additional provisions that were not included in the text of 4AMLD. The Fifth Directive has been extended to cover all forms of tax advisory service, lettings agents, and art dealers. The main changes are: (i) focused on enhanced powers for direct access to information and increased transparency around beneficial ownership information and trusts and (ii) crypto-currencies become regulated entities under the scope of the directive.

- Enhanced powers for direct access to information and increased transparency

While many member states already conduct due diligence and report suspicious transactions, the Fifth Directive makes it a legal requirement. 5AMLD prescribes the following specific enhanced due diligence measures for business relationships and transactions involving high-risk third countries[4]:

– obtaining additional information on the customer, ultimate beneficial owner ("UBO"), and the intended nature of the business relationship;

[4]As of 13 February 2019, the European Commission considers the following to be high-risk third countries: Afghanistan; American Samoa; The Bahamas; Botswana; DPR Korea; Ethiopia; Ghana; Guam; Iran; Iraq; Libya; Nigeria; Pakistan; Panama; Puerto Rico; Samoa; Saudi Arabia; Sri Lanka; Syria; Trinidad and Tobago; Tunisia; US Virgin Islands; Yemen.

- obtaining information on the source of funds and wealth of the customer and UBO and the reasons for the intended or performed transactions;
- obtaining approval of senior management for establishing or continuing the business relationship; and
- conducting enhanced monitoring of the business relationship by increasing the number and timing of controls applied and selecting patterns of transactions that need further examination.

The Fifth Directive goes further by allowing public access to these records, even without having to demonstrate any kind of "legitimate interest." Trusts also are required to meet greater transparency obligations, including the beneficial ownership requirements. The threshold for identifying beneficial ownership is reduced from 25 to 10% for entities posing significant money laundering or tax evasion risks. The Fifth Directive requires enhanced due diligence when dealing with transactions from high-risk countries, and obtaining evidence of the source of funds and source of wealth, information on beneficial ownership and background to the intended transaction.

- crypto-currencies become regulated entities

The new legislation covers two types of crypto-currency business:

- "providers engaged in exchange services between virtual currencies and fiat currencies" (i.e., crypto-currency exchanges) and
- "custodian wallet providers" (i.e., crypto-currency wallet services) where the service holds its users' private keys.

The aforementioned crypto-currency businesses are obligated to implement measures to counter money laundering and terrorist fund-raising, such as customer due diligence (including KYC) and transaction monitoring. They are also required to maintain comprehensive records and report suspicious transactions, as traditional financial institutions, such as banks.

2. The Sixth Directive

Approximately six months after the adoption of the 5th EU Anti-Money Laundering Directive (5AMLD), the European Parliament published further rules to strengthen the fight against money laundering through the 6th EU Money Laundering Directive. The Sixth EU Anti-Money Laundering Directive ("6AMLD") came into force at the EU level on December 2, 2018, and EU member states are required to implement it by December 3, 2020. It focuses on standardizing the approach of EU member states to the offense of money laundering and expanding the scope for potential liability for money laundering and the range of sanctions that EU member states are required to impose under local law. 6AMLD requires EU member states to incorporate corporate liability for money laundering into national law for both the primary money laundering offenses, and for failures in a legal person's supervision or control leading to money laundering on its behalf. The key amendments under 6AMLD include, inter alia:

- Unified list of predicate offenses

The 6AMLD lists 22 specific predicate offenses for money laundering which all EU member states must criminalize (i.e., environmental offenses, cybercrime, and direct and indirect tax offenses). To that end, EU member states and regulated firms would need to develop an in-depth understanding of the predicate offenses, the relevant risk factors and typologies involved.

- Aiding and abetting, attempting and inciting

6AMLD broadens the scope of money laundering offenses to include aiding, abetting, and attempting to commit an offense of money laundering as a criminal offense.

- Extension of criminal liability to legal persons

6AMLD extends criminal liability to legal persons (e.g., companies or incorporated partnerships) as well as individuals in certain positions (representatives, decision-makers or those with authority to exercise control) who commit offenses for the benefit of their organization, including where the offense was made possible by the lack of supervision or control of the individual.

- Increased international cooperation for the prosecution of money laundering

In cases where two member states claim jurisdiction over the prosecution of an offense, 6AMLD requires that they collaborate and agree to prosecute in a single Member State. More, 6AMLD contains other measures for a "more efficient and swifter cross-border cooperation between competent authorities," as well as requirements for member states to have "effective investigative tools."

- Tougher punishments

6AMLD increases the minimum prison sentence for money laundering offenses for individuals from one year to four years, in addition to a variety of other "dissuasive" sanctions. It also includes punishments for legal persons, including exclusion from public benefits or aid; a temporary or even permanent ban from doing business; compulsory winding-up; and a temporary or permanent closure of establishments used to commit the offense.

- Requirement for dual criminality for specified offenses

6AMLD requires member states to criminalize money laundering arising from six specified predicate offenses,[5] even if the conduct constituting the predicate offense was lawful in the jurisdiction in which it was committed.

4.12 AML Challenges

The implementation of AML regulations faces multiple facet challenges on the part of criminal organizations which try to undermine the effort. They use virtual currencies, purchase of real estates, and arts to hide their illicit activities.

[5]The six specified offenses are: participation in an organized criminal group and racketeering; terrorism; trafficking in human beings and migrant smuggling; sexual exploitation (including of children); illicit trafficking in narcotics and psychotropic substances; and corruption.

4.12.1 Virtual Currencies

Virtual currencies offer yet another alternative to cash. Criminals use virtual currencies to conduct illicit transactions because these currencies offer potential anonymity. This is because virtual currency transactions are not necessarily tied to a real-world identity and enable criminals to quickly move criminal proceeds among countries. Transactions denominated in CVC are subject to FinCEN regulations regardless of whether the CVC are represented by a physical or digital token, whether the type of ledger used to record the transactions is centralized or distributed, or the type of technology utilized for the transmission of value. The term “virtual currency” refers to a medium of exchange that can operate like currency but does not have all the attributes of “real” currency. CVC is a type of virtual currency that either has an equivalent value as currency or acts as a substitute for currency, and is therefore a type of “value that substitutes for currency.”[6]

However, certain activities are excluded from the definition of “money transmitter.” Under FinCEN regulations, a person is not considered a money transmitter if that person only:

(a) provides the delivery, communication, or network access services used by a money transmitter to support money transmission services;
(b) acts as a payment processor to facilitate the purchase of, or payment of a bill for, a good or service through a clearance and settlement system by agreement with the creditor or seller;
(c) operates a clearance and settlement system or otherwise acts as an intermediary solely between BSA-regulated institutions;
(d) physically transports currency, other monetary instruments, other commercial paper, or other value that substitutes for currency as a person primarily engaged in such business, such as an armored car, from one person to the same person at another location or to an account belonging to the same person at a financial institution, provided that the person engaged in physical transportation has no more than a custodial interest in the currency, other monetary

[6]FIN-2019-G001 (May 9, 2019): Application of FinCEN’s Regulations to Certain Business Models Involving Convertible Virtual Currencies, p. 7.

instruments, other commercial paper, or other value at any time during the transportation;

(e) provides prepaid access; or

(f) accepts and transmits funds only integral to the sale of goods or the provision of services, other than money transmission services, by the person who is accepting and transmitting the funds.

4.12.2 Purchase of Real Estates

Criminals can easily convert their illicit proceeds into clean funds by purchasing real estate and other assets. Corrupt foreign government officials in Nigeria, the Democratic Republic of Congo,[7] Equatorial Guinea Republic,[8] and many others, who steal from their own people, extort

[7]The Democratic Republic of the Congo's (DRC) efforts to counter money laundering and terrorist financing (AML/CFT) are inadequate. Kleptocrats and terrorists from all around the world are utilizing the DRC's banking system as an ideal platform to launder the proceeds of their illicit activities. Unless the authorities of the DRC undertake significant effort to combat that these deficiencies potentially empower criminals, corrupt officials, and terrorists and threaten the integrity of the international financial system. That is, the DRC's government, if any, should enact laws prohibiting banks from opening anonymous accounts and encourage banks to adopt stricter controls on accounts managed by politically exposed persons (PEPs).

In June 2019, the US Department of the Treasury's Office of Foreign Assets imposed sanctions on Corneille Nangaa, the head of Congo's Independent National Electoral Commission, Norbert Basengezi his deputy and Marcellin Basengezi, for their alleged "persistent corruption" and delaying the vote that originally had been scheduled for late 2016. The DRC has become a platform for narco-traffickers since Joseph Kabila acceded to power in 2001. Prior to the recent sanctions, the US Treasury Department imposed sanctions on Israeli businessman Dan Gertler in December 2017, alleging he used his friendship with Kabila to amass a fortune through corrupt and opaque mining and oil deals. In July 2019, the FinCEN recommended banks operating in the DRC to the lenders put in place rigorous control and monitoring of the accounts of politically exposed people, given the widespread corruption in the DRC.

[8]A recent case involving Teodoro Nguema Obiang Mangue, the Second Vice President of Equatorial Guinea, highlights the challenge of successfully prosecuting money laundering schemes when parties have concealed the true ownership of bank accounts and assets. In that case, Nguema Obiang reported an official government salary of less than $100,000 a year during his 16 years in public office. Nguema Obiang, however, used his position and influence to amass more than $300 million in assets through fraud and corruption, money which he used to buy luxury real estate and vehicles, among other things. Nguema Obiang then orchestrated a scheme to fraudulently open and use bank accounts at financial institutions in California to funnel millions of dollars into the United States. Because US banks

businesses, or seek and accept bribery payments, have funneled their illicit gains into the US financial system. The flow of kleptocracy proceeds into the US financial system distorts our markets and threatens the transparency and integrity of our financial system. Moreover, kleptocracy erodes trust in government and private institutions, undermines confidence in the fairness of free and open markets, and breeds contempt for the rule of law, which threatens our national security.

4.12.3 The AML and Art Markets

Art Market Operators are at risk of being misused by persons seeking to launder the proceeds of criminal activity, thereby creating potentially serious reputational, legal, and financial consequences for the art trade.[9] As a means of combating anti-money laundering the art market operators should implement a reasonably designed risk-based approach by which they identify the criteria to measure potential money laundering risks, such as: (i) the identification of the money laundering risks of its clients, services, and transactions will allow art market operators (ii) the determination and implementation of proportionate measures and controls to mitigate these risks.[10]

The application of a risk-based approach to address money laundering in the art market will require the art market operator to establish its risk profile, taking account of the following, which is a non-exhaustive list[11]:

- countries where sales are conducted;
- jurisdictions where the Art Market Operator obtains its inventory;
- markets;

were unwilling to deal with Nguema Obiang out of concerns that his funds derived from corruption, Nguema Obiang used nominees to create companies that opened accounts in their names, thus masking his relationship to the accounts and the source of the funds brought into the United States. The Department ultimately reached a settlement of its civil forfeiture actions against assets owned by Nguema Obiang. However, the Department needs effective legal tools to directly target these types of fraudulent schemes and protect the integrity of the US financial system from similar schemes.

[9] Basel Art Trade Anti-Money Laundering Principles (2018), p. 1.

[10] Basel Art Trade Anti-Money Laundering Principles (2018), p. 4.

[11] Basel Art Trade Anti-Money Laundering Principles (2018), p. 4.

- delivery channels;
- services offered to clients;
- types of transactions;
- client profiles;
- the location of contracting parties;
- the source of funds;
- financing methods;
- the value of the art objects; and
- any other factors that the Art Market Operator may determine relevant when establishing its own risk profile, which it will then use to develop appropriate measures to mitigate the AML risks of its business.

The Art Market Operator efforts in combating AML are rendered more difficult as the client—beneficial ownership, for reasons either legitimate or not, can be obscured behind multiple layers of intermediaries, often located in opaque jurisdictions. To that end, the "Know Your Customer (KYC)" requirements however go beyond the basic knowledge of buyer and seller as referred to in any contract between them. Client identity verification involves obtaining supporting evidence that reinforces the claim of identity. Verification of identity will depend on the type of business relationship, as follows[12]:

- Natural persons: Identity will be verified on the basis of official identity papers or other reliable, independent source documents, data, or information as may be appropriate under the circumstances.
- Corporations, partnerships, foundations: Identity will be verified on the basis of documentary evidence of due organization and existence.
- Trusts: Identity will be verified on the basis of appropriate evidence of formation and existence or similar documentation. The identity of the trustees will be established and verified.

In the context of client identification, the following are categories of persons that may require enhanced due diligence:

[12] Basel Art Trade Anti-Money Laundering Principles (2018), p. 6.

- persons residing in and/or having funds sourced from countries identified by credible sources as having inadequate AML standards or representing high risk for crime and corruption;
- persons engaged in types of economic or business activities or sectors known to be susceptible to money laundering;
- certain categories of "Politically Exposed Persons"[13];
- persons who are not physically present.[14]

AML focuses mainly on transactions undertaken to disguise the proceeds of a crime. To that end, the Art Market Operator should:

- only accept payments from reputable financial institutions in countries that have implemented reasonable measure to address money laundering, countering the financing of terrorism and tax evasion;
- adopt a policy of not accepting payments from third parties; and
- not accept cash or multiple cash payments for high-value transactions.

Cash transfers are generally to be discouraged wherever possible. Where cash transactions are permitted and exceed EUR 10,000 (or equivalent local currency) or the amount specified in applicable legal and regulatory standards, the Art Market Operator should conduct enhanced due diligence on the buyer.[15] More, whenever the source of funds gives rise to grounded suspicions of money laundering and in the absence of plausible explanation, the Art Market Operator must report those suspicions to the appropriate authorities.

Finally, Art Market Operators are required to keep records of the following[16]:

[13] Refers to individuals holding or, as appropriate, having held, senior, prominent, or important public positions with substantial authority over policy, operations, or the use or allocation of government-owned resources, such as senior government officials, senior executives of government corporations, senior politicians, important political party officials, as well as their close family and close associates.

[14] Business relationships that are conducted through the Internet, telephone, or similar technology or are otherwise through non-face-to-face interactions will need to be assessed by the Art Market Operator prior to transactions taking place and, in some circumstances, enhanced due diligence may be appropriate for such relationships.

[15] Basel Art Trade Anti-Money Laundering Principles (2018), p. 9.

[16] Basel Art Trade Anti-Money Laundering Principles (2018), p. 10.

- clients' identification as well as documents;
  obtained in connection with the verification of identity and the results of enhanced due diligence searches;
- evidence of searches carried out in relation to the provenance of the art object; and
- any deviations from the risk-based approach. These records shall be maintained for a prescribed lapse of time (typically at least 5 years from completion of the transaction or the end of the business relationship, though some countries require substantially longer than this).

4.13 Closing the Loopholes

Several proposals are under consideration in order to enhance the efficiency of AML laws.

4.13.1 The Beneficial Ownership Identification

- The misuse of legal entities posed a significant money laundering risk. The pervasive use of shell companies, front companies, nominees, or other means to conceal the true beneficial owners of assets is a significant loophole in this country's Anti-Money Laundering (AML) regime.[17] Opaque corporate structures facilitate anonymous access to the financial system for every type of criminal and terrorist activity. Narco-traffickers, corrupt leaders, rogue states, terrorists, and fraudsters of all kinds establish domestic shell companies to mask and further criminal activity, to invest and buy assets with illicit proceeds, and to prevent law enforcement and others from efficiently and effectively investigating tips or leads.[18] One of the most public revelations into alleged illicit actors' use of shell companies to conceal

[17] Statement of Steven M. D'Antuono Acting Deputy Assistant Director, Criminal Investigative Division Federal Bureau of Investigation Before the United States Senate Committee on Banking, Housing, and Urban Affairs For a Hearing Entitled "Combatting Illicit Financing by Anonymous Shell Companies" (May 21, 2019).

[18] The UN Office on Drugs and Crimes estimates that global illicit proceeds total more than $2 trillion annually, and proceeds of crime generated in the United States were estimated to total approximately $300 billion in 2010.

ownership was the former Panamanian law firm Mossack Fonseca.[19] Had beneficial ownership information been available, and more quickly accessible to law enforcement and others, it would have been harder and more costly for the aforementioned criminals to hide their illicit activities. Identification of the beneficial ownership of these shell corporations would allow AML enforcement agencies to be more effective and efficient in preventing these crimes from occurring in the first place. For instance, a New York company that was used to conceal Iranian assets, including those designated for providing financial services to entities involved in Iran's nuclear and ballistic missile program.[20] A clearer system of information and identification on the actors behind shell companies is more than necessary to efficiency of the Office of Foreign Assets Control's (OFAC) sanctions, the Financial Crimes Enforcement Network's anti-money laundering authorities.[21] That is, the collection of beneficial ownership information at the time of company formation would significantly reduce the amount of time currently required to research who is behind anonymous shell companies, and at the same time, prevent the flight of assets and the destruction of evidence. In the United States, the inexistence of federal corporate laws and corporate structures are formed pursuant to state-level registration requirements, and while states require varying levels of information on the officers, directors, and managers, none require information regarding the identity of individuals who ultimately own or control legal entities upon formation of these entities.[22] The Bank Secrecy Act (BSA) of 2018.

[19] International Consortium of Investigative Journalists (2018): New Panama Papers Leak Reveals Firm's Chaotic Scramble to Identify Clients, Save Business Amid Global Fallout.

[20] Testimony for the Record Kenneth A. Blanco Director Financial Crimes Enforcement Network U.S. Department of the Treasury Committee on Banking, Housing and Urban Affairs United States Senate (May 21, 2019).

[21] Testimony for the Record Kenneth A. Blanco Director Financial Crimes Enforcement Network U.S. Department of the Treasury Committee on Banking, Housing and Urban Affairs United States Senate (May 21, 2019).

[22] Statement of Steven M. D'Antuono Acting Deputy Assistant Director, Criminal Investigative Division Federal Bureau of Investigation Before the United States Senate Committee on Banking, Housing, and Urban Affairs For a Hearing Entitled "Combating Illicit Financing by Anonymous Shell Companies" (May 21, 2019), p. 1.

The Bank Secrecy Act (BSA) establishes program, recordkeeping and reporting requirements for national banks, federal savings associations, federal branches, and agencies of foreign banks. As of April 1, 2013, financial institutions must use the Bank Secrecy Act BSA E-Filing System in order to submit Suspicious Activity Reports. Under the Bank Secrecy Act (BSA) and related anti-money laundering laws, banks must:

- establish effective BSA compliance programs;
- establish effective customer due diligence systems and monitoring programs;
- screen against Office of Foreign Assets Control (OFAC) and other government lists;
- establish an effective suspicious activity monitoring and reporting process;
- develop risk-based anti-money laundering program.

A financial institution is required to file a suspicious activity report no later than 30 calendar days after the date of initial detection of facts that may constitute a basis for filing a suspicious activity report. If no suspect was identified on the date of detection of the incident requiring the filing, a financial institution may delay filing a suspicious activity report for an additional 30 calendar days to identify a suspect. In no case shall reporting be delayed more than 60 calendar days after the date of initial detection of a reportable transaction.

Under the Bank Secrecy Act (BSA), financial institutions are required to assist US government agencies in detecting and preventing money laundering, such as:

- keep records of cash purchases of negotiable instruments;
- file reports of cash transactions exceeding $10,000 (daily aggregate amount); and
- report suspicious activity that might signal criminal activity (e.g., money laundering or tax evasion).

The BSA was amended to incorporate the provisions of the USA PATRIOT Act which requires every bank to adopt a customer identification program as part of its BSA compliance program.

A coordinated effort among AML enforcement agencies is needed. Collecting beneficial ownership information at company formation with all US allies can assist to that end.[23] FATF's Guidance on Transparency and Beneficial Ownership states that[24] countries should take measures to prevent the misuse of legal persons [such as shell companies, corporate structures, and other entity structures] for money laundering and terrorist financing by ensuring that legal persons are sufficiently transparent. In its 2016 Mutual Evaluation Report (MER) of the United States' Anti-Money Laundering and Counter-Terrorist Financing Regime, the FATF highlighted the lack of beneficial ownership information issue as one of the most critical gaps in the United States' compliance with FATF standards.[25] Furthermore, in a 2018 report titled Concealment of Beneficial Ownership, FATF found that, "the lack of [available beneficial ownership in select] countries is a major vulnerability, and professionals operating in countries that have not implemented appropriate regulations [...] represent an unregulated 'back-door' into the global financial system."[26]

Moving forward, the United States may consider similar approach to the one implemented at the level of the European Union under its Fifth Anti-Money Laundering Directive in 2018. Section 25 of the directive deals directly and unequivocally with the requirement that member states acquire and retain corporate beneficial ownership states:

> "Member States are currently required to ensure that corporate and other legal entities incorporated within their territory obtain and hold adequate, accurate and current information on their beneficial ownership. The need for accurate and up-to-date information on the beneficial owner is a key factor in tracing criminals who might otherwise be able to hide their identity behind a corporate structure. The globally interconnected financial system makes it possible to hide and move funds around the world, and money launderers and terrorist financers as well as other criminals have increasingly made use of that possibility."

[23]The FATF is an independent intergovernmental body that develops and promotes policies to protect the global financial system against money laundering, terrorist financing and the financing of proliferation of weapons of mass destruction.

[24]FATF Recommendations 24 and 25.

[25]Statement of Steven M. D'Antuono Acting Deputy Assistant Director, Criminal Investigative Division Federal Bureau of Investigation Before the United States Senate Committee on Banking, Housing, and Urban Affairs For a Hearing Entitled "Combating Illicit Financing by Anonymous Shell Companies" (May 21, 2019), p. 2.

[26]Idem, p. 3.

4.13.2 Coordination, Collaboration, and Information Sharing

Although each bank must ensure that it has an adequate and well-trained personnel in BSA regulatory requirements and has put in place an effective and efficient internal BSA/AML policies, procedures, and processes, it is important that collaborative arrangements be designed and implemented in accordance with the bank's risk profile for money laundering and terrorist financing. The Financial Action Task Force is recommending domestic financial regulators to share additional information beyond the required information. Such an effort can have wider benefits by strengthening the understanding of risks and vulnerabilities. It can also ensure better compliance and leveraging of capacities by the private sector and preventing criminals from exploiting individual financial institutions' lack of awareness of their activity with other institutions.[27]

[27] FATF (2017): Private Sector Information Sharing, p. 22.

PART II

Actors: Regulators and Banks

CHAPTER 5

The Regulators

5.1 General

The United States operates under a dual banking system in which a bank may choose to be chartered by the federal government or by a state. Banks chartered at the state level are subject to supervision by both federal and state supervisors. The eight major US federal financial regulators can be categorized into those focused on prudential banking regulation promoting safety and soundness, including the Federal Reserve, FDIC, OCC, and NCUA; those focused on financial markets, including the SEC and the CFTC; one focused on housing finance, the FHFA; and one focused on consumer financial protection, the CFPB.[1] More, every US bank is subject to regulation, supervision, and examination by a primary federal banking supervisor[2]:

- for national banks and federal savings banks: the OCC;
- for state banks that choose to be members of the Federal Reserve System (state member banks) and bank holding companies: the Federal Reserve;
- for state banks that choose not to become members of the Federal Reserve System (nonmember banks): the FDIC.

[1] U.S. Department of the Treasury (2017): A Financial System that Creates Economic Opportunities—Banks and Credit Unions, p. 24.

[2] BIS-Basel Committee on Banking Supervision (2014): Assessment of Basel III Regulations—United States of America, p. 9.

F. I. Lessambo, *The U.S. Banking System*,
https://doi.org/10.1007/978-3-030-34792-5_5

5.2 Primary Federal Regulators

5.2.1 The Federal Reserve

The Federal Reserve Bank is the central bank of the United States. The Federal Reserve System is a curious mixture of public and private, federal and regional.[3] It does not conduct commercial banking activities, rather the Federal Reserve role consists of maintaining stable economic growth. The Federal Reserve originated from the Owen-Glass[4] bill introduced in both houses of Congress and become law on December 1913. From its inception, the Federal Reserve was assigned three key purposes: (i) to provide an elastic supply of currency; (ii) to provide a means to discount commercial credits; and (iii) to supervise and regulate the nation's banks. Later on, due to changes in our modern economy and needs, the Federal Reserve is assigned to provide full employment as well. The US Federal Reserve System and its Federal Reserve Board is the most powerful central bank in the world.[5]

The Federal Reserve is the primary prudential regulator for a variety of lending institutions, including bank holding companies, certain US branches of foreign banks, and state-chartered banks that are members of the Federal Reserve System.[6] Under the Gramm-Leach-Bliley Act,[7] the Federal Reserve serves as the umbrella regulator for financial holding companies, which are allowed to engage in a broad array of financially related activities (i.e., insurance).

5.2.1.1 *The Organizational Structure of the Federal Reserve System*

As of to date, the Federal Reserve is organized as follow:

[3] Nouriel Roubini and D. Backus (1998): Lectures in Macroeconomics, Chapter 12: Monetary Policy and Commercial Banking.

[4] Representative Carter Glass (1858–1946) of Virginia, and Senator Robert Owen of Oklahoma played significant role in the debate surrounding the institution of the Federal Reserve System in the US Congress.

[5] James C. Baker (2002): The Bank for International Settlements, p. 149.

[6] Edward V. Murphy (2015): Who Regulates Whom and How? An Overview of U.S. Financial Regulatory Policy for Banking and Securities Markets, Congressional Research Service, p. 23.

[7] GLBA; P.L. 106-102.

- The Board of Governors;
- The Federal Open Market Committee;
- The Federal Reserve Banks; and
- The Board of Directors.

1. The Board of Governors (BOG)

The BOG represents the ultimate authority of the Federal Reserve System. It was established as a Federal agency and is composed of seven Governors, mostly professional economists, jurists, appointed by the President of the United States and confirmed by the Senate for a staggered 14-year terms. The Chairman (and Vice Chairman) are also appointed by the President with the advice and consent of the Senate, for four-year terms. The Board of Governors and its staff of about 1700 are located in Washington, DC.

> In selecting the members of the Board, not more than one of whom shall be selected from any one Federal Reserve District, the President shall have due regard to a fair representation of the financial, agricultural, industrial, and commercial interests, and geographical divisions of the country.[8]

However, in practice, the regional restriction placed by the Federal Reserve Act is loosely applied.[9] Ben Bernanke and Donald Kohn, for instance, represent the Atlanta and Kansas City Districts. Neither lived nor worked in these districts at the time of their appointments. Also, despite the requirement that the members of the Federal Reserve Board reflect a range of interests, the Board is dominated by economists and bankers.

The primary aim of the board is to determine and implement monetary policy. The board also exercises supervisory and regulatory activities over the Federal Reserve Banks, bank holding companies, and Federal Reserve System banks. The board decides the percentage of deposits member banks must hold as reserves. It reviews and approves the interest rate, or the discount rate, and charged member banks for Federal

[8] Federal Reserve Act, Section 10.

[9] Patricia S. Pollard (2003): A Look Inside Two Central Banks: The ECB and the Federal Reserve, The Fed of St. Louis, p. 15.

Reserve loans. Furthermore, there are three advisory groups that aid or assist the Board of Governors.[10]

At least four times per year, the twelve members of Federal Advisory Council meet with the members of the Board of Governors to discuss, assess general economic conditions.

2. The Federal Open Market Committee

The Federal Reserve System's vital element is the Federal Open Market Committee (FOMC). The FOMC comprises of the members of the Board of Governors, the President of the Federal Reserve Bank of New York, and Presidents of four other Federal Reserve Banks, who serve on a rotating basis.

3. The Federal Reserve Banks

The Federal Reserve Banks were established by Congress as the operating arms of the United States' central banking system. The 12 districts Federal Reserve banks are: Atlanta, Boston, Chicago, Cleveland, Dallas, Kansas City, Minneapolis, New York, Philadelphia, Richmond, San Francisco, and St. Louis. They operate under the general supervision of the Board of Governors located in Washington, DC. Each Federal Reserve Bank is composed of nine directors. Federal Reserve Banks generate their own income through interest earned on government securities acquired in the course of Federal Reserve monetary policy and through services provided to depository institutions, as required by the Monetary Control Act of 1980.

Each of the Federal Reserve Banks is organized into a "corporation" whose shares are sold to the commercial banks and thrifts operating within its jurisdiction or district. However, they are neither publicly traded corporations nor for-profit corporations. Each year they return to the US Treasury all earnings in excess of Federal Reserve operating and other expenses. The directors of each Federal Reserve Bank are classified

[10]These three advisory groups are: (1) Federal Advisory Council, consisting of one member from each Reserve Bank. Its major concerns involve banking and economic issues, (2) Consumer Advisory Council, consisting of thirty specialists in consumer and financial matters, and (3) Thrift Institutions Advisory Council, consisting of people representing thrift institutions. This Council is concerned with issues affecting those institutions.

into class A, B, and C, depending on how they have been appointed: Three class A directors are selected by the member banks; three class B directors are also elected by member banks to represent the non-banking sector of the economy; and three class C directors are appointed by the Board of Governor and represent non-bank public.

Furthermore, the Federal Reserve Bank of New York is seen as the "primus inter pares" since it not only sits in the world's financial center but also serves as the FOMCs operating arm, conducting open market operations and foreign exchange intervention. Congress chartered these banks and, consequently, has oversight responsibilities for them. It is also worthy to mention that the board of governors have authority to set the interest rates that the twelve banks charge "their member banks for loans as well as determine the amount of reserves that banks must keep on hand, in order to stabilize the economy and prevent wide fluctuations. In addition, the board sets margin requirements for financial securities traded on the stock exchanges. It also establishes maximum interest rates on time deposits and savings deposits for its member banks."[11]

4. The Board of Directors

Each Federal Reserve Bank and the branches thereof are supervised by a board of directors. Each board has three classes of directors (A, B, and C) with three members in each class. These directors contribute local business experience, community involvement, and leadership and reflect the diverse interests of each district. Each board has nine members. Six of the directors are elected by member commercial banks. Three of the directors are appointed by the Board of Governors. From among these three, the Board of Governors selects a chairman and a deputy chairman of the given Bank's board.

5.2.1.2 Role and Functions of the Federal Reserve

The original rationale behind the Federal Reserve Act of December 23, 1913, was to make certain that there will always be an available supply of money and credit in the United States with which to meet unusual banking requirements. Banks of a new class, to be known as Federal Reserve Banks, were to be established and upon these banks is to rest the heavy

[11] http://www.answers.com/topic/fed-federal-reserve-system#cite_note-mpb-85.

responsibility of supporting the structure if credit in periods of financial strain.[12] This makes sense since there is always a foundation that the US economy can turn to in times of financial distress. Historically, the banks had to depend on the loan contraction and the selling of securities. In future, they will resort to the Federal Reserve banks, securing additional funds from these by rediscounting commercial loans.[13] This new system would lend a helping hand in alleviating the financial pressure on the banking institutions. Other reasons stated in the Federal Reserve Act were to furnish an elastic currency, to afford means of rediscounting commercial paper, to establish a more effective supervision of banking in the United States, and for other purposes.[14]

5.2.1.3 The Federal Reserve Policies and Processes

Federal Reserve has several duties that it must follow[15]:

1. Conducting the nation's monetary policy by influencing the monetary and credit conditions in the economy in pursuit of maximum employment, stable prices, and moderate long-term interest rates. This is an important task that the Federal Reserve must perform to ensure that the US economy is stabilized without running into any financial crisis.
2. Regulating and supervision banking institutions to ensure the safety and soundness of the nation's banking and financial system and to protect the credit rights of consumers. This duty protects consumers so that they are not being exploited by the financial institutions.
3. Maintaining the stability of the financial system and containing systemic risk that may arise in financial markets. This goes hand in hand with the aforementioned duties that reduced the risk while preserving a balance.

[12] The Federal Reserve Act of 1913 O.M.W. Sprague (February 1914): *The Quarterly Journal of Economics* 28(2): 213–254. Published by: The MIT Press Stable, http://www.jstor.org/stable/1883621.

[13] The Federal Reserve Act of 1913 O.M.W. Sprague (February 1914): *The Quarterly Journal of Economics* 28(2): 213–254. Published by: The MIT Press Stable, http://www.jstor.org/stable/1883621.

[14] http://www.answers.com/topic/fed-federal-reserve-system#cite_note-mpb-85.

[15] http://www.federalreserve.gov/pf/pdf/pf_complete.pdf.

4. Providing financial services to depository institutions, the US government, and foreign official institutions, including playing a major role in operating the nation's payments system.

All the aforementioned duties emphasize the significance of the supervision and regulation of the Federal Reserve by Congress. In essence, these responsibilities state that the Federal Reserve controls and states the responsibility for the management of total spending, aggregate demand as well as inflation. In carrying out its monetary policy management (via manipulating reserves), the Federal Reserve influences interest rates—especially short-term rates—as well as foreign exchange rates and other financial market prices. And in times of financial crisis, the Federal Reserve's lender-of-last-resort function stabilizes the entire financial system.

5.2.1.4 The Federal Reserve Funding

The FED does not receive its funding from the US Congress. Rather, its funds come from its own investments. The FED receives interests from US Treasury through the open market operation, or on its foreign currency investments. In addition, it receives interest on loans it grants to member banks.

5.2.1.5 Independence of the Federal Reserve

Whether the Federal Reserve is independent or not is still a moot point. According to a study conducted by Mehta, the Federal Bank system of the US cannot be independent mainly because of the following reasons[16]:

> It is stated that the Federal Bank has a tremendous power concentration in the hands of select few, who make decisions for the entire country.

"Although the President has the power to appoint the members into FED's Board of Governors, the bulk of the FED is elected by members of the Board of Governors, Federal Reserve Bank branches, commercial banks, and financial institutions".[17] Furthermore, any error of judgment

[16] http://chir.ag/papers/ind-fed-final.shtml.

[17] http://chir.ag/papers/ind-fed-final.shtml.

by the FED has dire consequences on the overall economy. Those institutions have the tendency of co-opting their own members, regardless of their qualification, expertise in monetary, and tax policies require for the position. Given the crucial nature of its objectives, it is imperative that the Federal Reserve attracts talented civil servants who would bring knowledge and independence of spirit in the debates. For instance, as mentioned in the research paper by Mehta, if the FED were independent, it can run "monetary policies more smoothly and effectively."

In addition, FED's independence can give it power to "immediately avert any crisis" without having to delay or wait upon Congress sideline political show. Having an ability to make self-regulating decisions can work on behalf of the government and give lasting benefits to the United States. Even though the FED is perceived as an independence entity, it is not truly independent. The Federal Reserve is still liable and accountable to Congress and comes under government audit and review. The Federal Reserve officials report regularly to Congress on monetary policy, regulatory policy, and a variety of other issues, and they meet with senior Administration officials to discuss the Federal Reserve's and the federal government's economic programs. The FED also reports to Congress on its finances.[18] This makes sure that the Federal Reserve is constantly being checked and supervised by Congress which maintains equilibrium between checks and balances. While all these interactions, checks, and balances could lead to a higher quality delivery, the result is just the opposite.

The doctrine of central bank independence is meaningless when as in the United States, those to whom the Federal Reserve officers, appear are not well-equipped to understand the premises of the Federal Reserve monetary policy, or become complacent in monitoring the activities reported before them. Independence in a vacuum provides no benefits.

As Professor Stiglitz contrasts it:

> Brazil and India, neither of which have fully independent central banks, are among the good performers; the European Central Bank and the FED are among the poor performers.[19]

[18] http://www.frbsf.org/publications/federalreserve/monetary/structure.html.

[19] Joseph Stiglitz (2010): *Free Fall: America Free Markets, and the Sinking of the World Economy*, p. 142.

5.2.1.6 The Financial Statements of the Federal Reserve

The Reserve Banks' financial statements are audited annually by an independent public accounting firm retained by the Board of Governors. To ensure auditor independence, the Board requires that the external auditor be independent in all matters relating to the audit. That is, the external auditor shall not perform services for the Reserve Banks or others that would place it in a position of auditing its own work, making management decisions on behalf of the Reserve Banks, or in any other way impairing its audit independence. The financial statements of the Board of Governors are prepared in accordance with accounting principles generally accepted in the United States ("GAAP"). The Board of Governors' financial statements are audited annually by an independent public accounting firm retained by the Board's Office of Inspector General. The audit firm also provides a report on compliance and on internal control over financial reporting in accordance with government auditing standards. The Office of Inspector General also conducts audits, reviews, and investigations relating to the Board's programs and operations as well as of Board functions delegated to the Reserve Banks. The financial statements of the Federal Reserve Banks are prepared in accordance with the Financial Accounting Manual for Federal Reserve Banks ("Financial Accounting Manual"). The Board of Governors has developed specialized accounting principles and practices that it considers to be appropriate for the nature and function of a central bank.[20]

1. Consolidated Statements of Conditions

The Federal Reserve's balance sheet includes a large number of assets and liabilities. On every Thursday, the FED issues its weekly H.$.1 report, which provides consolidated statements of the condition of all the Federal Reserve banks. Over the years, the development and the implementation of new lending facilities have increased the complexity of the Federal Reserve balance sheet. The FED balance sheet provides a mine of information concerning the scale and the scope of the FED. The FED balance sheet expands when it buys assets and restricts when it sells assets.

[20]The primary difference between the accounting principles and practices in the Financial Accounting Manual and GAAP is the presentation of all System Open Market Account (SOMA) securities holdings at amortized cost rather than the fair value presentation required by GAAP.

The assets of the Federal Reserve balance sheet consist of for which the FED has to pay money, and include, inter alia:

- holdings of government securities;
- agency and mortgage-backed securities;
- discount window lending;
- lending to other institutions;
- assets of limited liability companies (LLCs) that have been consolidated onto the Federal Reserve's balance sheet; and
- foreign currency holdings associated with reciprocal currency.

Like the assets, the liabilities of the FED increase and decrease whenever the FED buys or sells its assets. The FED main liabilities include:

- Federal Reserve notes;
- Deposits of depository institutions;
- Deposits of the US Treasury;
- Foreign official deposits;
- Other deposits.

Combined Statements of Condition

As of December 31, 2017 and December 31, 2016
(in millions)

		2017	2016
ASSETS			
Gold certificates		$ 11,037	$ 11,037
Special drawing rights certificates		5,200	5,200
Coin		1,892	1,873
Loans	Note 4	134	63
System Open Market Account:	Note 5		
Treasury securities, net (of which $28,053 and $25,195 is lent as of December 31, 2017 and 2016, respectively)		2,545,733	2,567,422
Government-sponsored enterprise debt securities, net (of which $0 and $44 is lent as of December 31, 2017 and 2016, respectively)		4,752	16,648
Federal agency and government-sponsored enterprise mortgage-backed securities, net		1,817,700	1,795,003
Foreign currency denominated investments, net		21,316	19,442
Central bank liquidity swaps		12,067	5,563
Accrued interest receivable		24,744	25,598
Other assets		13	8
Investments held by consolidated variable interest entity (of which $1,720 and $1,742 is measured at fair value as of December 31, 2017 and 2016, respectively)	Note 6	1,722	1,742
Prepaid pension benefit costs	Note 9	14	-
Bank premises and equipment, net	Note 7	2,571	2,564
Items in process of collection		81	118
Other assets		1,001	1,056
Total assets		$ 4,449,977	$ 4,453,337
LIABILITIES AND CAPITAL			
Federal Reserve notes outstanding, net		$ 1,570,727	$ 1,462,939
System Open Market Account:	Note 5		
Securities sold under agreements to repurchase		563,958	725,210
Other liabilities		558	1,012
Liabilities of consolidated variable interest entity (of which $8 and $32 is measured at fair value as of December 31, 2017 and 2016, respectively)	Note 6	9	33
Deposits:			
Depository institutions		1,954,431	1,759,675
Treasury, general account		228,933	399,190
Other deposits		83,018	58,413
Interest payable to depository institutions and others		1,006	403
Accrued benefit costs	Notes 9 and 10	2,332	3,118
Deferred credit items		1,001	922
Accrued remittances to the Treasury		2,337	1,725
Other liabilities		278	255
Total liabilities		4,408,588	4,412,895
Capital paid-in		31,389	30,442
Surplus (including accumulated other comprehensive loss of $3,334 and $3,985 at December 31, 2017 and 2016, respectively)		10,000	10,000
Total capital		41,389	40,442
Total liabilities and capital		$ 4,449,977	$ 4,453,337

The accompanying notes are an integral part of these combined financial statements.

Consolidated Statements of Operations

The Federal Reserve statements of operations include the following items:

- Interest income;
- Interest expense;
- Non-interest income;
- Operating expenses.

Combined Statements of Operations

For the years ended December 31, 2017 and December 31, 2016
(in millions)

		2017	2016
INTEREST INCOME			
Loans	Note 4	$ 1	$ 1
System Open Market Account:	Note 5		
Treasury securities, net		64,267	63,845
Government-sponsored enterprise debt securities, net		416	959
Federal agency and government-sponsored enterprise mortgage-backed securities, net		48,912	46,299
Foreign currency denominated investments, net		(17)	(7)
Central bank liquidity swaps		14	9
Investments held by consolidated variable interest entity	Note 6	15	9
Total interest income		113,608	111,115
INTEREST EXPENSE			
System Open Market Account:	Note 5		
Securities sold under agreements to repurchase		3,365	1,122
Other		7	4
Deposits:			
Depository institutions and others		25,849	12,020
Term Deposit Facility		13	24
Total interest expense		29,234	13,170
Net interest income		84,374	97,945
NON-INTEREST INCOME			
System Open Market Account:	Note 5		
Treasury securities gains (losses), net		28	(15)
Federal agency and government-sponsored enterprise mortgage-backed securities gains, net		8	19
Foreign currency translation gains (losses), net		1,894	(103)
Other		27	35
Investments held by consolidated variable interest entity losses, net	Note 6	(9)	(19)
Income from services		442	434
Reimbursable services to government agencies		698	677
Other		68	64
Total non-interest income		3,156	1,092
OPERATING EXPENSES			
Salaries and benefits		3,085	2,979
Occupancy		325	327
Equipment		184	175
Net periodic pension expense	Note 9	525	565
Other		682	624
Assessments:			
Board of Governors operating expenses and currency costs		1,464	1,410
Bureau of Consumer Financial Protection		573	596
Total operating expenses		6,838	6,676
Net income before providing for remittances to the Treasury		80,692	92,361
Earnings remittances to the Treasury	Note 3o	80,559	91,467
Net income after providing for remittances to the Treasury		133	894
Change in prior service costs related to benefit plans	Notes 9 and 10	59	231
Change in actuarial gains (losses) related to benefit plans	Notes 9 and 10	592	(414)
Total other comprehensive income (loss)		651	(183)
Comprehensive income		$ 784	$ 711

The accompanying notes are an integral part of these combined financial statements.

Consolidated Statements of Changes in Capital

Combined Statements of Changes in Capital

For the years ended December 31, 2017 and December 31, 2016
(in millions, except share data)

		Surplus			
	Capital paid-in	Net income retained	Accumulated other comprehensive income (loss)	Total surplus	Total capital
Balance at December 31, 2015 (590,166,055 shares)	$ 29,508	$ 13,802	$ (3,802)	$ 10,000	$ 39,508
Net change in capital stock issued (redeemed) (18,682,206 shares)	934	-	-	-	934
Comprehensive income:					
Net income	-	894	-	894	894
Other comprehensive loss	-	-	(183)	(183)	(183)
Dividends on capital stock	-	(711)	-	(711)	(711)
Net change in capital	934	183	(183)	-	934
Balance at December 31, 2016 (608,848,261 shares)	$ 30,442	$ 13,985	$ (3,985)	$ 10,000	$ 40,442
Net change in capital stock issued (redeemed) (18,923,950 shares)	947	-	-	-	947
Comprehensive income:					
Net income	-	133	-	133	133
Other comprehensive income	-	-	651	651	651
Dividends on capital stock	-	(784)	-	(784)	(784)
Net change in capital	947	(651)	651	-	947
Balance at December 31, 2017 (627,772,211 shares)	$ 31,389	$ 13,334	$ (3,334)	$ 10,000	$ 41,389

The accompanying notes are an integral part of these combined financial statements.

5.2.1.7 Reforming the Federal Reserve

Over the years, there have been numerous proposals pursuant to the Federal Reserve reforms. In a commentary by Otho Smith, professor at University of Mississippi, Smith asserts to make sure that the Federal Reserve Bank is performing its jobs effectively, there may be some changes that must be mandated in the systems and policies of the FED. There has been debate to reduce the number of regional banks from twelve to five, to be more efficient and ensure its supervisory responsibilities accurately.[21] Another proposal requires that the Federal Reserve be more transparent in its activities so that the general public can better understand the institution.

The FED functions in almost an opaque manner, under its mistaken assumption that the Freedom of information Act did not extent to it, at least in key respects.[22] Transparency would certainly assist the

[21] http://mpra.ub.uni-muenchen.de/18977/1/MPRA_paper_18977.pdf.

[22] Joseph Stiglitz (2010): *Free Fall: America Free Markets, and the Sinking of the World Economy*, p. 52.

FED in its mission, given the significance of its mandate and its impact of Americans' life. The recent decision by a Federal District Court of District of Columbia Washington against the institution constitutes a step in the right direction, if the Circuit Court of Appeals and finally the US Supreme Court are still looking at the best interest of the United States and even the world. The FED decision effects not only the US financial markets, but also other financial markets over the world. Ultimately, the proposed reforms are intended to (a) make the FED more accountable to the public, (b) give the responsible people greater incentives to participate in their assigned activities, and (c) define the FED's goals more specifics.[23] As time passes, the demands of the people vary and one cannot follow the same rules and regulations that were written almost a century ago since they become almost obsolete. It is vital for the Federal Reserve to be at par with current times so that the laws are more practical and sensible. All the aforementioned proposed reforms by the respective parties are justified. The Federal Reserve should have a new and fresh outlook on the way it has been functioning and if there are any reforms that make the policies and processes contemporary and more proficient; Federal Bank should definitely adapt those so that it works more effectively and efficiently. Finally, the Federal Reserve needs to focus more on "the issue of US national debt and asset prices instead of a narrow measure of inflation," said Marc Sumerlin.[24] The Federal Reserve should take into account asset prices in its assessment of overall financial stability. From the European Central Bank experience, it is clear that a constant monitoring of asset prices helps to identify shocks that might hit the economy. Prior to the Wall Street and Consumer Protection Act of 2010, the FED did not incorporate asset prices of the banks and other financial institutions under its scrutiny into its monetary analysis. A clear monitoring of asset prices could prevent or at least mitigate the sub-prime mortgage. That is the FED would have to broaden its view on the inflation to add or consider commodity prices and keep credit growth in check.[25] Monetary policies should not be limited to a

[23]http://mpra.ub.uni-muenchen.de/18977/1/MPRA_paper_18977.pdf.

[24]Marc Sumerlin, The Fed's dual Mandate is not the problem, in WSJ, December 28, 2010.

[25]Marc Sumerlin, Opcit.

single variable—the consumer index price—but rather upon a series of variable such as the price of assets and the exchange rates.[26]

5.2.2 *The Office of the Controller of Currency*

The Office of the Comptroller (OCC) was created in 1863 as part of the Department of the Treasury to supervise federally chartered banks under the National Bank Act and federal savings associations chartered under the Home Owners Loan Act of 1933. The 1863 law was a response to the mismatch of local banks, local money, and conflicting regulatory standards that prevailed before the Civil War.[27] The OCC is the primary prudential regulator for federally chartered banks and thrifts. The head of the OCC, the Comptroller of the Currency, is also a member of the board of the FDIC and a voting member of FSOC. Like the other prudential regulators described below, the OCC has examination powers to enforce its responsibilities for the safety and soundness of nationally chartered banks, and strong enforcement powers, including the ability to issue cease and desist orders and revoke the charter of covered firms. The OCC charters, supervises, and regulates more than 1200 national banks, federal savings associations, and federal branches of foreign banks (collectively, "banks") that cover virtually the entire range of bank asset sizes and business models. Supervised banks range in size from very small community banks to the largest most globally active US banks. The vast majority of them, about 968, have less than $1 billion in assets, while more than 60 have greater than $10 billion in assets. Together, they hold $12.7 trillion in assets—almost 70% of all the assets of the commercial US banks.[28] In addition to institution-level examinations, the OCC

[26] Otto Hieronymi (2009): *Globalization and the Reform of the International Banking and Monetary System*, Palgrave Macmillan, p. 26.

[27] US Department of the Treasury—Office of the Comptroller of Currency: A Short History, p. 1, https://www.occ.treas.gov/about/what-wedo/history/OCC%20history%20final.pdf.

[28] Testimony of Grovetta N. Gardineer (Senior Deputy Comptroller for Bank Supervision Policy and Community Affairs office of the before the Committee on Banking, Housing, and Urban Affairs), United State Senate (May 21, 2019).

oversees systemic risk among nationally chartered banks and thrifts. One example of OCC systemic surveillance is the regular survey of credit underwriting practices. This survey compares underwriting standards over time and assesses whether OCC examiners believe the credit risk of nationally chartered bank portfolios is rising or falling. In addition, the OCC publishes regular reports on the derivatives activities of US commercial banks.

The OCC regulates depository banks and thrifts that have a federal charter (subsidiaries if in a holding company structure).

5.2.3 *The Federal Deposit Insurance Corporation*

The FDIC is given the authority to place failing financial institutions that pose a significant risk to the financial stability of the United States into receivership and require capital instruments issued by failing banks to be written off or otherwise fully absorb losses before taxpayers are exposed to loss (Title II, Section 210 of the Dodd–Frank Act). The FDIC's mission is to maintain stability and public confidence in the nation's financial system by insuring deposits, examining and supervising financial institutions for safety and soundness and consumer protection, and managing failed institutions placed into receivership.[29] The FDIC regulates banks with a state charter that are not members of the Federal Reserve System (subsidiaries if in a holding company structure). The FDIC is the primary federal prudential regulator of state-chartered banks that are not members of the Federal Reserve System. It has, to some extent, similar examination and enforcement powers for the firms it regulates, as the OCC has for federally chartered banks. In addition to its role as a prudential bank regulator, the FDIC administers a deposit insurance fund and resolves failing depositories and certain systemic non-banks.[30] The FDIC provides deposit insurance to all federally insured banks and thrifts, except credit unions. The FDIC administers the Deposit Insurance Fund, which is the primary mechanism used to protect covered deposits at US financial institutions from loss. The

[29] FDIC Mission, Vision, and Values, http://www.fdic.gov/about/mission/index.html.

[30] Edward V. Murphy (2015): Who Regulates Whom and How? An Overview of U.S. Financial Regulatory Policy for Banking and Securities Markets, Congressional Research Service, p. 21.

Deposit Insurance Fund is financed through fees assessed on the insured institutions, with assessments based on the amount of deposits requiring insurance, the amount of assets at each institution, and the degree of risk posed by each institution to the insurance fund. To minimize withdrawals from the Deposit Insurance Fund, the FDIC is assigned backup supervisory authority over approximately 3000 federally insured depository institutions whose primary regulators are the Federal Reserve, OCC, and, until recently, OTS. Among other measures, the FDIC is authorized to conduct a "special examination" of any insured institution "to determine the condition of such depository institution for insurance purposes."[31] To facilitate and coordinate its oversight obligations with those of the primary bank regulators and ensure it is able to protect the Deposit Insurance Fund, the FDIC has entered into an inter-agency agreement with the primary bank regulators.[32] The 2002 version of that agreement, in effect until 2010, stated that the FDIC was authorized to request to participate in examinations of large institutions or higher-risk financial institutions, recommend enforcement actions to be taken by the primary regulator, and if the primary regulator failed to act, take its own enforcement action with respect to an insured institution.

5.2.4 *The National Credit Union Administration*

The National Credit Union Administration (NCUA), originally part of the Farm Credit Administration, became an independent agency in 1970.[33] Created by the US Congress in 1970, the NCUA is an independent federal agency that insures deposits at federally insured credit unions, protects the members who own credit unions, and charters and regulates federal credit unions.[34] The agency operates its headquarters

[31] 12 U.S.C. § 1820(b)(3).

[32] The interagency agreement is entitled, "Coordination of Expanded Supervisory Information Sharing and Special Examinations." During the time period of the Subcommittee's investigation, the 2002 version of the interagency agreement, signed by the FDIC, Federal Reserve, OCC, and OTS, was in effect. In July 2010, the federal financial regulators agreed to adopt a stronger version, discussed later in this Report.

[33] P.L. 91-206, 84 STAT. 49.

[34] www.ncua.org.

in Alexandria, Virginia; its Asset Management and Assistance Center in Austin, Texas, to liquidate credit unions and recover assets; and five regional offices, which carry out the agency's supervision and examination program.

1. Organization of the NCUA

The Board of the NCUA has three members, appointed by the President of the United States, and confirmed by the US Senate. The selected members must have the "general interest of the public, and no more than two members can belong to the same political party." The President selects a Chairperson from the three members of the Board. Candidates for appointment must have a financial services background and have limited to no time on the board of a credit union. Board members can serve a term of 6 years or less based on the services requested by the Board, the President or as Congress allows. Board members are responsible for adopting rules as needed to conduct business transactions of the credit union. The members are required to meet at least once a year before April 1 and as Congress requests throughout the year. Minutes of the Board meeting are recorded and maintained for additional review whenever needed by Congress or the President. Congress must approve new regulations or policies created by the National Credit Union Administration Board before implementation. The Chairperson of the Board is the official representative and speaker for the NCUA, as well as responsible for adopting and implementing regulations of the NCUA Board.

2. NCUA functions

The NCUA protects the safety and soundness of the credit union system by identifying, monitoring, and reducing risks to the National Credit Union Share Insurance Fund. Backed by the full faith and credit of the United States, the Share Insurance Fund provides up to $250,000 of federal share insurance to millions of account holders in all federal credit unions and the overwhelming majority of state-chartered credit unions.[35]

[35] www.ncua.org.

As of September 2016, there were 5573 federally insured credit unions, with assets totaling more than $1.38 trillion, and net loans of $957.3 billion. The NCUA plays a role in helping to ensure broader financial stability as a member of the Federal Financial Institutions Examination Council, which is responsible for developing uniform principles, standards, and report forms, and for promoting uniformity in the supervision of depository financial institutions. The NCUA's Chairman is also a voting member of the Financial Stability Oversight Council,[36] an interagency body tasked with identifying and responding to emerging risks and threats to the financial system.

3. Credit union insurance

The NCUA insures share accounts I federally insured credit unions for $250,000 per qualifying account. The NCUA adds together all single accounts and insures them up to $250,000. Joint accounts are accounts owned by two or more members. It should also be noted that FDIC and NCUA insurances are basically identical, save for the names they assign to different types of accounts. Neither the FDIC nor the NCUA cover robberies or thefts that may occur within a qualifying account. Stolen funds are covered by a "blanket bond" policy.[37]

5.3 State Regulators (Agencies)

State bank regulators operate similarly to the OCC, but at the state level for state-chartered banks. Their oversight works in conjunction with the Federal Reserve and the FDIC. To avoid duplication and regulatory burden, federal and state banking regulators coordinate exam schedules and often alternate exams. The federal agency regulators and state regulators have a hand in bank supervision because of some of the products and services banks may provide. This approach is called functional regulation.

[36]The Council is charged with identifying risks to the financial stability of the United States; promoting market discipline; and responding to emerging risks to the stability of the United States' financial system. The Council consists of 10 voting members and 5 nonvoting members and brings together the expertise of federal financial regulators, state regulators, and an independent insurance expert appointed by the President.

[37]Blanket bond covers embezzlement, defalcation, earthquake, fire, flood, robberies, and other cases in which funds have been stolen.

5.4 Activities-Based Regulators (Agencies)

Activities-based regulators commonly refer to "as non-bank financial regulators" regulate banks activities that fall within the ambit of their missions. The most important are: (i) the Securities and Exchange Commission ("SEC"); (ii) the Commodity Futures Trading Commission ("CFTC"); (iii) the Consumer Financial Protection Bureau ("CFPB").

5.4.1 The Securities and Exchange Commission (SEC)

The SEC was created as an independent agency in 1934 to enforce newly written federal securities laws (P.L. 73-291, 48 Stat. 881). Although the SEC is concerned with ensuring the safety and soundness of the firms it regulates, its primary concern is maintaining fair and orderly markets and protecting investors from fraud. The SEC generally 20 does not have the authority to limit risks taken by non-bank financial institutions or the ability to prop up a failing firm, with some exceptions. Two types of firms come under the SEC's jurisdiction: (1) all corporations that sell securities to the public and (2) securities broker/dealers and other securities markets intermediaries.

Firms that sell securities—stocks and bonds—to the public are required to register with the SEC. Registration entails the publication of detailed information about the firm, its management, the intended uses for the funds raised through the sale of securities, and the risks to investors. The initial registration disclosures must be kept current through the filing of periodic financial statements: annual and quarterly reports (as well as special reports when there is a material change in the firm's financial condition or prospects).

5.4.2 The Commodities and Futures Trading Commission (CFTC)

The CFTC was created in 1974 to regulate commodities futures and options markets, which at the time were poised to expand beyond their traditional base in agricultural commodities to encompass contracts based on financial variables, such as interest rates and stock indexes. The CFTC's mission is to prevent excessive speculation, manipulation of commodity prices, and fraud. Like the SEC, the CFTC oversees industry self-regulatory organizations (SROs)—the futures exchanges and the

National Futures Association—and requires the registration of a range of industry firms and personnel, including futures commission merchants (brokers), floor traders, commodity pool operators, and commodity trading advisers. The Dodd–Frank Act greatly expanded the CFTC's jurisdiction by eliminating exemptions for certain over-the-counter derivatives. As a result, swap dealers, major swap participants, swap clearing organizations, swap execution facilities, and swap data repositories are required to register with the CFTC. These entities are subject to business conduct standards contained in statute or promulgated as CFTC rules.

5.4.3 The Consumer Financial Protection Bureau (CFPB)

Title X of Dodd–Frank created the Consumer Financial Protection Bureau to bring the consumer protection regulation of depository and non-depository financial institutions into closer alignment. The bureau is an independent entity within the Federal Reserve with authority over an array of consumer financial products and services (including deposit taking, mortgages, credit cards and other extensions of credit, loan servicing, check guaranteeing, collection of consumer report data, debt collection, real estate settlement, money transmitting, and financial data processing). CFPB serves as the primary federal consumer financial protection supervisor and enforcer of federal consumer protection laws over many of the institutions that offer these products and services. However, the bureau's regulatory authority varies based on institution size and type. Regulatory authority differs for (1) depository institutions with more than $10 billion in assets, (2) depository institutions with $10 billion or less in assets, and (3) non-depositories. The Dodd–Frank Act also explicitly exempts a number of different entities and consumer financial activities from the bureau's supervisory and enforcement authority. Among the exempt entities are:

- merchants, retailers, or sellers of nonfinancial goods or services, to the extent that they extend credit directly to consumers exclusively for the purpose of enabling consumers to purchase such nonfinancial goods or services;
- automobile dealers;
- real estate brokers and agents;

- financial intermediaries registered with the SEC or CFTC;
- insurance companies; and
- depository institutions with $10 billion or less in assets

5.4.4 *The Financial Crimes and Enforcement Network (FinCEN)*

FinCEN is a bureau within the Department of the Treasury, which mission is to safeguard the financial system from illicit use, combat money laundering, and promote national security through the collection, analysis, and dissemination of financial intelligence and strategic use of financial authorities.[38] FinCEN serves two roles: FinCEN serves in two roles: (i) It is the Financial Intelligence Unit (FIU) for the United States, and (ii) it is the lead anti-money laundering/countering the financing of terrorism (AML/CFT) regulator for the federal government. FinCEN receives approximately 55,000 new financial institution filings each day. The majority of the financial intelligence FinCEN collects comes from two reporting streams: one on large cash transactions exceeding $10,000 and the other on suspicious transactions identified by financial institutions. Targeting third-party money launderers, the intermediaries who help turn dirty money clean, remains a top priority for FinCEN. As part of an incremental approach to regulating the real estate industry, FinCEN issued Geographic Targeting Orders (GTOs) in January 2016 requiring certain US title insurance companies to record and report the beneficial ownership information of legal entities making "all-cash" or rather "non-mortgaged" purchases of high-value residential real estate in Manhattan and in Miami-Dade County, Florida. To combat cybersecurity challenges, FinCEN has established a number of initiatives, both internally and externally, to address new and evolving cybersecurity threats.

5.5 Conclusion

Oscillating between over-regulation and under-regulation over the time, a well-balance approached is needed. Excessive regulation creates barriers to entry for mid-sized and community banks and protect the positions of

[38] US Department of the Treasury—FinCEN (May 24, 2016): Stopping Terror Finance: A Coordinated Government Effort United States House of Representatives Committee on Financial Services Task Force to Investigate Terrorism Financing (Testimony of Testimony of Jennifer Shasky Calvery).

the largest banks. Asset thresholds for increased regulatory requirements create inappropriate incentives, and "one-size –fits-all" regulatory standards undermine a diversification of the business models.[39] Conversely, ill-thought de-regulation as under the current administration poses significant risks to the overall economy.

[39] US Department of the Treasury: A Financial System That Creates Economic Opportunities—Banks and Credit Unions, p. 41.

CHAPTER 6

Commercial Banks and Savings Banks

6.1 General

From 1933 to 1999, the activities of commercial banks were distinctive from those of investment banks. The Glass–Steagall Act of 1933 sought to bring stability back to US financial markets with reforms such as separating commercial banking from investment banking, limiting commercial banks to debt security investments of only investment-grade quality, and prohibiting commercial banks from underwriting risky securities. Both commercial banks and savings & loans provide banking and loan products to consumers. However, there are some differences between the two. Commercial banks, also called national banks, tend to place a greater emphasis on business customers than S&Ls, underwriting billions of dollars in loans for construction projects, expansion plans, acquisitions, and other events. Many of their clients are large corporations and governments. A number of commercial banks also offer investment banking services.

6.2 Commercial Banks

Commercial banks accept customer deposits and offer commercial loans. Most of the banks are small, yet the vast majority of assets are held by less than 125 banks. These banks can be state member banks of the Federal Reserve System or state non-member banks under the jurisdiction for local state banking commissions. The primary difference is that a

F. I. Lessambo, *The U.S. Banking System*,
https://doi.org/10.1007/978-3-030-34792-5_6

state member bank invests in the stock of the Federal Reserve and, prior to the recent recession and financial crisis, has access to specific Federal Reserve borrowing facilities. By law, commercial and savings banks can only engage in traditional banking activities (e.g., making loans, accepting deposits, and providing services for a fee). Banks can serve as referral agents to third parties for insurance and investment services, but cannot engage in insurance underwriting or investment banking. The only exception exists for large banks that establish a financial holding company and are permitted by regulatory approval to set up separate subsidiaries to handle insurance and investment activity. In such cases, the bank must be a separate subsidiary without any involvement with the non-bank subsidiaries under the financial holding company.

6.2.1 Types of Commercial Banks

Commercial banks are classified as either retail banks or wholesale banks.

6.2.1.1 Retail Banking Activities

Retail banks focus on individual consumer's banking relationships. Therefore, individual demand, saving, and time deposits comprise most of liabilities while consumers and small businesses loans linked to key individuals are a higher fraction of the loan portfolio. Retail banking is the cluster of products and services that banks provide to consumers and small businesses through branches, the Internet, and other channels. Banks very often organize their retail activities along three complementary dimensions: customers served, products and services offered, and the delivery channels linking customers to products and services.[1] Institutions organize their retail activities in different ways. Nonetheless, consumers and small businesses constitute the core retail banking clientele. Retail banking units provide various services to customers and small businesses. These services are, for individuals, sales of investment products, insurance brokerage, and financial and retirement planning.[2]

[1]Timothy Clark, Astrid Dick, and others (2007): The Role of Retail Banking in the US Banking Industry-Risk, Return, and Industry Structure, FRBNY Economic Policy Review, December 2007, pp. 39–40.

[2]Timothy Clark, Astrid Dick, and others (2007): The Role of Retail Banking in the US Banking Industry-Risk, Return, and Industry Structure, FRBNY Economic Policy Review, December 2007, p. 42.

To small businesses, retail banking activities include merchant and payments services, cash handling, insurance brokerage, and payroll and employee benefits services. Retail banking is seen as a significant source of revenue and profits to many large banking institutions. The re-emergence of retail banking activities is due to the fact that banks considered them to be a source of stable revenue/profits. Such stability is considered valuable for large banks seeking to offset the volatility of riskier business.[3] However, retail banking will likely be a stable and growing business as long as the consumer sector which feeds it remains strong and stable.

6.2.1.2 Wholesale Banking Activities

Wholesale banks deal primarily with commercial consumers so that they typically operate with fewer consumers deposits, more purchased liabilities, and hold proportionately more business loans to large firms. Wholesale banking pertains to banking services between merchant banks and other financial institutions. This type of banking deals with larger clients, such as large corporations and other banks. Wholesale banking services include currency conversion, working capital financing, large trade transactions, and other types of services. Banking services that are considered "wholesale" are reserved only for government agencies, pension funds, corporations with strong financial statements (i.e., balance sheet, statement of income, and statement of cash flows), and other institutional customers of similar size and stature. These services are made up of cash management, equipment financing, large loans, merchant banking, and trust services, among others. Wholesale banking also refers to the borrowing and lending between institutional banks. This type of lending occurs on the interbank market and often involves extremely large sums of money.

6.2.2 Financial Statements of Commercial Banks

The reported financial statements for banks are, to many respects, different from most companies that investors analyze. For instance, there are no accounts receivables or inventory to assess whether sales are

[3]Timothy Clark, Astrid Dick, and others (2007): The Role of Retail Banking in the US Banking Industry-Risk, Return, and Industry Structure, FRBNY Economic Policy Review, December 2007, p. 50.

increasing or declining. More, there are several unique features of bank financial statements that include how the balance sheet and income statement are laid out.

6.3 Commercial Banks and Monetary Policy

Commercial banks are financial institutions that hold customer deposits, extend personal and business loans, or provide other financial services. Their role in money supply is to offer financing that helps individuals, or businesses make large purchases for which they do not have cash on hand. Commercial banks are intermediaries between the central bank (FED) and the ultimate money borrowers. The Federal Reserve can influence the money supply through commercial banks by changing money reserves or discount rates. Money reserves indicate the overall amount of money commercial banks must retain rather than loaning out. Discount rates work in a similar fashion. Low rates increase the money supply while high rates decrease the money supply.

6.4 Commercial Banks and Credit Policy

Banks issue commercial credit to companies, which then access funds as needed to help meet their financial obligations. Companies use commercial credit to fund daily operations and new business opportunities, purchase equipment, or cover unexpected expenses. Bank lending plays an important role in determining the magnitude of the effect of monetary policy on the economy.[4] The important role played by banks in this transmission mechanism arises from the reserve requirement constraint faced by banks.[5] A commercial bank lending volume contracts when monetary policy is tightened by the Federal Reserve. That is, the loan supply is reduced as the loan portfolios are more responsive to monetary policy. However, the loan portfolios of well-capitalized banks seem to be

[4]Joe Peek and Eric S. Rosengren (2013): The Role of Banks in the Transmission of Monetary, Public Policy Discussion Papers, no. 13-5, Federal Reserve Bank of Boston, MA.

[5]Joe Peek and Eric S. Rosengren (2013): The Role of Banks in the Transmission of Monetary, Public Policy Discussion Papers, no. 13-5, Federal Reserve Bank of Boston, MA, p. 4.

less sensitive to monetary policy shocks.[6] More, the lending channel has been loosened in recent years by developments in financial markets that allow banks to be less dependent on reservable deposits to fund their lending.[7] Several factors may explain such a loosening: (i) the growth in loan securitization, (ii) the expansion of the secondary mortgage market,[8] and (iii) the increasing globalization of banking.[9]

6.5 Commercial Banks and Consumer Protection Policy

The Dodd–Frank Wall Street Reform and Consumer Protection Act, of July 2010 provides consumers' protection. However, the Dodd–Frank is not the sole protection granted to commercial bank customers. Several other laws, regulations, and guidelines do exist.[10] The CFPB was created to provide a single point of accountability for enforcing federal consumer financial laws and protecting consumers in the financial marketplace. Prior to its creation, that responsibility was divided among several agencies.

On May 9, 2019, the Consumer Financial Protection Bureau (CFPB) issued a Notice of Proposed Rulemaking (NPRM) to implement the Fair Debt Collection Practices Act (FDCPA). The proposal aims to provide consumers with clear protections against harassment by debt collectors and straightforward options to address or dispute debts. Among other things, the NPRM would set clear, bright-line limits on the number of calls debt collectors may place to reach consumers on a weekly basis;

[6] R.P. Kishan and T.P. Opiela (2000): Bank Size, Bank Capital, and the Bank Lending Channel, *Journal of Money, Credit and Banking* 32(1): 121–141.

[7] Joe Peek and Eric S. Rosengren (2013): The Role of Banks in the Transmission of Monetary, Public Policy Discussion Papers, no. 13-5, Federal Reserve Bank of Boston, MA, p. 12.

[8] E. Loutskina and P. Strahan (2009): Securitization and the Declining Impact of Bank Finance on Loan Supply-Evidence from Mortgage Originations, *Journal of Finance* 64(2): 861–889.

[9] That is, banks with international operations are more able to insulate their lending activities from domestic liquidity shock, such as monetary policy tightening.

[10] Credit Card Accountability, Responsibility, and Disclosure Act of 2009 (Credit CARD Act of 2009), 2009 Truth in Lending Act (TILA), 1968.

clarify how collectors may communicate lawfully using newer technologies; and require collectors to provide additional information to consumers to help them identify debts and respond to collection attempts.

6.6 Savings Banks

Savings banks are financial institution whose primary purpose consists of accepting savings deposits and paying interest on those deposits. Put differently, savings banks provide a place for people to save their money and accrue interest on their money over time. They originated in Europe during the eighteenth century with the aim of providing access to savings products to all levels in the population. Savings banks frequently originated as part of philanthropic efforts to encourage saving among people of modest means. The earliest municipal savings banks developed out of the municipal pawnshops of Italy. Local savings banks were established in the Netherlands through the efforts of a philanthropic society that was founded in 1783, the first bank opening there in 1817. During the same time, private savings banks were developing in Germany, the first being founded in Hamburg in 1778. The first British savings bank was founded in 1810 as a Savings and Friendly Society by a pastor of a poor parish; it proved to be the forerunner of the trustee savings bank. The origin of savings banking in the United States was similar; the first banks were nonprofit institutions founded in the early 1800s for charitable purposes. With the rise of other institutions performing the same function, mutual savings banks remained concentrated in the northeastern United States.

CHAPTER 7

Investment Banks

7.1 General

Historically, investment banks helped raise capital for business and other endeavors by helping to design, finance, and sell financial products like stocks or bonds. When a corporation needed capital to fund a large construction project, for example, it often hired an investment bank either to arrange a bank loan or to raise capital by designing, financing, and marketing an issue of shares or corporate bonds for sale to investors. Investment banks performed these services in exchange for fees. Today, investment banks also participate in a wide range of other financial activities, including providing broker–dealer and investment advisory services, and trading commodities and derivatives. Investment banks also often engage in proprietary trading, meaning trading with their own money and not on behalf of a customer. Many investment banks are structured today as affiliates of one or more banks. Under the Glass-Steagall Act of 1933, certain types of financial institutions had been prohibited from commingling their services. For example, with limited exceptions, only broker–dealers could provide brokerage services; only banks could offer banking; and only insurers could offer insurance. Each financial sector had its own primary regulator who was generally prohibited from regulating services outside of its jurisdiction.[1] Glass-Steagall also contained

[1] Federal law has never established a "super-regulator" with jurisdiction to police compliance and conduct across banking, brokerage, investment advisory, and insurance sectors, and that remains the case today.

F. I. Lessambo, *The U.S. Banking System*,
https://doi.org/10.1007/978-3-030-34792-5_7

prohibitions against proprietary trading.[2] One reason for keeping the sectors separate was to ensure that banks with federally insured deposits did not engage in the type of high risk activities that might be the bread and butter of a broker–dealer or commodities trader. Another reason was to avoid the conflicts of interest that might arise, for example, from a financial institution pressuring its clients to obtain all of its financial services from the same firm. A third reason was to avoid the conflicts of interest that arise when a financial institution is allowed to act for its own benefit in a proprietary capacity, while at the same time acting on behalf of customers in an agency or fiduciary capacity. Glass-Steagall was repealed in 1999, after which the barriers between banks, broker–dealers, and insurance firms fell. US financial institutions not only began offering a mix of financial services, but also intensified their proprietary trading activities. The resulting changes in the way financial institutions were organized and operated made it more difficult for regulators to distinguish between activities intended to benefit customers versus the financial institution itself. The expanded set of financial services investment banks were allowed to offer also contributed to the multiple and significant conflicts of interest that arose between some investment banks and their clients during the financial crisis.

7.2 Investment Banks in the World

The aforementioned are the largest full-service global investment banks; full-service investment banks usually provide both advisory and financing banking services, as well as sales, market making, and research on a broad array of financial products, including equities, credit, rates, currency, commodities, and their derivatives. Investment banking is comprised of three main areas: investment banking division (IBD), sales and trading (S&T), and asset management. The large global banks typically offer all three services, with smaller banks usually focusing more on the IBD side covering advisory and mergers and acquisitions (M&A). Investment banks help companies and governments and their agencies to raise money by issuing and selling securities in the primary market. They assist public and private corporations in raising funds in the capital

[2] See Section 16 of the Banking Act of 1933, Pub. L. 73-66 (also known as the Glass-Steagall Act).

Table 7.1 Top investment banks in the world

	Top investment banks in the world
1	Goldman Sachs
2	Bank of America Merrill Lynch
3	Morgan Stanley
4	Citigroup
5	Barclays Investment Bank
6	Credit Suisse
7	Deutsche Bank
8	Wells Fargo Securities
9	RBC Capital Markets
10	UBS
11	HSBC
12	Jefferies Group
13	BNP Paribas
14	Mizuho
15	Lazard
16	Nomura
17	Evercore Partners
18	BMO Capital Markets
19	Mitsubishi UFJ Financial Group

markets (both equity and debt), Principal Businesses of Investment Banks (Table 7.1).

7.3 Roles and Duties of an Investment Bank

Investment banks typically play a variety of significant roles when dealing with their clients, including that of market maker, underwriter, placement agent, and broker–dealer. Each role brings different legal obligations under federal securities law.

7.3.1 Market Maker

A "market maker" is typically a dealer in financial instruments that stands ready to buy and sell for its own account a particular financial instrument on a regular and continuous basis at a publicly quoted price.[3]

[3]Section 3(a)(38) of the Securities Exchange Act of 1934 states: "The term 'market maker' means any specialist permitted to act as a dealer, any dealer acting in the capacity of block positioner, and any dealer who, with respect to a security, holds himself out (by

A major responsibility of a market maker is filling orders on behalf of customers. Market makers do not solicit customers; instead they maintain, buy, and sell quotes in a public setting, demonstrating their readiness to either buy or sell the specified security, and customers come to them. For example, a market maker in a particular stock typically posts the prices at which it is willing to buy or sell that stock, attracting customers based on the competitiveness of its prices. This activity by market makers helps provide liquidity and efficiency in the trading market for the security.[4] It is common for a particular security to have multiple market makers who competitively quote the security. Market makers generally use the same inventory of assets to carry out both their market-making and proprietary trading activities. Market makers are allowed, in certain circumstances specified by the SEC, to sell securities short in situations to satisfy market demand when they do not have the securities in their inventory in order to provide liquidity. Market makers have among the most narrow disclosure obligations under federal securities law, since they do not actively solicit clients or make investment recommendations to them. Their disclosure obligations are generally limited to providing fair and accurate information related to the execution of a particular trade.[5]

Market makers are also subject to the securities laws' prohibitions against fraud and market manipulation. In addition, they are subject to legal requirements relating to the handling of customer orders, for example using best execution efforts when placing a client's buy or sell order.[6]

entering quotations in an inter-dealer communications system or otherwise) as being willing to buy and sell such security for his own account on a regular or continuous basis."

[4]See SEC website, http://www.sec.gov/answers/mktmaker.htm; FINRA website, FAQs, "What Does a Market Maker Do?" http://finra.atgnow.com/finra/categoryBrowse.do.

[5]SEC (2011): "Study on Investment Advisers and Broker–Dealers," study conducted by the US Securities and Exchange Commission, at 55, http://www.sec.gov/news/studies/2011/913studyfinal.pdf.

[6]See Responses to Questions for the Record from Goldman Sachs at P SI_ Q FR _G S0046.

7.3.2 Underwriter and Placement Agent

If an investment bank agrees to act as an "underwriter" for the issuance of a new security to the public, such as an RMBS, it typically purchases the securities from the issuer, holds them on its books, conducts the public offering, and bears the financial risk until the securities are sold to the public. By law, securities sold to the public must be registered with the SEC. Underwriters help issuers prepare and file the registration statements filed with the SEC, which explain to potential investors the purpose of a proposed public offering, the issuer's operations and management, key financial data, and other important facts. Any offering document, or prospectus, given to the investing public in connection with a registered security must also be filed with the SEC.

If a security is not offered to the general public, it can still be offered to investors through a "private placement." Investment banks often act as the "placement agent," performing intermediary services between those seeking to raise money and investors. Placement agents often help issuers design the securities, produce the offering materials, and market the new securities to investors. Offering documents in connection with private placements are exempt from SEC registration and are not filed with the SEC. In the years leading up to the financial crisis, RMBS securities were registered with the SEC, while CDOs were sold to investors through private placements. Both of these securities were also traded in a secondary market by market makers. Investment banks sold both types of securities primarily to large institutional investors, such as other banks, pension funds, insurance companies, municipalities, university endowments, and hedge funds. Whether acting as an underwriter or placement agent, a major part of the investment bank's responsibility is to solicit customers to buy the new securities being offered. Under the securities laws, investment banks that act as an underwriter or placement agent for new securities are liable for any material misrepresentation or omission of a material fact made in connection with a solicitation or sale of those securities to investors.[7] The obligation of an underwriter and placement

[7]See Sections 11 and 12 of Securities Act of 1933. See also Rule 10b-5 of the Securities Exchange Act of 1934.

See also, e.g., SEC v. Capital Gains Research Bureau, Inc., 375 U.S. 180, 201 (1963) ("Experience has shown that disclosure in such situations, while not onerous to the advisor, is needed to preserve the climate of fair dealing which is so essential to maintain public confidence in the securities industry and to preserve the economic health of the country.").

agent to disclose material facts to every investor it solicits comes from two sources: the duties as an underwriter specifically, and the duties as a broker–dealer generally. With respect to duties relating to being an underwriter, the US Court of Appeals for the First Circuit observed that underwriters have a "unique position" in the securities industry:

> [T]he relationship between the underwriter and its customer implicitly involves a favorable recommendation of the issued security. ... Although the underwriter cannot be a guarantor of the soundness of any issue, he may not give it his implied stamp of approval without having a reasonable basis for concluding that the issue is sound.[8]

In addition, Section 11 of the Securities Act of 1933 makes underwriters liable to any investor in any registered security if any part of the registration statement "contained an untrue statement of a material fact or omitted to state a material fact required to be stated therein or necessary to make the statements therein not misleading."[9]

7.3.3 Broker–Dealer

Broker–dealers also have affirmative disclosure obligations to their clients. With respect to the duties of a broker–dealer, the SEC has held:

> [W]hen a securities dealer recommends a stock to a customer, it is not only obligated to avoid affirmative misstatements, but also must disclose material adverse facts to which it is aware. That includes disclosure of 'adverse interests' such as 'economic self- interest' that could have influenced its recommendation.[10]

See also SEC Study on Investment Advisers and Broker–Dealers at 51 (citations omitted) ("Under the so- called 'shingle' theory ... , a broker-dealer makes an implicit representation to those persons with whom it transacts business that it will deal fairly with them, consistent with the standards of the profession. ... Actions taken by the broker-dealer that are not fair to the customer must be disclosed in order to make this implied representation of fairness not misleading.").

[8] SEC v. Tambone, 55 0 F.3d 10 6 (1st Cir. 20 08).

[9] Section 11 of the Securities Act of 1933, codified at 15 U.S.C. § 77 a.

[10] In the Matter of Richmark Capital Corporation, Securities Exchange Act R el. No. 48 758 (November 7, 2003) (citing Chasins v. Smith Barney & Co., Inc., 438 F.3d 1167, 1172 (2 d Cir. 1970) ("The investor ... must be permitted to evaluate overlapping

To help broker–dealers understand when they are obligated to disclose material adverse facts to investors, the Financial Industry Regulatory Authority (FINRA) has further defined the term "recommendation":

> [A] broad range of circumstances may cause a transaction to be considered recommended, and this determination does not depend on the classification of the transaction by a particular member as 'solicited' or 'unsolicited.' In particular a transaction will be considered to be recommended when the member or its associated person brings a specific security to the attention of the customer through any means, including, but not limited to, direct telephone communication, the delivery of promotional material through the mail, or the transmission of electronic messages.[11]

There is no indication in any law or regulation that the obligation to disclose material adverse facts is diminished or waived in relation to the level of sophistication of the potential investor.[12]

7.4 Types of Investment Banks

The firms engaged in the investment banking industry are commonly classified into three categories: bulge bracket banks, middle-market banks, and boutique banks. Boutique banks are often further divided into regional boutiques and elite boutique banks. Elite boutique banks sometimes have more in common with bulge bracket banks than they do with regional boutiques. The classification of investment banks is primarily based on size; however, "size" can be a relative term in this context and may refer to the size of the bank in terms of the number of employees or offices, or to the average size of M&A deals handled by the bank.

motivations through appropriate disclosures, especially where one motivation is economic self- interest")).

[11] FINRA Notice No. 96-60.

[12] See FINRA Rules 22 10(d)(1)(A) and 2 211(a)(3) and (d)(1) (by rule all institutional sales material and correspondence may not "omit any material fact or qualification if the omission, in the light of the context of the material presented, would cause the communications to be misleading.").

7.4.1 *Regional Boutique Banks*

The smallest of the investment banks, both in terms of firm size and typical deal size, are the banks referred to as regional boutique banks. Regional boutiques usually have no more than a handful to a few dozen employees. Because of the small size of most regional boutiques, they do not typically offer all the services offered by bulge bracket investment banks, and may simply specialize in a single area, such as handling M&As in a particular market sector.

Regional boutiques may have clients that include major corporations headquartered in their areas, but they more commonly serve smaller firms and organizations. Most regional boutique banks focus on capital raising or M&A (buy and sell side engagements) but the large regional i-banks will provide a full suite of services including equity and debt capital markets, leverage finance and restructuring services. Examples of larger well known regional investment banks would be Lazard, Rothschild, Houlihan Lokey, Jefferies & Co. The main criterion for being defined as a boutique investment bank is that it does not offer full-service investment banking, but does offer at least one investment banking financial service.

7.4.2 *Elite Boutique Banks*

The term Elite Boutique encompasses several factors of a banks strengths. Some of the most important factors are pay, exit opportunities, and culture. All of these factors are firm specific. The firms that have the most to offer in these categories are termed Elite Boutiques. The top seven elite boutique investment banks include: PJT, Evercore, Moelis, Lazard, Greenhill, Perella Weinberg, Houlihan Lokey, and Piper Jaffray. Very often, they still lack the kind of global presence of a major investment bank such as JPMorgan Chase & Company. Elite boutiques are often like regional boutiques in that they usually do not provide a complete range of investment banking services and may limit their operations to handling M&A-related issues. They are more likely than regionals to offer restructuring or asset management services. Most elite boutique banks begin as regional boutiques and then gradually work up to elite status through handling successions of larger and larger deals for more prestigious clients.

7.4.3 Middle-Market Banks

Middle-market investment banks are financial institutions or intermediaries that deal mostly with mid-market firms, specifically for raising debt or equity capital as well as M&A. Middle market firms are mid-size businesses having annual revenues from $10 million up to $500 million and 100–2000 employees. Middle-market investment banks are distinguished from the others by the following attributes:

- *Deal size*: Deals or transactions with mid-market firms generally range from $10 million to $500 million
- *Geographic focus*: Middle market investment banks typically have a strong local presence but lack international exposure as compared to a bulge bracket bank that has a multitude of overseas branches and offices worldwide
- *Services*: Services offered include the following: merger and acquisition advisory services, debt and equity capital fundraising, and corporate restructuring
- *Client focus*: Mid-market banks often deal with relatively smaller, private firms, offer more tailored or personalized services, and focus on working with companies in a particular market sector or industry.

Mid-market firms are generally classified into the following three categories:

- *National full-service middle market firms*: Expand their services to combine investment banking, wealth management, equity research, and brokerage and private equity services.
- *National Advisory-only firms*: This category primarily includes big accounting firms that provide merger and acquisition advisory services in addition to audit and accounting services.
- *Single-industry specialists*: Focus their services on middle market companies within a single industry, such as real estate management companies or retail stores. May also be sector-specific rather than industry-specific, e.g., healthcare, consumer products. An example is Brown Gibbons Lang & Co.

The top seven middle market investment banks include: William Blair & Co., Robert W. Baird & Co., Houlihan Lokey, Lincoln International, Stifel, Harris William & Co., and KPMG Corporate Finance.

7.4.4 *Bulge Bracket Banks*

The "bulge bracket" is a slang term to describe the largest and most profitable multi-national investment banks in the world whose banking clients are normally huge institutions, corporations, and governments. The bulge bracket banks are the major, international investment banking firms with easily recognizable names such as Goldman Sachs, Deutsche Bank, Credit Suisse Group AG, Morgan Stanley and Bank of America. The bulge bracket firms are the largest in terms of numbers of offices and employees, and also in terms of handling the largest deals and the largest corporate clients. The overwhelming majority of clients are Fortune 500, if not Fortune 100, firms. Bulge bracket investment banks regularly handle multibillion-dollar M&A deals, although, depending on the overall state of the economy or the particular client, a bulge bracket bank may sometimes handle deals valued in the low hundred millions. Each of the bulge bracket banks operates internationally and has a large global, as well as domestic, presence. The major investment banks provide their clients with the full range of investment banking services, including trading, all types of financing, asset management services, equity research and issuance, and the bread and butter of investment banking, M&A services. Most bulge bracket banks also have commercial and retail banking divisions and generate additional revenue by cross-selling financial products.

7.5 Investment Banks: Financial Statements

Goldman Sachs is the most prestigious investment bank. The nearly 150-year-old institution is a public company with $917 billion in assets as of 2017. Historically known for its list of wealthy corporate and hedge fund clients, Goldman Sachs has moved into consumer finance three years ago with its Marcus business.

7.5.1 *The Balance Sheet*

THE GOLDMAN SACHS GROUP, INC. AND SUBSIDIARIES

Consolidated Statements of Financial Condition

	As of December	
$ in millions	**2017**	2016
Assets		
Cash and cash equivalents	**$110,051**	$121,711
Collateralized agreements:		
Securities purchased under agreements to resell (includes **$120,420** and $116,077 at fair value)	**120,822**	116,925
Securities borrowed (includes **$78,189** and $82,398 at fair value)	**190,848**	184,600
Receivables:		
Brokers, dealers and clearing organizations	**24,676**	18,044
Customers and counterparties (includes **$3,526** and $3,266 at fair value)	**60,112**	47,780
Loans receivable	**65,933**	49,672
Financial instruments owned (at fair value and includes **$50,335** and $51,278 pledged as collateral)	**315,988**	295,952
Other assets	**28,346**	25,481
Total assets	**$916,776**	$860,165
Liabilities and shareholders' equity		
Deposits (includes **$22,902** and $13,782 at fair value)	**$138,604**	$124,098
Collateralized financings:		
Securities sold under agreements to repurchase (at fair value)	**84,718**	71,816
Securities loaned (includes **$5,357** and $2,647 at fair value)	**14,793**	7,524
Other secured financings (includes **$24,345** and $21,073 at fair value)	**24,788**	21,523
Payables:		
Brokers, dealers and clearing organizations	**6,672**	4,386
Customers and counterparties	**171,497**	184,069
Financial instruments sold, but not yet purchased (at fair value)	**111,930**	117,143
Unsecured short-term borrowings (includes **$16,904** and $14,792 at fair value)	**46,922**	39,265
Unsecured long-term borrowings (includes **$38,638** and $29,410 at fair value)	**217,687**	189,086
Other liabilities and accrued expenses (includes **$268** and $621 at fair value)	**16,922**	14,362
Total liabilities	**834,533**	773,272
Commitments, contingencies and guarantees		
Shareholders' equity		
Preferred stock; aggregate liquidation preference of **$11,853** and $11,203	**11,853**	11,203
Common stock; **884,592,863** and 873,608,100 shares issued, and **374,808,805** and 392,632,230 shares outstanding	**9**	9
Share-based awards	**2,777**	3,914
Nonvoting common stock; no shares issued and outstanding	**-**	-
Additional paid-in capital	**53,357**	52,638
Retained earnings	**91,519**	89,039
Accumulated other comprehensive loss	**(1,880)**	(1,216)
Stock held in treasury, at cost; **509,784,060** and 480,975,872 shares	**(75,392)**	(68,694)
Total shareholders' equity	**82,243**	86,893
Total liabilities and shareholders' equity	**$916,776**	$860,165

Source: SEC- GS 10 K Form (2017)

1. Analysis of the statement of financial position

- Statement of financial position

The main components of the above bank's balance sheet are:

- Assets
  - Cash and cash equivalents
  - Collateral agreements (securities purchases, securities borrowed)
  - Notes and Loan Receivables
  - Long-term assets

- Liabilities and Shareholders' equity
  - Long-term liabilities
  - Common stock
  - Retained earnings
  - Comprehensive income

Goldman Sachs total assets for 2018 were $931.796B, a 1.64% increase from 2017.

Goldman Sachs total assets for 2017 were $916.776B, a 6.58% increase from 2016.

Goldman Sachs total assets for 2016 were $860.165B, a 0.14% decline from 2015.

7.5.2 *The Statement of Income*

THE GOLDMAN SACHS GROUP, INC. AND SUBSIDIARIES

Consolidated Statements of Earnings

	Year Ended December		
in millions, except per share amounts	**2017**	2016	2015
Revenues			
Investment banking	**$ 7,371**	$ 6,273	$ 7,027
Investment management	**5,803**	5,407	5,868
Commissions and fees	**3,051**	3,208	3,320
Market making	**7,660**	9,933	9,523
Other principal transactions	**5,256**	3,200	5,018
Total non-interest revenues	**29,141**	28,021	30,756
Interest income	**13,113**	9,691	8,452
Interest expense	**10,181**	7,104	5,388
Net interest income	**2,932**	2,587	3,064
Net revenues, including net interest income	**32,073**	30,608	33,820
Operating expenses			
Compensation and benefits	**11,853**	11,647	12,678
Brokerage, clearing, exchange and distribution fees	**2,540**	2,555	2,576
Market development	**588**	457	557
Communications and technology	**897**	809	806
Depreciation and amortization	**1,152**	998	991
Occupancy	**733**	788	772
Professional fees	**965**	882	963
Other expenses	**2,213**	2,168	5,699
Total non-compensation expenses	**9,088**	8,657	12,364
Total operating expenses	**20,941**	20,304	25,042
Pre-tax earnings	**11,132**	10,304	8,778
Provision for taxes	**6,846**	2,906	2,695
Net earnings	**4,286**	7,398	6,083
Preferred stock dividends	**601**	311	515
Net earnings applicable to common shareholders	**$ 3,685**	$ 7,087	$ 5,568
Earnings per common share			
Basic	**$ 9.12**	$ 16.53	$ 12.35
Diluted	**$ 9.01**	$ 16.29	$ 12.14
Average common shares			
Basic	**401.6**	427.4	448.9
Diluted	**409.1**	435.1	458.6

Source: SEC- GS 10 K Form (2017)

1. Analysis of the income statement

By and large, Goldman Sachs income statement is made of the following items:

- Interest income
- Non-interest income
- Interest expenses

Goldman Sachs annual revenue for 2018 was $36.616B, a 11.87% increase from 2017.

Goldman Sachs annual revenue for 2017 was $32.73B, a 6.3% increase from 2016.

Goldman Sachs annual revenue for 2016 was $30.79B, a 8.96% decline from 2015.

7.5.3 *Statements of Changes in Shareholders' Equity*

THE GOLDMAN SACHS GROUP, INC. AND SUBSIDIARIES

Consolidated Statements of Changes in Shareholders' Equity

	Year Ended December		
$ in millions	**2017**	2016	2015
Preferred stock			
Beginning balance	**$ 11,203**	$ 11,200	$ 9,200
Issued	**1,500**	1,325	2,000
Redeemed	**(850)**	(1,322)	–
Ending balance	**11,853**	11,203	11,200
Common stock			
Beginning balance	**9**	9	9
Issued	**–**	–	–
Ending balance	**9**	9	9
Share-based awards			
Beginning balance, as previously reported	**3,914**	4,151	3,766
Cumulative effect of the change in accounting principle related to forfeiture of share-based awards	**35**	–	–
Beginning balance, adjusted	**3,949**	4,151	3,766
Issuance and amortization of share-based awards	**1,810**	2,143	2,308
Delivery of common stock underlying share-based awards	**(2,704)**	(2,068)	(1,742)
Forfeiture of share-based awards	**(89)**	(102)	(72)
Exercise of share-based awards	**(189)**	(210)	(109)
Ending balance	**2,777**	3,914	4,151
Additional paid-in capital			
Beginning balance	**52,638**	51,340	50,049
Delivery of common stock underlying share-based awards	**2,934**	2,282	2,092
Cancellation of share-based awards in satisfaction of withholding tax requirements	**(2,220)**	(1,121)	(1,198)
Preferred stock issuance costs, net of reversals upon redemption	**8**	(10)	(7)
Excess net tax benefit related to share-based awards	**–**	147	406
Cash settlement of share-based awards	**(3)**	–	(2)
Ending balance	**53,357**	52,638	51,340
Retained earnings			
Beginning balance, as previously reported	**89,039**	83,386	78,984
Cumulative effect of the change in accounting principle related to:			
Debt valuation adjustment, net of tax	**–**	(305)	–
Forfeiture of share-based awards, net of tax	**(24)**	–	–
Beginning balance, adjusted	**89,015**	83,081	78,984
Net earnings	**4,286**	7,398	6,083
Dividends and dividend equivalents declared on common stock and share-based awards	**(1,181)**	(1,129)	(1,166)
Dividends declared on preferred stock	**(587)**	(577)	(515)
Preferred stock redemption discount/(premium)	**(14)**	266	–
Ending balance	**91,519**	89,039	83,386
Accumulated other comprehensive loss			
Beginning balance, as previously reported	**(1,216)**	(718)	(743)
Cumulative effect of the change in accounting principle related to debt valuation adjustment, net of tax	**–**	305	–
Beginning balance, adjusted	**(1,216)**	(413)	(743)
Other comprehensive income/(loss)	**(664)**	(803)	25
Ending balance	**(1,880)**	(1,216)	(718)
Stock held in treasury, at cost			
Beginning balance	**(68,694)**	(62,640)	(58,468)
Repurchased	**(6,721)**	(6,069)	(4,195)
Reissued	**34**	22	32
Other	**(11)**	(7)	(9)
Ending balance	**(75,392)**	(68,694)	(62,640)
Total shareholders' equity	**$ 82,243**	$ 86,893	$ 86,728

Source: SEC- GS 10 K Form (2017)

7.5.4 *The Statement of Cash Flows*

THE GOLDMAN SACHS GROUP, INC. AND SUBSIDIARIES

Consolidated Statements of Cash Flows

	Year Ended December		
$ in millions	**2017**	2016	2015
Cash flows from operating activities			
Net earnings	**$ 4,286**	$ 7,398	$ 6,083
Adjustments to reconcile net earnings to net cash provided by/(used for) operating activities:			
Depreciation and amortization	**1,152**	998	991
Deferred income taxes	**5,458**	551	425
Share-based compensation	**1,769**	2,111	2,272
Loss/(gain) related to extinguishment of subordinated borrowings	**(114)**	3	(34)
Changes in operating assets and liabilities:			
Receivables and payables (excluding loans receivable), net	**(30,082)**	(15,813)	19,132
Collateralized transactions (excluding other secured financings), net	**10,025**	78	(14,825)
Financial instruments owned (excluding available-for-sale securities)	**(11,327)**	15,253	16,078
Financial instruments sold, but not yet purchased	**(5,296)**	1,960	(16,835)
Other, net	**6,387**	(5,639)	(3,806)
Net cash provided by/(used for) operating activities	**(17,742)**	6,900	9,481
Cash flows from investing activities			
Purchase of property, leasehold improvements and equipment	**(3,185)**	(2,876)	(1,833)
Proceeds from sales of property, leasehold improvements and equipment	**574**	381	228
Net cash acquired in/(used for) business acquisitions	**(2,383)**	14,922	(1,808)
Purchase of investments	**(9,853)**	–	–
Proceeds from sales and paydowns of investments	**2,887**	1,512	1,019
Loans receivable, net	**(17,156)**	(4,669)	(16,180)
Net cash provided by/(used for) investing activities	**(29,116)**	9,270	(18,574)
Cash flows from financing activities			
Unsecured short-term borrowings, net	**(501)**	(1,506)	(369)
Other secured financings (short-term), net	**(405)**	(808)	(867)
Proceeds from issuance of other secured financings (long-term)	**7,401**	4,186	10,349
Repayment of other secured financings (long-term), including the current portion	**(4,726)**	(7,375)	(6,502)
Purchase of APEX, senior guaranteed securities and trust preferred securities	**(237)**	(1,171)	(1)
Proceeds from issuance of unsecured long-term borrowings	**58,347**	50,763	44,595
Repayment of unsecured long-term borrowings, including the current portion	**(30,756)**	(36,557)	(29,520)
Derivative contracts with a financing element, net	**1,684**	2,115	(47)
Deposits, net	**14,506**	10,058	14,639
Preferred stock redemption	**(850)**	–	–
Common stock repurchased	**(6,772)**	(6,078)	(4,135)
Settlement of share-based awards in satisfaction of withholding tax requirements	**(2,223)**	(1,128)	(1,204)
Dividends and dividend equivalents paid on common stock, preferred stock and share-based awards	**(1,769)**	(1,706)	(1,681)
Proceeds from issuance of preferred stock, net of issuance costs	**1,495**	1,303	1,993
Proceeds from issuance of common stock, including exercise of share-based awards	**7**	6	259
Cash settlement of share-based awards	**(3)**	–	(2)
Net cash provided by financing activities	**35,198**	12,102	27,507
Net increase/(decrease) in cash and cash equivalents	**(11,660)**	28,272	18,414
Cash and cash equivalents, beginning balance	**121,711**	93,439	75,025
Cash and cash equivalents, ending balance	**$110,051**	$121,711	$ 93,439

Source: SEC- GS 10 K Form (2017)

1. Analysis of the cash flows statement

GS statement of cash flows is composed of:

- Cash flows from operating activities: include cash generated from/(used in)operations, Taxation received, Taxation paid
- Cash flows from investing activities: include capital expenditure for fixed assets

- Cash flows from financing activities: include receipts from issuing ordinary share capital, Interest paid on long-term subordinated loans.

Goldman Sachs annual free cash flow for 2018 was $16.15B, a 177.51% decline from 2017.

Goldman Sachs annual free cash flow for 2017 was $-20.837B, a 619.63% decline from 2016.

Goldman Sachs annual free cash flow for 2016 was $4.01B, a 49.09% decline from 2015.

CHAPTER 8

Merchant Banks

8.1 General

The modern "merchant bank" is a misnomer. In modern British usage it is the same as an investment bank. To a modern American, merchant bank is used to refer to banks activities in buying and selling nonfinancial companies, or when banks act like private equity or venture capital firms in buying a company or investing in a start-up.[1] The origin of merchant banks is quite different. The history of merchant banks can be traced back to Italy in the late Medieval times as well in France in the seventeenth and eighteenth centuries. Merchant banks began operating as organized money markets consisting of merchants financing the transactions of other merchants. French merchant, Marchand Banquer, invested all his profits by integrating the banking business into his merchant activities and became a merchant banker.

In the UK, merchant banks started in the early eighteenth century. The oldest merchant bank in the UK is Barings Bank, which was established by a German-originated family of bankers and merchants. It was founded in 1762 and was the second oldest merchant bank in the world after Berenberg Bank. The bank was, at one time, referred to as the sixth great European power after Germany, Russia, UK, Austria, and France after it helped finance the US government during the 1812 War. The

[1] Steven Davidoff Solomon (2016): Fed Proposes Ban on Merchant Banking, a Practice With Little Risk, NYT, September 13, 2016.

F. I. Lessambo, *The U.S. Banking System*,
https://doi.org/10.1007/978-3-030-34792-5_8

growth of trade and industries in the nineteenth century led to the emergence of merchant banks in the United States. The first merchant banks in the United States were JP Morgan & Co and Citi Bank. The industry was mainly dominated by German-Jewish immigrant bankers and Yankee houses with close ties to expatriate Americans who settled in London as merchant bankers. However, with the growth of the financial world, corporations overshadowed family-owned businesses in the banking business. The corporations included merchant banking as one of their areas of interest, a characteristic that banks hold until today. The business was riskier as the family-run bank could lose all its investments due to storms, occasional wars or even piracy. The business blossomed during the next follow centuries, merchant banking spread across Europe and then to the United States, becoming the occupation of the big banking houses like J.P. Morgan.[2] Merchant banking is deemed a profitable business as it allows banks to take part in the business of their clients—getting to know them better and having more of a stake in their success. The modern merchant banks offer a wide range of activities: issue management, portfolio management, credit syndication, acceptance credit, counsel on mergers and acquisitions, insurance, etc.

8.2 Size of Merchant Bank in the Financial Industry

Merchant Banking Services Market Size in the US tantamount to $12.7 bn in 2019, with a size growth of 9.2% in 2019 and an annualized market size growth of 8.8% from 2014 to 2019. The below graphic illustrates the merchant banking services in the United States and the market size growth from 2014 to 2019.

8.3 Merchant Bank Activities

Merchant banks conduct underwriting, loan services, financial advising, and fundraising services for large corporations and high-net-worth individuals. They do not provide regular banking services such as checking accounts and do not take deposits.

Merchant banks are different from investment banks and commercial banks. Compared to investment banks, merchant banks merely fulfills

[2] Steven Davidoff Solomon (2016): Fed Proposes Ban on Merchant Banking, a Practice with Little Risk, NYT, September 13, 2016.

capital requirements of the companies in the form of share ownership, rather than granting loans, whereas investment banks are the middleman between the issuer of securities and the investing public, and also provides various financial services to the clients. They are also distinct from commercial banks in that they do not extend loans nor collect deposits from customers. Merchant banks perform a number of functions, including the following[3]:

- Promotional Activities

A merchant bank functions as a promoter of industrial enterprises in India. He helps the entrepreneur in conceiving an idea, identification of projects, preparing feasibility reports, obtaining government approvals, and incentives, etc. Some of the merchant banks also provide assistance for technical and financial collaborations and joint ventures.

- Equity Underwriting

Large companies often employ the services of merchant banks in acquiring capital through the stock market. Merchant banks provide equity underwriting services. Equity underwriting is achieved by evaluating the amount of stock to be issued, the value of the business, the use of proceeds, and the timing of issuance of the new stock. Merchant banks handle all the necessary processes and liaison with the appropriate marketing division to advertise the stock.

- Credit Syndication

Merchant banks help in processing loan applications for short and long-term credit from financial institutions. They provide these services by estimating total costs involved, developing a financial plan for the entire project, as well as adopting a loan application for commercial lenders. More, they assist in choosing the ideal financial institutions to provide credit facilities and act on the terms of the loan application with the financiers. Merchant banks also ensure the lender's willingness to participate, organize bridge finance, and engage in legal formalities

[3]Corporate Finance Institute.

regarding investment to be approved and checking the working capital requirements.

- Portfolio Management

Merchant banks provide portfolio management services to institutional investors (i.e., pension funds) and other investors. They help in the management of securities to enhance the value of the underlying investment. Very often, merchant banks assist their clients in the purchase and sale of securities to help them attain their investment objectives.

- Leasing and Finance

Many merchant bankers provide leasing and finance facilities to their customers. Some of them even maintain venture capital funds to assist the entrepreneurs. They also help companies in raising finance by way of public deposits.

- Servicing of Issues

Merchant banks have also started to act as paying agents for the service of debt securities and to act as registrars and transfer agents. Thus, they maintain even the registers of shareholders and debenture holders and arrange to pay dividend or interest due to them

- Other Specialized Services

In addition to the basic activities involving marketing of securities, merchant banks also provide corporate advisory services on issues like mergers and amalgamations, tax matters, recruitment of executives and cost and management audit, etc. Many merchant bankers have also started making of bought out deals of shares and debentures. The activities of the merchant bankers are increasing with the change in the money market.

8.4 Financial Statement of Merchant Banks

The following are the financial statements of Merchants Financial Group as of December 31, 2016:

Merchants Financial Group, Inc. and Subsidiary

Consolidated Balance Sheets
December 31, 2016 and 2015
(In Thousands, Except Share Information)

Assets		**2016**		2015
Cash and cash equivalents (Note 2)	$	**28,849**	$	36,965
Securities (Notes 3 and 10)		**141,291**		187,614
Loans held for sale (Note 4)		**28,152**		23,288
Loans and direct financing leases, net (Notes 5, 10, 14 and 16)		**1,299,197**		1,217,941
Operating lease assets, net (Note 6)		**4,351**		-
Premises and equipment, net (Note 7)		**28,962**		29,811
Investment in restricted stock		**5,116**		7,815
Other real estate and other personal property owned (Note 8)		**3,016**		3,005
Accrued interest receivable and other assets		**10,683**		9,819
Cash value of life insurance		**35,769**		34,958
Mortgage servicing rights, net (Note 4)		**13,169**		12,652
Intangibles (Note 1)		**24,408**		25,335
Total assets	$	**1,622,963**	$	1,589,203

Liabilities and Stockholders' Equity				
Liabilities				
Deposits (Note 9):				
Noninterest-bearing	$	**319,733**	$	286,553
Interest-bearing		**1,031,790**		952,291
Total deposits		**1,351,523**		1,238,844
Federal funds purchased		**25,588**		105,232
Borrowings (Note 10)		**16,181**		21,411
Notes payable (Note 11)		**12,000**		15,000
Subordinated debentures (Note 12)		**41,254**		41,754
Accrued interest payable and other liabilities (Note 13)		**26,304**		27,973
Total liabilities		**1,472,850**		1,450,214
Commitments, Contingencies and Credit Risk (Note 14)				
Stockholders' Equity (Note 17)				
Common stock, par value $0.025 per share; 4,000,000 shares authorized; shares issued: 2,730,601 in 2016 and 2015		**68**		68
Additional paid-in capital		**8,976**		8,647
Retained earnings		**142,892**		131,702
Accumulated other comprehensive income (loss) (Note 3)		**(290)**		1,055
Unearned ESOP shares (Note 15)		**(1,533)**		(2,483)
Total stockholders' equity		**150,113**		138,989
Total liabilities and stockholders' equity	$	**1,622,963**	$	1,589,203

1. Analysis of the balance sheet

The balance sheet of a merchant bank is quite similar to the balance sheet of any banking institution and reflects the core activities of the merchant bank. For instance:

- Cash and cash equivalent: Cash flows from loans, federal funds purchased, deposits and short-term borrowings. The bank maintains cash in deposit accounts which, at times, may exceed federally insured limits.
- Securities: Three types of securities are: (i) held-to-maturity, which are securities the firm has both the positive intent and ability to hold to maturity. They are reported at amortized cost. Amortization of premiums and accretion of discounts, computed by the interest method over their contractual lives, are included in interest income; and (ii) Securities classified as available-for-sale include debt securities that the Company intends to hold for an indefinite period of time, but not necessarily to maturity. Securities available for sale are carried at fair value with unrealized gains or losses reported net of the related deferred tax effect in other comprehensive income. The amortization of premiums and accretion of discounts, computed by the interest method over their contractual lives, are recognized in interest income. Realized gains or losses, determined on the basis of the amortized cost of specific securities sold, are included in net income.
- Loans held for sale: are loans originated with the intent to sell them in the secondary market. They consist of first mortgage loans that are secured by residential real estate.
- Loans and direct lease financing receivable (loans): consist of the bank leasing operations of various types of equipment and trucks used in manufacturing, construction, and agricultural.
- Investment in restricted stocks: consist of stocks bought from and sold to the Federal Home Loan Bank based upon its $100 par value. These stocks do not have readily determinable fair values and are carried at cost, and evaluated for impairment in accordance with guidance for depository and lending institutions. Investment in restricted stock also includes stocks of the Federal Reserve Bank and are carried at cost.

However, merchant banks operate trust and investment services. Assets of the trust and investment departments, other than trust cash on deposit at the bank, are not included in these consolidated financial statements because they are not assets of the Company.

Merchants Financial Group, Inc. and Subsidiary

Consolidated Statements of Income
Years Ended December 31, 2016 and 2015
(In Thousands, Except Per Share Information)

	2016	2015
Interest income:		
Loans	$ 54,878	$ 49,535
Securities	4,432	6,055
Direct financing leases	4,569	4,501
Other	1,068	982
	64,947	61,073
Interest expense:		
Deposits	3,361	3,259
Notes payable and short-term borrowings	1,055	890
Subordinated debt owed to trust	971	991
	5,387	5,140
Net interest income	59,560	55,933
Provision for loan and lease losses (Note 5)	3,227	1,933
Net interest income after provision for loan and lease losses	56,333	54,000
Noninterest income:		
Trust department	1,579	1,531
Service charges and other fees	5,448	5,475
Loan servicing fees	6,436	6,193
Net gain on sale of loans	6,151	4,440
Net gain on sale of available-for-sale securities (Note 3)	350	91
Net gain (loss) on sale of other real estate and other personal property owned including writedowns (Note 8)	344	(64)
Other noninterest income	3,053	2,735
	23,361	20,401
Noninterest expenses:		
Salaries and employee benefits (Note 15)	35,455	33,266
Occupancy	7,322	6,487
Mortgage servicing rights (Note 4)	3,957	3,284
Other noninterest expenses	10,896	10,268
	57,630	53,305
Income before income taxes	22,064	21,096
Provision for income taxes (Note 13)	7,909	7,640
Net income	$ 14,155	$ 13,456
Earnings per common share (Note 1)	$ 5.30	$ 5.04

2. Analysis of the Income Statement

The items of the income statement are (i) for revenue: loans, securities, direct financing leases, and other; and (ii) for expenses: deposits, notes payable, and short-term borrowings, and subordinated debt owned by the Trust. Non-interest income and expenses (i.e., salaries, provisions for income taxes) are also included.

Merchants Financial Group, Inc. and Subsidiary

Consolidated Statements of Comprehensive Income
Years Ended December 31, 2016 and 2015
(In Thousands)

		2016		2015
Net income	$	14,155	$	13,456
Other comprehensive loss, net of reclassification adjustments and income tax effect:				
Change in unrealized losses on securities		(1,514)		(1,928)
Unrealized gain on interest rate swap		169		-
Total other comprehensive loss		(1,345)		(1,928)
Comprehensive Income	$	12,810	$	11,528

See Notes to Consolidated Financial Statements.

3. Analysis of the Comprehensive income statement

Certain changes in assets and liabilities, such as unrealized gains and losses on available-for-sale securities, are reported on the consolidated statement of comprehensive income. Such items, along with net income, are components of comprehensive income. Gains and losses on available-for-sale securities are reclassified to net income as the gains or losses are realized upon sale of the securities.

Merchants Financial Group, Inc. and Subsidiary

Consolidated Statements of Stockholders' Equity
Years Ended December 31, 2016 and 2015
(In Thousands, Except Per Share Information)

	Common Stock	Additional Paid-In Capital	Retained Earnings	Accumulated Other Comprehensive Income (Loss)	Unearned ESOP Shares	Total
Balance, December 31, 2014	$ 68	$ 8,242	$ 120,998	$ 2,983	$ (1,103)	$ 131,188
Net income	-	-	13,456	-	-	13,456
Other comprehensive loss (Note 3)	-	-	-	(1,928)	-	(1,928)
ESOP shares purchased	-	-	-	-	(2,510)	(2,510)
ESOP shares released for allocation (Note 15)	-	405	-	-	1,130	1,535
Cash dividends declared ($1.03 per share)	-	-	(2,752)	-	-	(2,752)
Balance, December 31, 2015	68	8,647	131,702	1,055	(2,483)	138,989
Net income	-	-	14,155	-	-	14,155
Other comprehensive loss (Note 3)	-	-	-	(1,345)	-	(1,345)
ESOP shares purchased	-	-	-	-	(449)	(449)
ESOP shares released for allocation (Note 15)	-	329	-	-	1,399	1,728
Cash dividends declared ($1.11 per share)	-	-	(2,965)	-	-	(2,965)
Balance, December 31, 2016	$ 68	$ 8,976	$ 142,892	$ (290)	$ (1,533)	$ 150,113

See Notes to Consolidated Financial Statements.

Merchants Financial Group, Inc. and Subsidiary

Consolidated Statements of Cash Flows
Years Ended December 31, 2016 and 2015
(In Thousands)

	2016	2015
Cash Flows From Operating Activities		
Net income	$ 14,155	$ 13,456
Adjustments to reconcile net income to net cash provided by operating activities:		
Securities gains, net (Note 3)	(350)	(91)
Net amortization and accretion of bond premiums and discounts	1,769	2,387
Provision for loan and lease losses (Note 5)	3,227	1,933
Gain on sale of loans	(6,151)	(4,440)
Net change in fair value of loans held for sale	(283)	(30)
Proceeds from sales of loans held for sale	490,427	447,009
Originations and purchases of loans held for sale	(491,164)	(437,435)
Mortgage servicing rights amortization and provision change (Note 4)	3,957	3,284
Depreciation expense	2,023	1,605
Net charge-offs/write-downs of OREO and other personal property owned (Note 8)	616	64
Loss on disposal of fixed assets	392	-
Deferred income taxes (Note 13)	2,620	(1,019)
Release of shares to ESOP	1,728	1,535
Increase in cash value of life insurance	(811)	(4,534)
Gain on sale of OREO and other personal property owned (Note 8)	(960)	-
Gain on buyback of trust preferred securities	(105)	-
Other	(3,064)	3,990
Net cash provided by operating activities	18,026	27,714
Cash Flows From Investing Activities		
Cash flows from securities (Note 18)	42,397	65,741
(Purchase) sale of restricted stock	2,699	(1,421)
Net increase in loans and direct financing leases	(87,117)	(143,655)
Purchase of operating lease assets	(4,709)	-
Purchases of premises and equipment	(3,728)	(3,049)
Proceeds from sale of premises and equipment	2,520	609
Purchased mortgage servicing rights	(2,167)	(1,745)
Proceeds from sales of OREO and foreclosed assets	2,967	128
Net cash used in investing activities	(47,138)	(83,392)
Cash Flows From Financing Activities		
Net increase in deposits	112,679	31,840
Net increase (decrease) in federal funds purchased	(79,644)	43,610
Net decrease in short-term borrowings (Note 10)	(5,230)	(19,008)
Repayment of long-term borrowings	(3,000)	-
Buyback of trust preferred securities	(395)	-
ESOP shares purchased	(449)	(2,510)
Cash dividends paid	(2,965)	(2,752)
Net cash provided by financing activities	20,996	51,180
Decrease in cash and cash equivalents	(8,116)	(4,498)
Cash and Cash Equivalents		
Beginning	36,965	41,463
Ending	$ 28,849	$ 36,965

See Supplemental Cash Flow Disclosures (Note 18)

4. Analysis of the cash flow statements

The cash flow statement includes cash flow from securities, cash payment for interests, cash payments for income taxes, as well as cash flow from investing, and financing activities.

CHAPTER 9

Credit Union

9.1 General

Credit union charter is granted by the federal government or by the state governments. The credit union system is comprised of approximately 5800 credit unions with assets totaling $1.3 trillion. Ninety-five percent of credit unions in the system have assets of less than $1 billion.[1] Credit unions in the United States serve 100 million members, comprising 43.7% of the economically active population. US credit unions are not-for-profit, cooperative, tax-exempt organizations.[2] Federally charted credit unions, properties, franchises, capital, reserves, surpluses, and income are exempt from all taxation imposed by the US federal or by any state, territorial, or local taxing authority. However, any real property and any tangible personal property of such federal credit unions are subject to federal, state, territorial, and local taxation to the same extent as other similar property is taxed. Navy Federal Credit Union is the largest US credit union, with over $97 billion in assets and over 8.23 million members. Its return on average assets was 1.65% in 2018 as of

[1] US Department of the Treasury (2017): A Financial System That Creates Economic Opportunities—Banks and Credit Unions, p. 23.

[2] Credit unions in the United States are exempt from federal and state income taxes (but not from other forms of tax, such as payroll, sales, or property taxes). Credit union members themselves pay income tax on dividends earned through financial participation in the credit union.

F. I. Lessambo, *The U.S. Banking System*,
https://doi.org/10.1007/978-3-030-34792-5_9

May 30, 2019. Historically, credit unions were formed around a single church, place of work, labor union, or town. Thus, membership was limited to those who were in the field of membership. To that end, the Federal Credit Union Act of 1934 limited membership to "groups having a common bond or occupation" or association, or to groups within a well-defined neighborhood, community, or rural district. President Trump named effective January 26, 2017, J. Mark Mc Walters as new acting Chairman of the National Credit Union Associations (NCUA). Credit unions in the United States are chartered by either the federal government or a state government. The states of Delaware, South Dakota, and Wyoming do not regulate credit unions at the state level; in those states, only a federal charter required in order to operate. All federal credit unions and 95% of state-chartered credit unions have "share insurance" (deposit insurance) of at least $250,000 per member through the National Credit Union Share Insurance Fund (NCUSIF). This deposit insurance is backed by the full faith and credit of the US government and is administered by the National Credit Union Administration. As of December 2006, the NCUSIF had a higher insurance fund capital ratio than the fund for the Federal Deposit Insurance Corporation (FDIC). US credit unions also typically have higher equity capital ratios than US banks. As of the end of 2016, the National Credit Union Share Insurance Fund insured more than $1 trillion in deposits at 5785 not-for-profit cooperative US credit unions.

9.2 Role in the Economy

The primary role of the credit unions is to satisfy the depository and borrowing needs of their members. They are not-for-profit cooperative financial institutions, and since 1935, the credit unions have been exempt from federal income tax which allows them to offer higher rates on deposits and lower interest rates on loans to all members. Members benefit from the credit unions easy access to a loan with a low-interest rate which increases their spending. On the other hand, depositors benefit higher interest on their membership deposits. Earning higher profits from deposits incite investors to increase their investments, which affect the GDP positively. The presence of credit unions in the economy not only helps members to get a better rate but also serves as a check on the interest rate commercial banks and other saving institutions offer their customers. A recent study conducted by the National Association of Federally Insured Credit Unions highlighted that removing the tax exemption from credit unions will affect the US economy negatively.

> Our analysis indicates that removing the credit union tax exemption would cost the federal government $38 billion in lost income tax revenue over the next ten years. The GDP would be reduced by $142 billion, and 883,000 jobs would be lost over the course of the next decade as well.[3]

9.3 Regulatory Requirements

Credit unions are required to calculate a risk-based net worth (RBNW) that establishes whether the credit union is considered "complex" or not under the regulatory framework. A credit union is defined as "complex" if the credit union's quarter-end total assets exceed $50 million and its RBNW requirement exceeds 6%. More, the Federal Reserve Bank requires that a credit maintain a minimum average reserve balance during a 14-day maintenance period. The minimum average balance requirement is calculated and provided by the FRB for each 14-day maintenance period.

9.4 The National Credit Union Administration as the Regulator

Federally chartered credit unions are subject to the regulation of the National Credit Union Administration (NCUA). State-chartered credit unions are examined and supervised by state regulators and the National Credit Union Administration. The NCUA is funded through their fees and assessments, further creating the National Credit Union Share Insurance Fund (NCUSIF) and the Central Liquidity Facility (CLF). Both organizations "aid credit unions in providing insurance, liquidity, and liquidation.[4]"

[3] Robert and Douglas, 2017, p. 2.

[4] B.A. Good (1996): The Credit Union Industry—An Overview. Federal Reserve Bank of Cleveland Economic Commentary, May 15.

- The NCUA Insurance

The NCUA provides credit unions with similar coverage as the Federal Deposit Insurance Corporation provides to commercial banks, up to $250,000 deposit coverage for federal and state credit union members. A state-chartered credit union can choose whether or not to have depositary coverage, or the state requirements will indicate whether or not depositary coverage is needed. According to the National Credit Union Administration, Industry at a Glance, as of September 2016, the industry's current equity ratio is 1.27a considerable amount of coverage for credit unions in case of liquidity issue or financial issues that may arise. The financial requirement of the NCUSIF is similar to that of the FDIC.

- The NCUA Board and Members

Credit unions are monitored and regulated by the National Credit Union Administration, "an independent agency" in the executive branch of the government.[5] The Board of the National Credit Union Administration has three members, appointed by the President of the United States, and must be confirmed by the Senate. The selected members must have the "general interest of the public, and no more than two members can belong to the same political party.[6]" The President selects a Chairperson from the three members of the Board. Candidates for appointment must have a financial services background and have limited to no time on the board of a credit union. Board members can serve a term of 6 years or less based on the services requested by the Board, the President or as Congress allows. Board members are responsible for adopting rules as needed to conduct business transactions of the credit union. The members are required to meet at least once a year before April 1 and as Congress requests throughout the year. Minutes of the meeting are recorded and maintained for additional review when needed by Congress or the President. Congress must approve new regulations or policies created by the National Credit Union Administration

[5] B. Good (1996): The Credit Union Industry—An Overview. Federal Reserve Bank of Cleveland Economic Commentary, May 15.

[6] NCUA, 2013.

Board before implementation. The Chairperson of the Board is the official representative and speaker for the NCUA, as well as responsible for adopting and implementing regulations of the NCUA Board.

- Establishing a credit union

Establishing credit unions requires seven or more people to "individually or collectivity before some officer competent to administer the oath of an organization certificate" the following as per the National Credit Union Administration Section 1753 within a proposal indicating the:

- Name of the credit union;
- Location and territory of operation;
- Name and address of individual proposing the credit union and number of shares;
- Par value of shares;
- Specified information regarding the field of membership;
- Credit unions terms of existence;
- Proposed benefits and advantages the credit union will provide to its members.

The proposed name of the individual must include the position each holds and their responsibilities. The completed proposal is submitted to the NCUA for approval. The Board will review the submission to ensure that the proposed credit union has met the Board's requirements. The requirement includes whether or not the proposed individuals are suitable to manage/advise the credit union and whether the credit union will be financially sound to operate as a credit union. A credit union approved by the NCUA Board is required to pay a fee. There are annual fees and additional charges based on the services and assets of the credit union, both of which are determined by the schedule established by the board. Credit unions are required to maintain a recording of their accounting practices and regulatory implementation, both of which should be readily accessible to the National Credit Union Administration Board upon request for examination. All credit union's fiscal year ends on December 31.

- Organization of a Credit Union

Each credit union consists of a Credit Committee, Board of Directors, and Supervisory Committee. The Board of Directors appoints the Supervisory Committee.

1. The Board of Directors

The group is required to have a minimum of three members and no more than five members. Once appointed, the Board has ten days to notify the NCUA of the member's name and address. Members of the Committee are not compensated. There are exceptions due to health, which would merit compensation, outlined in the credit union's bylaws. The Board of Directors meets monthly, after the annual members meeting. The Board of Directors then elects a member of the board to receive compensation; only one member of the board will receive compensation. The Board of Directors of a credit union is responsible for the general direction and control of the affairs of the federal credit union. The Board of Directors is responsible for the following:

- filling vacancies on the board;
- the appointment of members to the credit Committee and the supervisory Committee;
- supervising the investment Committee if the bank chooses to invest funds.

The Board determines the number of shares for the credit union, establish par value, authorize interest refund to members, and additional provision disclosed in the National Credit Union Administration Sections 1760–1761b.

2. The Credit Committee

The Credit Committee is created when the bylaws of the credit union indicate that a Committee is needed. The members of the Committee can either be appointed by the Credit Unions Board of Directors or voted upon by the members at least one officer must be a Loan Officer, no more than one Loan Officer may be appointed to the Committee. The Credit Committee meets no more than once a month or as needed by Congress. The Committee must review larger loans or loans that the credit union may need for approval. The Committee may grant approval authority to the Loan Officer; however, if an appeal occurs, the Committee will review the loan, and a majority vote will reverse the approval. Guidelines for the conduct and abilities of the Credit Committee are indicated in Section 1760 of the National Credit Union Administration guidelines.

3. The Supervisory Committee

The Supervisory Committee conducts an annual audit of the credit union. A report of the audit is provided to the NCUA and the Credit Union Members. The Committee has the power to suspend members from the Board of Directors and other Committees for failure to meet the credit union bylaws or federal regulations. A meeting can be held seven to fourteen days after a suspension of a Committee or Board member to review any violations the Supervisory Committee may have noted. The Committee may review any members account, in accordance with their audit process to verify account stating no more than once a year per credit union member as needed guidelines of the conduct and abilities of the Credit Committee are indicated in Section 1761d, of the National Credit Union Administration guidelines.

- Credit Union Membership

Credit unions have three types of memberships: (i) single common bond, (ii) multiple common bond, and (iii) the community credit union. Membership to the credit union is defined as "at least one of its stock" with payment of an initial installment and uniform entrance fee if required by the credit union, indicated in the credit unions bylaws (NCUA, 2013).

1. Single Common Bond Credits

Single common bond credits union are defined as a group of members with a common bond such as an association or occupation, for example, the Navy Federal Credit Union; all the members are Navy personnel.

2. The Multiple Common Bond Credits

The multiple common bond credits consist of more than one type of common group of occupation or association without a numerical limitation, for example, the Municipal Credit Union. The Municipal Credit Union has city workers as members that vary in occupation such as police officers and teachers, however, are within the same credit union. Community Credit Union consists of members being a part of the same organization within a "well-defined location, community, neighborhood or rural district" (NCUA, 2013). A credit union may request additional group coverage within their credit union; however, they must receive approval from the NCUA before extending an offer of membership to the group. Membership guidelines are located in Section 1759 of the National Credit Union Administration regulations. Member meetings are held annually based on the bylaws of the established credit union, and each member has one vote.

3. The Community Credits

Consist of persons or organizations within a well-defined local community, neighborhood, or rural district.

9.5 Financial Statements of Credit Unions

To illustrate the financial statements of credit unions, we use the statements of the biggest credit union, the Navy Federal Credit Union FY 2017–2018.

Consolidated Statements of Financial Condition

		As of December 31,		
(dollars in thousands)		2018		2017
ASSETS				
Cash and cash equivalents	$	1,362,428	$	4,472,369
Available-for-sale debt securities		16,574,816		15,268,843
Held-to-maturity securities		400,831		401,716
Equity securities		194,426		–
Mortgage loans awaiting sale		1,193,288		1,409,583
Loans to members, net of allowance for loan losses of $1,475,942 and $1,285,699, respectively		72,389,939		64,591,895
Accounts receivable and accrued interest		824,890		762,756
Property, plant and equipment, net		1,930,167		1,615,320
Investments in FHLB		569,975		675,022
NCUSIF deposit		635,843		559,842
Mortgage servicing rights		479,638		392,533
Goodwill		58,905		58,905
Other assets		347,300		356,977
Total assets	**$**	**96,962,446**	**$**	**90,565,761**
LIABILITIES AND MEMBERS' EQUITY				
Deposit accounts				
Checking	$	13,531,358	$	12,230,488
Savings		16,664,659		15,096,996
Money market savings		14,344,397		12,981,183
Certificates		19,790,889		17,163,989
Individual retirement accounts		6,086,231		5,534,087
Total deposit accounts		**70,417,534**		**63,006,743**
Liabilities				
Borrowed funds		13,308,239		15,779,939
Accounts payable and accrued expenses		1,304,400		1,104,184
Other liabilities		527,591		444,267
Total deposit accounts and liabilities		**85,557,764**		**80,335,133**
Members' equity				
Equity		12,149,541		10,551,156
Accumulated other comprehensive loss		(744,859)		(320,528)
Total members' equity		**11,404,682**		**10,230,628**
Total liabilities and members' equity	**$**	**96,962,446**	**$**	**90,565,761**

The accompanying notes are an integral part of these consolidated financial statements.

1. Analysis of the Statement

The balance sheet of the Navy Federal Credit Union is composed of assets, liabilities, and members' equity. The assets are: cash and cash equivalents, securities (held-to-maturity, available-for-sale, and equity security). The liabilities are: deposits accounts (checking, savings, and mortgage market savings), borrowed funds, account payable, and other liabilities. The equity is composed of members' equity solely. From FY 2017 to 2018, there has been a significant increase in the balance sheet.

Consolidated Statements of Income

	For the Years Ended December 31,	
(dollars in thousands)	2018	2017
Interest income		
Loans to members	$ 4,939,073	$ 4,238,969
Investment securities	420,946	359,441
Other investments	38,314	30,844
Total interest income	**5,398,333**	**4,629,254**
Dividends and interest expense		
Dividends on deposits	642,614	497,865
Interest on borrowed funds	340,006	299,181
Total dividends and interest expense	**982,620**	**797,046**
Net interest income	**4,415,713**	**3,832,208**
Provision for loan losses	(1,446,604)	(1,241,976)
Net interest income after provision for loan losses	**2,969,109**	**2,590,232**
Non-interest income		
Net gain on mortgage loans	167,632	194,853
Net (loss)/gain on investments	(9,519)	18,904
Mortgage servicing revenue	132,594	110,509
Interchange income	461,918	400,753
Fee and other income	724,292	671,229
Total non-interest income	**1,476,917**	**1,396,248**
Non-interest expense		
Salaries and employee benefits	1,394,426	1,300,816
Office operations and equipment	382,229	322,704
Servicing expense	347,510	321,780
Professional and outside services	211,667	174,594
Marketing	165,432	150,545
Depreciation and amortization	224,134	154,252
Other	175,357	214,815
Total non-interest expense	**2,900,755**	**2,639,506**
Net income	**$ 1,545,271**	**$ 1,346,974**

The accompanying notes are an integral part of these consolidated financial statements.

2. Analysis of the statement of income

Navy Federal Credit Union statement of income for FY 2017–2018 is essentially made of interest income (loan to members, investment securities, and other investments), non-interest income (net gain on mortgage loans, etc.), and dividend and interest expenses.

Consolidated Statements of Comprehensive Income

	For the Years Ended December 31,	
(dollars in thousands)	2018	2017
Net income	**$ 1,545,271**	**$ 1,346,974**
Other comprehensive (loss)/income		
Change in unrecognized pension and postretirement amounts	(81,024)	54,295
Change in net unrealized (losses)/gains on AFS debt securities	(291,831)	89,355
Change in unrecognized (losses)/gains on derivatives	(13,100)	11,029
Total other comprehensive (loss)/income	**(385,955)**	**154,679**
Total comprehensive income	**$ 1,159,316**	**$ 1,501,653**

The accompanying notes are an integral part of these consolidated financial statements.

Consolidated Statements of Changes in Members' Equity

(dollars in thousands)	Equity	Accumulated Other Comprehensive Income/(Loss)	Total Members' Equity
Balance at December 31, 2016	**$ 9,202,546**	**$ (475,207)**	**$ 8,727,339**
Other comprehensive income	–	154,679	154,679
Net income	1,346,974	–	1,346,974
Discretionary transfer	1,636	–	1,636
Balance at December 31, 2017	**$ 10,551,156**	**$ (320,528)**	**$ 10,230,628**
Cumulative effects from adoption of new accounting standards	53,114	(38,376)	14,738
Other comprehensive loss	–	(385,955)	(385,955)
Net income	1,545,271	–	1,545,271
Discretionary transfer	–	–	–
Balance at December 31, 2018	**$ 12,149,541**	**$ (744,859)**	**$ 11,404,682**

The accompanying notes are an integral part of these consolidated financial statements.

3. Analysis of the statement of comprehensive income

Navy Federal Credit Union comprehensive income includes: change in unrecognized pension and postretirement, change in net unrealized (losses)/gains on available-for-sale debt securities, and change in unrecognized (losses)/gains on derivatives.

Consolidated Statements of Cash Flows

(dollars in thousands)	For the Years Ended December 31, 2018	2017
Operating activities		
Net income	**$ 1,545,271**	**$ 1,346,974**
Adjustments to reconcile net income to net cash provided by operating activities:		
Provision for loan losses	1,446,604	1,241,976
Depreciation and amortization	224,134	154,252
Non-cash adjustments and gain on disposal of property, plant and equipment	(91,924)	(352)
Loss on valuation of equity securities	8,677	–
Loss/(gain) on sale of AFS securities	1,013	(18,904)
Amortization of loan origination fees and costs	13,728	4,498
Loss on valuation of mortgage servicing rights	46,909	42,480
Mortgage loans originated for sale	(7,667,792)	(7,042,646)
Gain on sale of mortgages	(167,632)	(194,853)
Mortgage loan sales proceeds	7,714,985	6,918,130
Accretion and amortization of investment securities	50,875	61,154
Change in accounts receivable and accrued interest	(61,333)	42,814
Change in mortgage servicing rights	(134,014)	(115,486)
Change in other assets	(145,523)	(46,691)
Change in accounts payable and accrued expenses	182,849	72,508
Change in other liabilities	67,958	37,519
Net cash provided by operating activities	**3,034,785**	**2,503,373**
Investing activities		
Purchase of AFS debt securities	(3,456,124)	(5,843,978)
Purchase of HTM securities	–	(99,383)
Proceeds from maturities, paydowns and calls of AFS debt securities	1,129,531	2,277,357
Proceeds from sales of AFS debt securities	844,762	2,406,638
Proceeds from maturities, paydowns and calls of HTM securities	1,022	9,531
Issuance of loan receivable	(750)	–
Net redemptions/(purchases) of FHLB stock	105,235	(86,466)
Proceeds from sale of loans originated for investment	–	946,526
Net increase in loans to members	(9,230,193)	(9,051,483)
Purchases of property, plant and equipment	(422,995)	(433,080)
Increase in NCUSIF deposit	(76,002)	(63,892)
Proceeds from sale of real estate owned and other assets	42,009	43,626
Net cash used in investing activities	**(11,063,505)**	**(9,894,604)**
Financing activities		
Net increase in deposit accounts	7,410,791	7,122,831
Net decrease in securities sold under repurchase agreements	–	(30,000)
Proceeds from borrowed funds	28,085,002	15,875,002
Repayments of borrowed funds	(30,556,702)	(13,840,502)
Payments of capital lease and financing obligations	(20,312)	–
Net cash provided by financing activities	**4,918,779**	**9,127,331**
Net (decrease)/increase in cash and cash equivalents	(3,109,941)	1,736,100
Cash and cash equivalents at beginning of year	**4,472,369**	**2,736,269**
Cash and cash equivalents at end of year	**$ 1,362,428**	**$ 4,472,369**
Supplemental cash flow information:		
Interest paid	$ 955,685	$ 799,775
Non-cash activities:		
Transfers from loans to other assets	28,182	19,187
Loans securitization	356,859	99,881
Accrued additions and improvements of property, plant and equipment	17,367	28,345
Financed property, plant and equipment purchases	6,327	–

The accompanying notes are an integral part of these consolidated financial statements.

4. Analysis of the statement of cash flows

Navy Federal Credit Union statement of cash flows is made of (i) statement from operating activities, (ii) cash flows from financing activities, and (iii) cash flows from investing activities. The cash flow from operating activities has increased significantly from 2017 to 2018. This is a good indication that Navy is blossoming through its main or core activities.

CHAPTER 10

Public Bank—Bank of North Dakota

10.1 General

Bank of North Dakota (BND) is owned and operated by the State of North Dakota under the supervision of the Industrial Commission as provided by Chapters 6–9 of the North Dakota Century Code. BND is a unique institution combining elements of banking, fiduciary, investment management services, and other financial services, and state government with a primary role in financing economic development. The state and its agencies are required to place their funds in the bank, but local governments are not required to do so. Since the initial investment of $2 million in 1919, BND has returned more than $1 billion to the state through the general fund, infrastructure, disaster relief, and other special programs. Throughout its history, the Bank has identified and played a key role in solving the funding needs of the state such as succession planning for family farms and ranches. The Bank's profits are used in three ways: appropriation through the North Dakota Legislature, mission-driven loan programs, and BND's capital. The Legislature appropriates the transfer of capital to the state's general fund. Every legislative session, the state's budget needs are reviewed and the amounts designated from BND's capital vary based on the needs of the state and BND's goal to maintain liquidity and capital. The Bank's profits are also used to support its mission-driven loan programs. Pending legislative approval, BND funds interest rate buy-downs and off-balance sheet programs that help drive economic development and infrastructure projects

F. I. Lessambo, *The U.S. Banking System*,
https://doi.org/10.1007/978-3-030-34792-5_10

across the state. Bank of North Dakota works essentially as a banker's bank implying that the greater part of its loan is done in partnership with local banks and credit unions. About portion of the bank's $3.9 billion loan portfolio comprises of business and agricultural loans that are initiated by a local financial institution and funded to a limited extent by BND. By taking an interest in these loans, BND extends the loan limit of North Dakota's community group banks, giving them included strength in competing against big out-of-state banks.[1] The Bank also serves as a central clearing agency and provides many other services to North Dakota banks and other financial institutions. Among the many programs, the Bank administers are the Guaranteed Student Loan Program, the Community Water Facility Loan Fund, and the Beginning Farmer Loan Program.

10.2 History of BND

The Bank of North Dakota was established by legislative action in 1919 to promote agriculture, commerce, and industry in North Dakota. During the early 1900s, North Dakota's economy was based on agriculture, specifically wheat. Frequent drought and harsh winters did not make it easy to earn a living. The arduous growing season was further complicated by grain dealers outside the state who suppressed grain prices, farm suppliers who increased their prices, and banks in Minneapolis and Chicago which raised the interest rates on farm loans, sometimes up to 12%. North Dakota farmers faced these high double-digit interest rates. The loans almost always came due during the harvest, which forced farmers to sell more wheat when prices were cheapest. Making matters worse, just about every grain elevator along the railroad was operated by the big grain companies, which offered the same price and the same grade rating-always lower than the growers needed and wanted. The final insult was when the grain was weighed; the companies used a fan to blow on the pile, supposedly to remove dust. But the fan removed not only the dust but during the course of the year in some of the larger elevators, fifty thousand bushels of grain as well.[2] North Dakotans were frustrated and attempts to legislate fairer

[1] Stacy Mitchell (2015): Public Banks: Bank of North Dakota, Institute for local Self Reliance.

[2] Abby Rapoport (2013): The People's Bank-American Prospect, 24(2): 82–87.

business practices failed. A.C. Townley, a politician who was fired from the Socialist Party, organized the Non-Partisan League with the intent of creating a farm organization that protected the social and economic position of the farmer. In 1915, they began to team up with former socialist organizers eager to create a viable political operation. Calling themselves the Non-Partisan League, they began to challenge Republicans in primaries. The Non-Partisan League gained control of the Governor's office, majority control of the House of Representatives and one-third of the seats in the Senate in 1918. Their platform included state ownership and control of marketing and credit agencies. In 1919, the state legislature established Bank of North Dakota, and the North Dakota Mill and Elevator Association. BND opened July 28, 1919, with $2 million of capital. BND has responded to the state's needs since its inception.

Today, in partnership with more than 100 North Dakota financial institutions, BND fulfills its mission to promote the development of agriculture, commerce and industry in North Dakota. The operating policy stated that the Bank shall be "helpful to and to assist in the development of state and national banks and other financial institutions and public corporations within the state and not, in any manner, to destroy or to be harmful to existing financial institutions." The Bank's operating policy continues to serve as a guiding principle for the Bank's work in our state.

10.3 Missions and Regulatory Framework

BND has the statutory authority to engage in several banking activities. Its main focus is financing for economic development. The bank is involved in both direct lending and participation loans (lending by the bank through participation with another financial institution), with an emphasis on the latter. The bank offers commercial financing programs for farming, ranching, small business, start-up enterprises, community development, and other areas. The bank also administers a state student loan program and other educational financing programs, including a 529 college-savings program. The bank does have an account with the Federal Reserve Bank, thus deposits are not insured by the Federal Deposit Insurance Corporation; instead, deposits are guaranteed by the general fund of the state of North Dakota itself and the taxpayers of the state. One of the chief ways BND fulfills this mission is through lending operations. The bank's $3.9 billion loan portfolio has four main components: business, farm, residential, and student loans.

Fig. 10.1 Total loan portfolio (*Source* BND Financial Statements [2018])

- Total loan portfolio

A $3.9 billion loan portfolio includes agriculture loans, business loans, home loans, and student loans. The Bank of North Dakota grows the lending limit of North Dakota's community banks, giving them included quality in going up against huge out-of-state banks by partaking in these loans. There were 17,299 loans for $1.33 billion originated or renewed in 2018. BND's loan portfolio shrunk by $325 million, primarily due to strategic decisions that were made which impacted the student loan and home loan portfolios (Fig. 10.1).

- Agricultural Loan Portfolio

BND sustains several agricultural loans, including (i) Agriculture Partnership in Assisting Community Expansion (Ag PACE)[3] and (ii) Family Farm loan Program.[4] Most of BND's agriculture lending programs are initiated with the local financial institution. There are two exceptions to this: the Beginning Farmer Real Estate Loan and Established Farmer Real Estate Loan. The agricultural loan portfolio decreased by $3 million in 2018. However, increases in three specific agricultural loans: Beginning Farmer Real Estate, Beginning Farmer Chattel, and Ag PACE are positive indicators for the agricultural economy (Fig. 10.2).

- Business Loan Portfolio

All of BND's business lending programs work with the local lender as the borrower's first contact. The local lender initiates the loan application with BND on behalf of the borrower. In 2017, BND has introduced an Accelerated Growth Loan Program to assist North Dakota-based companies entering or anticipating a period of dynamic growth. These companies must establish a record of proven operations, experienced management, and the ability to generate cash flow but have limited assets for traditional bank financing. The business loan portfolio decreased by $32 million in 2018. The number of commercial loans originated and renewed is stable, but there was a decrease in the dollar amount of these loans. Significant growth was seen in PACE and Flex PACE programs due to the expansion of parameters which was instituted in 2017 (Fig. 10.3).

[3]This program has been built up to purchase down the interest rates on loans to farmers who are investing into other nontraditional agribusiness exercises to supplement cultivate income.

[4]Family Farm Loan Program: The North Dakota governing body has built up a program to help family farms. This program permits BND to take an interest in loans for qualified purposes up to 90% of the loan amount.

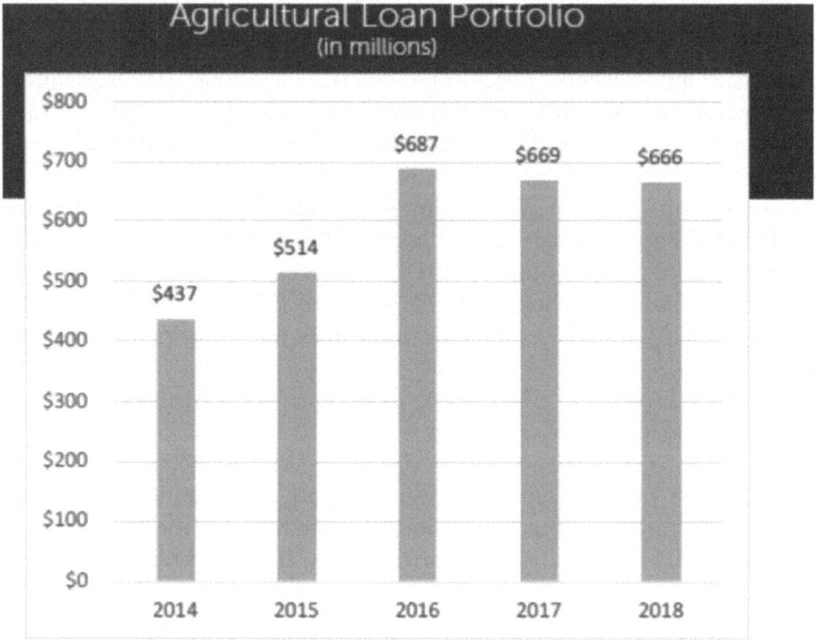

Fig. 10.2 Agricultural loan portfolio (*Source* BND Financial Statements [2018])

- Home Loan Portfolio

Bank of North Dakota's role in home loans is to help local lenders provide the best service possible to their customers. The local lender may: (i) originate a home loan with the borrower and sell it to BND, who will service the loan right here in ND, or (ii) refer the borrower to BND to originate the loan. The home loan portfolio decreased by $68 million, largely due to a newly implemented strategy to book fewer fixed-rate mortgages. This allows BND to meet the area of greatest need in the home loan arena: rural mortgage origination and purchase (Fig. 10.4).

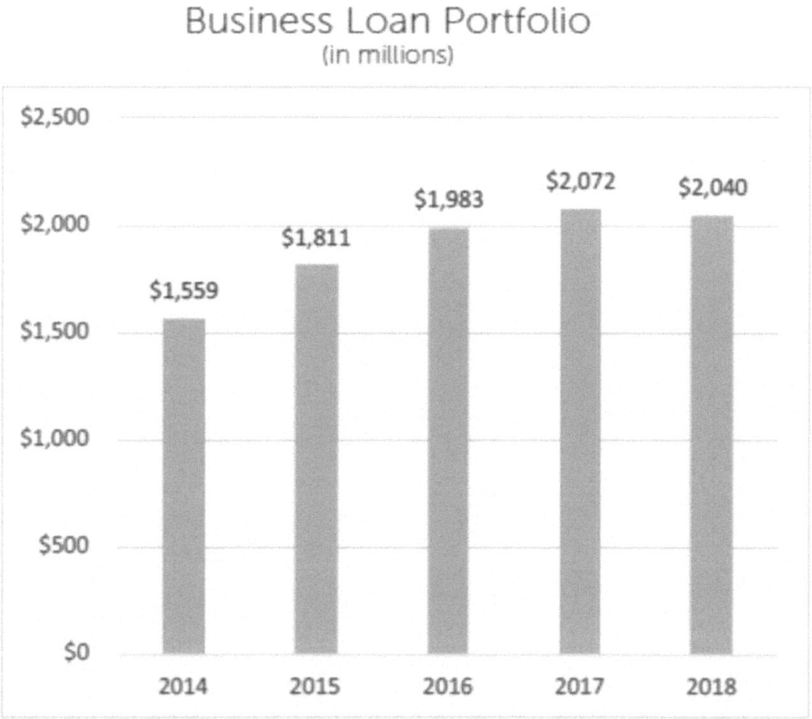

Fig. 10.3 Business loan portfolio (*Source* BND Financial Statements [2018])

- Student Loan Portfolio

Student's loans used to be the only loan program, in which the bank dealt directly with the borrowers. Effective January 1, 2018, Bank of North Dakota sold and transferred its Federal Student Loan portfolio to North Texas Higher Education Authority, Inc. (NTHEA). BND sold off the remaining $246 million of federal student loans in its portfolio. This sale, along with fewer residents benefiting from refinancing their student loans, led to a portfolio decrease of $222 million (Fig. 10.5).

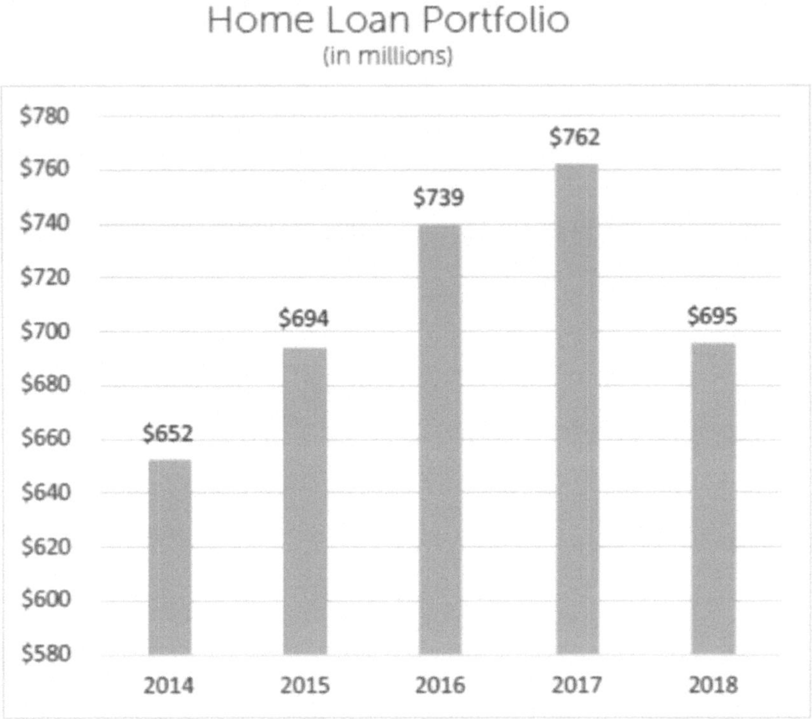

Fig. 10.4 Home loan portfolio (*Source* BND Financial Statements [2018])

It should be noted that, the Bank of North Dakota rarely makes direct loans; instead, when a community bank wants to give a sizable loan but lacks the capital, the state bank will partner on the loan and provide a backstop. Such partnerships help ensure that small-business owners, farmers, and ranchers can access lines of credit—and they strengthen community banks, which is why North Dakota has more local banks per capita than any other state.[5] Individuals may also open accounts at the bank, but BND does not market these services and does not have ATMs, branch offices, and other standard features common to retail banks. This is in keeping with the bank's mission to support local banks, rather than compete with them.

[5]Abby Rapoport (2013): The People's Bank-American Prospect, 24(2): 82–87.

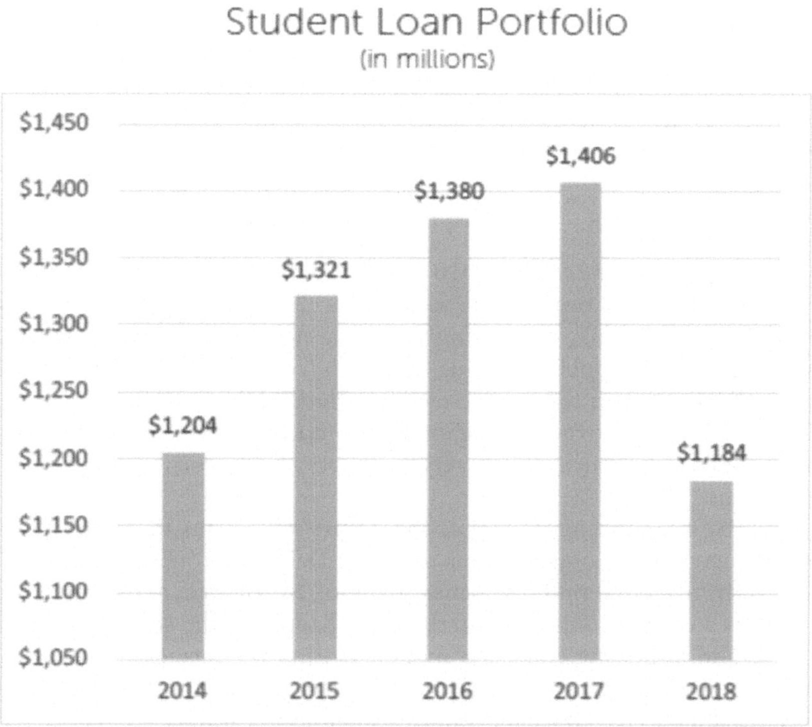

Fig. 10.5 Student loan portfolio (*Source* BND)

10.4 Organizational Structure of BND

BND is governed by the state's Industrial Commission, which consists of the governor, the attorney general, and the commissioner of agriculture. The North Dakota Industrial Commission is the body that oversees the management of several separate programs and resources, including the Bank of North Dakota, North Dakota Mill and Elevator, and the Department of Mineral Resources. The commission, in effect, serves as the bank's board of directors. Besides the Industrial Commission, BND management includes seven-member of the BND Advisory Board of Directors, which oversees the bank's operations. The governor appoints the board members who are then responsible for reviewing the bank's operations and making recommendations to the Industrial Commission concerning management, services, policies, and procedures. The daily management is entrusted in the BND Executive Committee, which consists of seven members including the President, the CEO; and leaders in lending; banking accounting and treasury; student loans; human resources; and information technology.

10.5 BND Financial Resilience

In the midst of the 2008–2010 financial crisis, Wall Street financial analysts and media began to praise the excellent record of this solitary publicly owned bank, attributing it to the achievement of the private oil industry. The public banking model is considered more beneficial and productive than the private model. The BND's costs are exceptionally low; not executives' exorbitant wages, no rewards, fees, or commissions; only one branch office; very low borrowing costs; and no FDIC premiums.

The bank's concentration is giving advances to loans to students and increasing credit to organizations in North Dakota, frequently in association with smaller community banks. Bank of North Dakota likewise goes about as a clearinghouse for interbank exchanges in the state by settling checks and dispersing coins and money. During the financial crisis, Bank of North Dakota expanded its loans and letter of credit to North Dakota banks that expected to create compressive liquidity arranges.

Since the Great Depression in the 1930s there was an economic downfall due to the stock market crash in 1929, which placed Wall Street into alarm, horror, and effected millions of investors. History repeated itself in 2008 causing the Bank Financial Crisis of the US Banking system despite the efforts of the Federal Reserve and Treasury Department. Due to housing prices felling approximately 31.8% and banks not receiving returns on investments, the conclusion was to issue subprime loans. This allowed banks to engage in trading and selling of derivatives, which cause an increase in mortgage issuance. The effects made house prices plummeted and left borrowers in default. Homeowners were locked into a home they could no longer afford nor was able to sell. When homeowner was no longer able to pay back on their mortgages, the banks had to cut lending because there were not enough payouts.

> … The recent market instability was caused by many factors, chief among them a dramatic change in the ability to create new lines of credit, which dried up the flow of money and slowed new economic growth and the buying and selling of assets. This hurt individuals, businesses, and financial institutions hard, and many financial institutions were left holding mortgage backed assets that had dropped precipitously in value and weren't bringing in the amount of money needed to pay for the loans. This dried up their reserve…

August of 2007 the Federal Reserve attempted to help the US banks system from the subprime mortgage by issuing $24 billion in liquidity, however by September 2008, Congress approved an additional $700 billion to bail out banks. In order for the economic to recover from the regression, Former President Obama and Congress approved $787 billion economic stimulus plan, providing a $75 billion plan to stop an estimated 7–9 million homeowner from foreclosures.[6]

Despite the bailout issuance given to US banks, one institution stood out with little to no assistant from the federal government and that is North Dakota, state own bank with continuous budget surplus since the banking crisis of 2008. Unlike other banks, BND has the advantage because they are fully invested within their home state of North Dakota. Its balance sheet is so strong that it recently reduced individual income taxes and property taxes by a combined $400 million, and is debating further cuts. It also has the lowest foreclosure rate and lowest credit card default rate in the country and it has had no bank failures in at least the last decade. The fact that the states monies are kept within it allows for capitalization on resources to full advantage.

[6]K. Amadeo (November 9, 2016). The Great Recession of 2008: Explanation with Dates. Retrieved February 14, 2017, from The Great Recession of 2008: Explanation with Dates.

10.6 Financial Statement Analysis for Bank of North Dakota

10.6.1 The Balance Sheet

BANK OF NORTH DAKOTA
BALANCE SHEETS
DECEMBER 31, 2018 AND 2017
(In Thousands)

	2018	2017
ASSETS		
Cash and due from banks	$ 470,227	$ 357,042
Federal funds sold	39,465	57,555
Cash and cash equivalents	509,692	414,597
Securities	1,912,743	1,665,252
Loans held for investment	4,584,233	4,661,432
Loans held for sale	-	247,846
Less allowance for loan losses	(92,750)	(84,958)
	4,491,483	4,824,320
Interest receivable	56,865	53,525
Bank premises, equipment, and software, net	10,249	10,919
Rebuilders loan program receivable	10,288	13,682
Other assets	24,514	21,007
Total assets	$ 7,015,834	$ 7,003,302
LIABILITIES AND EQUITY		
Deposits		
Non-interest bearing	$ 567,352	$ 555,020
Interest bearing	4,202,467	4,049,938
	4,769,819	4,604,958
Federal funds purchased and repurchase agreements	271,505	299,775
Short and long-term debt	1,103,436	1,263,569
Other liabilities	9,190	10,198
Total liabilities	6,153,950	6,178,500
Equity		
Capital	2,000	2,000
Capital surplus	72,000	72,000
Undivided profits	777,742	747,848
Accumulated other comprehensive income	10,142	2,954
Total equity	861,884	824,802
Total liabilities and equity	$ 7,015,834	$ 7,003,302

1. Analysis of the balance sheet

Total assets remained stable at $7 billion, and the core assets of the BND are the following:

- Assets
  - Cash and Due from banks
  - Securities: Loans held for investments and loans held for sale;
  - Interest receivable, and
  - Other assets
- Liabilities
  Total liabilities have slightly decreased but remain above $6 billion. Core liabilities are:
  - Deposits (non-interest bearing and interest bearing)
  - Interest bearing
- Equity
  ND ended the year with capital of $861 million, an increase of $37 million.

10.6.2 The Statement of Income

BANK OF NORTH DAKOTA
STATEMENTS OF INCOME
YEARS ENDED DECEMBER 31, 2018 AND 2017
(In Thousands)

	2018	2017
INTEREST INCOME		
Federal funds sold	$ 1,092	$ 569
Securities	40,225	30,321
Loans, including fees	198,686	188,810
Total interest income	240,003	219,700
INTEREST EXPENSE		
Deposits	17,341	10,469
Federal funds purchased and repurchase agreements	4,705	2,818
Short and long-term debt	24,396	24,578
Total interest expense	46,442	37,865
NET INTEREST INCOME	193,561	181,835
PROVISION FOR LOAN LOSSES	12,000	12,000
NET INTEREST INCOME AFTER PROVISION FOR LOAN LOSSES	181,561	169,835
NONINTEREST INCOME		
Service fees and other	7,170	6,335
Total noninterest income	7,170	6,335
NONINTEREST EXPENSE		
Salaries and benefits	16,870	16,608
Data processing	5,253	5,157
Occupancy and equipment	932	1,448
Other operating expenses	7,168	7,673
Total noninterest expenses	30,223	30,886
NET INCOME	$ 158,508	$ 145,284

BANK OF NORTH DAKOTA
STATEMENTS OF COMPREHENSIVE INCOME
YEARS ENDED DECEMBER 31, 2018 AND 2017
(In Thousands)

	2018	2017
Net income	$ 158,508	$ 145,284
Other comprehensive income (loss)		
Unrealized loss on securities available for sale	(703)	(10,498)
Unrealized gain on interest rate swap	7,632	861
Reclassification adjustment for losses realized in net income	259	355
Other comprehensive income (loss)	7,188	(9,282)
Comprehensive income	$ 165,696	$ 136,002

1. Analysis of the statements

BND has reported record profits in 2018, with $159 million in net earnings. This is the 15th straight year the bank has grown its profits to record levels.

10.6.3 *Statement of Equity*

BANK OF NORTH DAKOTA
STATEMENTS OF EQUITY
YEARS ENDED DECEMBER 31, 2018 AND 2017
(In Thousands)

	Capital	Capital Surplus	Undivided Profits	Accumulated Other Comprehensive Income (Loss)	Total
BALANCE, DECEMBER 31, 2016	$ 2,000	$ 72,000	$ 789,496	$ 12,236	$ 875,732
Net income			145,284		145,284
Unrealized loss on securities available for sale				(10,498)	(10,498)
Unrealized gain on interest rate swap				861	861
Reclassification adjustment for losses realized in net income				355	355
Transfers to other state funds			(186,932)		(186,932)
BALANCE, DECEMBER 31, 2017	2,000	72,000	747,848	2,954	824,802
Net income			158,508		158,508
Unrealized loss on securities available for sale				(703)	(703)
Unrealized gain on interest rate swap				7,632	7,632
Reclassification adjustment for losses realized in net income				259	259
Transfers to other state funds			(128,614)		(128,614)
BALANCE, DECEMBER 31, 2018	$ 2,000	$ 72,000	$ 777,742	$ 10,142	$ 861,884

10.6.4 *Statement of Cash Flows*

BANK OF NORTH DAKOTA
STATEMENTS OF CASH FLOWS
YEARS ENDED DECEMBER 31, 2018 AND 2017
(In Thousands)

	2018	2017
OPERATING ACTIVITIES		
Net income	$ 158,508	$ 145,284
Adjustments to reconcile net income to net cash from operating activities		
Depreciation and amortization	813	858
Provision for loan losses	12,000	12,000
Net amortization/(accretion) of securities	4,238	(7,455)
(Gain) loss on available-for-sale securities	(58)	55
Other than temporary impairment on equity securities	317	300
Gain on sale of residential and student loans	(1,620)	(108)
Write-off cost incurred for ND Financial Center	-	470
Loss (gain) on sale of foreclosed assets	(705)	43
Increase in interest receivable	(3,340)	(2,700)
Decrease (increase) in other assets	1,895	(5,756)
Increase in other liabilities	674	1,302
NET CASH FROM OPERATING ACTIVITIES	172,722	144,295
INVESTING ACTIVITIES		
Securities available for sale transactions		
Purchase of securities	(861,167)	(199,590)
Proceeds from sales, maturities, and principal repayments	603,033	599,311
Purchase of Federal Home Loan Bank stock	(250,080)	(140,600)
Sale of Federal Home Loan Bank stock	256,857	141,409
Purchase of other equity securities	(1,787)	(1,100)
Sale of other equity securities	712	602
Proceeds from sales of loans	283,647	7,561
Net (increase) decrease in loans	36,204	(137,172)
Purchases of premises and equipment	(143)	(305)
Payments from rebuilders loan program	3,394	3,793
Proceeds from sale of foreclosed assets	3,859	357
NET CASH FROM INVESTING ACTIVITIES	74,529	274,265
FINANCING ACTIVITIES		
Net increase (decrease) in non-interest bearing deposits	12,332	(108,136)
Net increase (decrease) in interest bearing deposits	152,529	(174,098)
Net increase (decrease) in federal funds purchased and repurchase agreements	(28,270)	57,295
Proceeds from issuance of short and long-term debt	6,377,000	3,515,001
Payment of short and long-term debt	(6,537,133)	(3,531,969)
Payment of transfers to other state funds	(128,614)	(186,932)
NET CASH USED FOR FINANCING ACTIVITIES	(152,156)	(428,839)
NET CHANGE IN CASH AND CASH EQUIVALENTS	95,095	(10,280)
CASH AND CASH EQUIVALENTS, BEGINNING OF YEAR	414,597	424,877
CASH AND CASH EQUIVALENTS, END OF YEAR	$ 509,692	$ 414,597

1. Analysis of the statement

The cash flows from operating, and financing activities have increased from \$144,295,000 to \$172,722.000, whereas the cash flows from investing activities have declined from \$274,265 to \$74,529,000.

10.7 Conclusion

Bank of North Dakota is only state-owned bank within the United States; it mission is to deliver quality, good financial services which sponsor agriculture, commerce, and industry within the state. It focuses on the development and investing by assisting 89 local banks by providing student loans and low interest rates to homeowners. Their dedication to the economy and citizens is an example or blueprint for how a state can serve the community. BND secret for survival opposed to other banks is the ability to maintain surplus and capitalize on all resources to their full advantage. BND practices should be duplicate for other states as an example on how we all can work together to improve our own (states) developments and growth.

PART III

Risks and Banking Regulation

CHAPTER 11

Risks in the Banking Industry

11.1 General

In order to offer shareholders a competitive rate of return, banks incur substantial risk, such as using a high amount of leverage, investing in assets riskier than the liability positions funding them, and maintaining minimal liquidity positions.

11.2 Typology of Risks

The following are the most common types of risks banks are exposed to: (i) credit risk, (ii) liquidity risk, (iii) interest rate risk, (iv) market risk, (v) off-balance sheet risk, (vi) foreign exchange risk, (vii) country or sovereign risk, (viii) technology risk, (ix) operational risk, and (x) insolvency risk. Needless to say that these risks are all interdependent.

11.2.1 Credit Risk

Credit risk refers to the possibility that a borrower will not repay principal and interest as promised in due time. Credit card loss rates are significantly higher than most other types of domestic loans. Credit risk is the most obvious risk in banking, and possibly the most important in terms of potential losses. The default of a small number of key customers could generate very large losses and in an extreme case could lead to a bank becoming insolvent. This risk relates to the possibility that loans will not

F. I. Lessambo, *The U.S. Banking System*,
https://doi.org/10.1007/978-3-030-34792-5_11

be paid or that investments will deteriorate in quality or go into default with consequent loss to the bank. Credit risk is not confined to the risk that borrowers are unable to pay; it also includes the risk of payments being delayed, which can also cause problems for the bank. Capital markets react to a deterioration in a company's credit standing through higher interest rates on its debt issues, a decline in its share price, and/or a downgrading of the assessment of its debt quality. As a result of these risks, bankers must exercise discretion in maintaining a sensible distribution of liquidity in assets and also conduct a proper evaluation of the default risks associated with borrowers. In general, protection against credit risks involves maintaining high credit standards, appropriate diversification, good knowledge of the borrower's affairs and accurate monitoring and collection procedures. In general, credit risk management for loans involves three main principles: (i) selection, (ii) limitation, and (iii) diversification.

- Selection

Selection means banks have to choose carefully those to whom they will lend money. The processing of credit applications is conducted by credit officers or credit Committees, and a bank's delegation rules specify responsibility for credit decisions. Limitation refers to the way that banks set credit limits at various levels.

- Limitation

Limit systems clearly establish maximum amounts that can be lent to specific individuals or groups. Loans are also classified by size and limitations are put on the proportion of large loans to total lending. Banks also have to observe maximum risk assets to total assets and should hold a minimum proportion of assets, such as cash and government securities, whose credit risk is negligible.

- Diversification

Credit management has to be diversified. Banks must spread their business over different types of borrower, different economic sectors, and geographical regions, in order to avoid excessive concentration of credit risk problems. Large banks therefore have an advantage in this respect.

The long-standing existence of the above procedures within banks is insufficient to address all credit risk problems. For example, the amount of a potential loss is uncertain since outstanding balances at the time of default are not known in advance. The size of the commitment is not sufficient to measure the risk, since there are both quantity and quality dimensions to consider. These are among the issues inherent in credit risk measurement and management which are examined in.

11.2.2 Liquidity Risk

Liquidity risk is the risk that an institution or bank may be unable to meet its short-term financial demands. Generally, liquidity risk is due to the inability to convert a security or an illiquid asset into cash without a loss of capital and/or income in the process.

The fundamental principle is that a bank must assiduously manage its liquidity risk and maintain sufficient liquidity to withstand a range of stress events. Liquidity is a critical element of a bank's resilience to stress, and as such, a bank must maintain a liquidity cushion, made up of unencumbered, high-quality liquid assets, to protect against liquidity stress events, including potential losses of unsecured and typically available secured funding sources.[1] A key element in the management of liquidity risk is the need for strong governance of liquidity risk, including the setting of a liquidity risk tolerance by the board. Also, a bank should appropriately price the costs, benefits, and risks of liquidity into the internal pricing, performance measurement, and new product approval process of all significant business activities. A bank's failure to effectively manage intraday liquidity could leave it unable to meet its payment obligations at the time expected, which could lead to liquidity dislocations that cascade quickly across many systems and institutions.[2] The longer-term liquidity needs of banks are more complex than the aforementioned

[1] A bank should develop methodologies to measure the effect of reputational risk in terms of other risk types, namely credit, liquidity, market, and other risks that they may be exposed to in order to avoid reputational damages and in order to maintain market confidence. This could be done by including reputational risk scenarios in regular stress tests. For instance, including non-contractual off-balance sheet exposures in the stress tests to determine the effect on a bank's credit, market and liquidity risk profiles.

[2] BIS—Basel Committee on Banking Supervision (2009): Enhancements to the Basel II Framework, p. 23.

seasonal and cyclical requirements. If loan growth exceeds deposit growth, banks must budget for longer-term liquidity. Such net growth can be financed by selling liquid assets or purchasing funds. The major problem with fulfilling such longer-term liquidity demands is that the supply of saleable assets and the amount of borrowing permissible are limited. In addition, a bank should always limit its use of bought-in liquidity, so as to have enough "borrowing capacity" if future unpredictable liquidity needs occur. Liquidity risk is often an inevitable outcome of banking operations. Since a bank typically collects deposits which are short term in nature and lends long term, the gap between maturities leads to liquidity risk and a cost of liquidity. The bank's liquidity situation can be captured by the time profiles of the projected sources and uses of funds, and banks should manage liquidity gaps within acceptable limits.

11.2.3 Interest Rate Risk

Interest rate risk relates to the exposure of banks' profits to interest rate changes which affect assets and liabilities in different ways. Banks are exposed to interest rate risk because they operate with unmatched balance sheets. If bankers believe strongly that interest rates are going to move in a certain direction in the future, they have a strong incentive to position the bank accordingly: When an interest rate rise is expected, they will make assets more interest-sensitive relative to liabilities, and do the opposite when a fall is expected. Assets and liabilities can obviously be mixed to increase or decrease project future exposures.

The impact of interest rate changes in the macro-economy on the risk exposure of banks is a matter of significant concern to both bankers and regulators. For example, a monetary environment that produces marked interest rate volatility may threaten banking stability. Because banks engage in maturity transformation, unexpected and significant market rate changes may lead to an unacceptable number of banks and other financial institutions encountering difficulties or even failing. Full awareness of such costs is needed in order to evaluate policy alternatives. At the same time, management needs to understand and manage its own exposure to interest rate risk.

With bank costs and revenues both being increasingly related to market interest rates, the net effects of interest rate changes on bank profits are becoming increasingly difficult to measure. Another important dimension of bank interest rate risk concerns other changes in the bank balance sheet that may be associated with the interest rate cycle. For example, a bank faced with significant profit variance related to market interest rate changes may alter its balance sheet volume and mix of earning assets in order to help stabilize earnings. Although some such volume and mix effects may be initiated by the bank itself, other factors may be external and uncontrollable in a deregulated banking environment. Faced with this complex set of relationships, the concept of interest rate risk and its measurement is becoming ever more sophisticated. Banks use the concept of matching to minimize their interest rate exposure. This requires the classification of assets and liabilities according to their interest rates. The aim of such matching is to show how each side of the bank's balance sheet is related to particular rates of interest, and how it is exposed to changes in market rates. There can never be perfect matching, because of three factors:

- Some risk is unavoidable (some interest rates are fixed or quasi-fixed, such as rates on cheque accounts and savings accounts, and these may be considered to be structurally mismatched with respect to variable interest rates on assets).
- Some interest rate risks have to be accepted to accommodate clients.
- There can be no certainty that the banks' borrowing costs in all cases will move in step with market rates.
- Market risk.

This relates to the risk of loss associated with adverse deviations in the value of the trading portfolio, which arises through fluctuations in, for example, interest rates, equity prices, foreign exchange rates, or commodity prices. It arises where banks hold financial instruments on the trading book, or where banks hold equity as some form large banks have dramatically increased the size and activity of their trading portfolios, resulting in greater exposure to market risk.

Bessis[3] defines market risk more narrowly as the risk of loss during the time required to effect a transaction (liquidation period). This risk has two components, relating to volatility and liquidity. First, even though the liquidation period is relatively short, deviations can be large in a

[3]Joel Bessis (2011): *Risk Management in Banking*, Wiley.

volatile market. Second, for instruments traded in markets with a low volume of transactions, it may be difficult to sell without suffering large discounts. Beyond the liquidation period, the risk is of a deficiency in monitoring the market portfolio, rather than a pure market risk.

Regulators are increasingly focusing on requiring banks to measure their market risk using an internally generated risk measurement model. The industry standard for dealing with market risk on the trading book is the value-at-risk (VaR) model pioneered by JP Morgan's. This model is used to calculate a VaR-based capital aim of VaR is to calculate the likely loss a bank might experience on its whole trading book. The validity of a bank's estimated VaR is assessed by backtesting, whereby actual daily trading gains or losses are compared to the estimated VaR over a particular period. Concerns would arise if actual results were frequently worse than the estimated VaR. A bank may measure its specific risk through by the "standardized approach."

11.2.4 Market Risk

Market risk is defined as the risk of losses arising from movements in market prices. The risks subject to market risk capital charges include but are not limited to: (a) default risk, interest rate risk, credit spread risk, equity risk, foreign exchange risk, and commodities risk for trading book instruments; and (b) foreign exchange risk and commodities risk for banking book instruments.[4]

In determining its market risk for regulatory capital requirements, a bank may choose between two broad methodologies: the standardized

[4]BIS—Basel Committee on Banking Supervision (2016): Minimum capital requirements for market risk, p. 5.

The risk charge under the sensitivities-based method must be calculated by aggregating the following risk measures: (i) Delta: A risk measure based on sensitivities of a bank's trading book to regulatory delta risk factors. Delta sensitivities are to be used as inputs into the aggregation formula, which delivers the capital requirement for the sensitivities-based method. (ii) Vega: A risk measure that is also based on sensitivities to regulatory vega risk factors to be used as inputs to a similar aggregation formula as for delta risks. (iii) Curvature: A risk measure which captures the incremental risk not captured by the delta risk of price changes in the value of an option. Curvature risk is based on two stress scenarios involving an upward shock and a downward shock to a given risk factor. The worst loss of the two scenarios is the risk position (defined in paragraph 48) to be used as an input into the aggregation formula which delivers the capital charge.

approach and internal models approach for market risk, subject to the approval of the national authorities.

1. The Standardized Approach (SA)

A bank must determine its regulatory capital requirements for market risk according to the standardized approach for market risk as required or set up by their supervisors' demand. The standardized approach capital requirement is the simple sum of three components: (i) the risk charges under the sensitivity-based method, (ii) the default risk charge, and (iii) the residual risk add-on.

2. The Internal Methods Approach

The use of an internal model for the purposes of regulatory capital determination is conditional upon the explicit approval of the bank's supervisory authority. The supervisory authority must give its approval if at a minimum:

(a) It is satisfied that the bank's risk management system is conceptually sound and is implemented with integrity;
(b) The bank has, in the supervisory authority's view, sufficient numbers of staff skilled in the use of sophisticated models not only in the trading area but also in the risk control, audit and, if necessary, back-office areas;
(c) The bank's models have, in the supervisory authority's judgment, a proven track record of reasonable accuracy in measuring risk;
(d) The bank regularly conducts sound stress tests in compliance with the set standards; and
(e) The positions included in the internal model for regulatory capital determination are held in approved trading desks that have passed the required test.

Moreover, banks using internal models for capital purposes are subject to the additional requirements, including the qualitative and the quantitative standards.

- Qualitative standards

Bank's supervisors must assess that banks have met the criteria before they are permitted to use a models-based approach. These qualitative criteria include[5]:

(a) The bank must have an independent risk control unit that is responsible for the design and implementation of the bank's risk management system. The unit must produce and analyze daily reports on the output of the bank's risk measurement model, including an evaluation of the relationship between measures of risk exposure and trading limits. This unit must be independent from business trading units and should report directly to senior management of the bank.
(b) The unit must conduct regular backtesting and profit and loss (P&L) attribution programs. Both of these exercises must be conducted at a trading desk level, while regular backtesting must also be conducted on the firm-wide internal model for regulatory capital determination level.
(c) A distinct unit must conduct the initial and ongoing validation of all internal models. Internal models must be validated on at least an annual basis.
(d) Board of directors and senior management must be actively involved in the risk control process and need to regard risk control as an essential aspect of the business to which significant resources are devoted. In this regard, the daily reports prepared by the independent risk control unit must be reviewed by a level of management with sufficient seniority and authority to enforce both reductions of positions taken by individual traders and reductions in the bank's overall risk exposure.
(e) Internal models used to calculate market risk charges are likely to differ from those used by banks in their day-to-day internal management functions. These valuation models must be an integral part of the internal identification, measurement, management, and internal reporting of price risks within the firm. As well,

[5] BIS—Basel Committee on Banking Supervision (2016): Minimum Capital Requirements for Market Risk, pp. 50–52.

internal risk models must, at a minimum, cover the positions covered by the regulatory models, although they may cover more.

(f) A routine and rigorous program of stress testing is required as a supplement to the risk analysis based on the output of the bank's risk measurement model. The results of stress testing must be reviewed at least monthly by senior management, used in the internal assessment of capital adequacy, and reflected in the policies and limits set by management and the board of directors. Where stress tests reveal particular vulnerability to a given set of circumstances, prompt steps must be taken to mitigate those risks appropriately.

(g) Banks need to have a routine in place for ensuring compliance with a documented set of internal policies, controls, and procedures concerning the operation of the risk measurement system. The bank's risk measurement system must be well documented.

(h) Any significant changes to a regulatory-approved model must be approved by the supervisor prior to being implemented.

(i) Risk measures must be calculated on the full set of positions, which are in the scope of application of the model. The risk measures must be based on a sound theoretical basis, calculated correctly, and reported accurately.

(j) An independent review of the risk measurement system must be carried out regularly by either the bank's own internal auditing process or an external auditor. This review must include the activities of both the business trading units and the independent risk control unit. The review must be sufficiently detailed to determine for any failings which desks are impacted. A review of the overall risk management process should take place at regular intervals (not less than once a year) and must specifically address, at a minimum:

- The organization of the risk control unit;
- The adequacy of the documentation of the risk management system and process;
- The accuracy and appropriateness of the risk measurement system (including any significant changes);
- The verification of the consistency, timeliness, and reliability of data sources used to run internal models, including the independence of such data sources;

- The approval process for risk pricing models and valuation systems used by front and back-office personnel;
- The scope of market risks captured by the risk measurement model;
- The integrity of the management information system;
- The accuracy and completeness of position data;
- The accuracy and appropriateness of volatility and correlation assumptions;
- The accuracy of valuation and risk transformation calculations; and
- The verification of the model's accuracy through frequent backtesting and P&L attribution. Supervisory framework for the use of backtesting in conjunction with the internal models approach to market risk capital requirements.

- Quantitative standards

Although banks are allowed some flexibility in devising the precise nature of their models, a set of minimum standards apply for the purpose of calculating their capital charge[6]: (i) an expected shortfall and (ii) empirical correlations within broad regulatory risk factor classes

(i) Expected shortfall: is computed on a daily basis for the bank-wide internal model for regulatory capital purposes. Expected shortfall can also be determined on a daily basis for each trading desk that a bank wishes to include within the scope for the internal model for regulatory capital purposes. In calculating the expected shortfall, a 97.5th percentile, one-tailed confidence level is to be used.
(ii) Empirical correlations across broad risk factor categories need to be constrained by the supervisory aggregation scheme and must be calculated and used in a manner consistent with the applicable liquidity horizons, clearly documented and able to be explained to supervisors on request.
(iii) Model validation standards: The validation must be conducted when the model is initially developed and when any significant

[6]BIS—Basel Committee on Banking Supervision (2016): Minimum Capital Requirements for Market Risk, p. 52.

changes are made to the model. Models need to be periodically revalidated, particularly when there have been significant structural changes in the market or changes to the composition of the portfolio which might lead to the model no longer being adequate. Model validation must not be limited to P&L attribution and backtesting, but must, at a minimum, also include the following:

(a) Tests to demonstrate that any assumptions made within the internal model are appropriate and do not underestimate risk. This may include the assumption of the normal distribution and any pricing models.
(b) Further to the regulatory backtesting programs, testing for model validation must use hypothetical changes in portfolio value that would occur were end-of-day positions to remain unchanged. It therefore excludes fees, commissions, bid-ask spreads, and intraday trading. Moreover, additional tests are required which may include, for instance:

  - Testing carried out for longer periods than required for the regular backtesting program; or
  - Testing carried out using the entire forecasting distribution using the *p*-value of the desk's profit or loss on each day. For example, the bank could be required to use in validation and make available to the supervisor the following information for each desk for each business day over the previous three years, with no more than a 60-day lag:

    (i) Two daily VaR's for the desk calibrated to a one-tail 99.0 and 97.5% confidence level, and a daily ES calibrated to 97.5;
    (ii) The daily profit or loss for the desk (i.e., the net change in price of the positions held in the portfolio at the end of the previous business day); and
    (iii) The *p*-value of the profit or loss on each day for the desk (i.e., the probability of observing a profit that is less than, or a loss that is greater than the amount reported according to the model used to calculate ES).

- Testing of portfolios must be done at both the trading desk and bank-wide level; and
- Testing of the necessary inputs for a DRC VaR measure at the 99.9% level;
- Ensuring that material basis risks are adequately captured. This should include mismatches between long and short positions by maturity or by issuer;
- Ensuring that the model captures concentration risk that may arise in an undiversified portfolio;
- Determining the eligibility of trading activities: The process for determining the eligibility of trading activities for the internal models-based approach is based on a three-stage approach[7]:

  (a) The first step is the overall assessment of both the bank's organizational infrastructure (including the definition and structure of trading desks) and its firm-wide internal risk capital model. These evaluations are based on both quantitative and qualitative factors.
  (b) The second step breaks the model approval process into smaller, more discrete, elements. At this stage, banks must nominate which trading desks are in-scope for model approval and which trading desks are out-of-scope. Desks that are out-of-scope must be capitalized according to the standardized approach on a portfolio basis. Desks that opt out of the internal models approach at this stage must remain ineligible for model inclusion for a period of at least one year.
  (c) The third step consists of risk factor analysis. This step determines which risk factors within the identified desks are eligible to be included in the bank's internal models for regulatory capital. For a risk factor to be classified as modellable by a bank, there must be continuously available "real" prices for a sufficient set of representative transactions.

11.2.5 Solvency Risk

This relates to the risk of having insufficient capital to cover losses generated by all types of risks and is thus effectively the risk of default of

[7]BIS (2016): Banking Committee on Banking Supervision—Minimum Capital Requirement for Market Risk, p. 60.

the bank. From a regulatory viewpoint, the issue of adequate capital is critically important for the stability of the banking system. To address solvency risk, it is necessary to define the level of capital which is appropriate for given levels of overall risk. The key principles involved can be summarized as follows:

- Risks generate potential losses.
- The ultimate protection for such losses is capital.
- Capital should be adjusted to the level required to ensure capability to absorb the potential losses generated by all risks.

To implement the latter, all risks should be quantified in terms of potential losses, and a measure of aggregate potential losses should be derived from the potential losses of all component risks.

11.2.6 Foreign Exchange Risk

The foreign exchange (FX) market is the most liquid sector of the global economy and generates the largest amount of cross-border payments on a daily basis, with an average daily turnover of $5.3 trillion. The FX market facilitates international trade and investments through the determination of exchange rates, conversion of national currencies, and transfer of funds. Therefore, a bank must have strong governance arrangements over its FX settlement-related risks, including a comprehensive risk management process and active engagement by the board of directors. To that end, a bank must set formal, meaningful counterparty exposure limits for FX trading and settlement that include limits for principal risk and replacement cost risk. Also, limits consistent with the bank's risk appetite need to be established by the credit risk management department, or equivalent, on a counterparty basis. Exceptions to established limits should be approved in advance by the appropriate authority in accordance with established policies and procedures. There must be clear and detailed escalation policies and procedures to inform senior management and the board, as appropriate, of potential FX issues and risks in a timely manner, and seek their approval when required.

11.2.7 Country/Sovereign Risk

Another type of risk that is important in international banking is country risk refers to the ability and willingness of borrowers within a country to meet their obligations. It is thus a credit risk on obligations advanced across borders. Assessment of country risk relies on the analysis of economic, social, and political variables that relate to the particular country in question. Although the economic factors can be measured objectively, the social and political variables will often involve subjective judgments. Country risk can be categorized under two headings. The first subcategory of country risk is sovereign risk, which refers to both the risk of default by a sovereign government on its foreign currency obligations, and the risk that direct or indirect actions by the sovereign government may affect the ability of other entities in that country to use their available funds to meet foreign currency debt obligations. In the former case, sovereign risk addresses the credit risk of national governments, but not the specific default risks of other debt issuers. Here, credit risk relates to two key aspects: economic risk, which addresses the government's ability to repay its obligations on time, and political risk, which addresses its willingness to repay debt. In practice, these risks are related, since a government that is unwilling to repay debt is often pursuing economic policies that weaken its ability to do so.

11.2.8 Technology Risk

Technology risk can be defined as the risk a bank faces from the use of computer systems in the daily basis: reconciliation of books of accounts, and storage and retrieval of information and reports. The risk can occur due to the choice of faulty or unsuitable technology and adoption of untried or obsolete technology. Major risk arises from breaches of security for access to the computer system, tampering with the system, and unauthorized use of it. Banks are facing greater threats from rapid changes occurring in the technological systems applicable to financial services.[8]

[8] Amalendu Ghosh (2012): Managing Risks in Commercial and Retail Banking, Chapter 3.

11.2.9 Operational Risk

Operational risk refers to the risk of loss resulting from inadequate or failed internal processes, people and systems or from external events. This definition includes legal risk, but excludes strategic and reputational risk.[9] Operational risk encompasses a broad swath of non-financial risks such as:

- Inadequate internal control;
- Cyber-security;
- Business conduct risk;
- Model risk management;
- Compliance risk management; and
- Payments, clearances, and settlement risks.

Common industry practice for sound operational risk governance often relies on three lines of defense:

(i) Business line management
The first line of defense is business line management. This means that sound operational risk governance will recognize that business line management is responsible for identifying and managing the risks inherent in the products, activities, processes, and systems for which it is accountable.[10]

(ii) An independent corporate operational risk management function
Independent corporate operational risk function (CORF) is typically the second line of defense, generally complementing the business line's operational risk management activities. A key function of the CORF is to challenge the business lines' inputs to, and outputs from, the bank's risk management, risk measurement, and reporting systems.

(iii) An independent review.[11]
To be effective, the review must be done by audit or by staff independent of the process or system under review, but may also involve suitably qualified external parties.

[9] Basel Committee on Banking Supervision (2011): Principles for the Sound Management of Operational Risk, p. 3.

[10] Basel Committee on Banking Supervision (2011): Principles for the Sound Management of Operational Risk, p. 4.

[11] Basel Committee on Banking Supervision (2011): Principles for the Sound Management of Operational Risk, p. 3.

11.2.10 *Moral Hazard Risk*

Moral hazard is the risk that the receiver of funds will not use the money as was intended or they may take unnecessary risks or not be vigilant in reducing risk.

Example:

- Many investors invested in American International Group (AIG) thinking that their money was relatively safe because they were investing in an insurance company that had the highest credit rating given by the credit rating agencies.
- However, AIG was also selling credit default swaps on mortgage-backed securities (MBSs) that started to default in large numbers in 2008 requiring them to post more collateral than they had. Why did AIG take such risks? Because the traders who sold the credit default swaps (CDSs) were receiving huge bonuses and they did not have to bear the risk—AIG did.
- But AIG was not concerned about risks because it was too big to fail, since they were selling most of these CDSs to banks and other investors.
- Hence, if AIG could not make the payments on the CDSs or post collateral as the CDS contracts required if AIG's credit rating dropped, then the government would have to bail them out; otherwise, many other banks would collapse if they did not receive the payments on their defaulted MBSs.

11.2.11 *Reputational Risk*

Reputational risk is the risk of damage to a bank's image and public standing that occurs due to some dubious actions taken by the bank. Reputation risk can be defined as "the risk arising from negative perception on the part of customers, counterparties, shareholders, investors or regulators that can adversely affect a bank's ability to maintain existing, or establish new, business relationships and continued access to sources of funding." A bank should identify potential sources of reputational risk to which it is exposed. These include the bank's business lines, liabilities, affiliated operations, off-balance sheet vehicles, and the markets in which it operates.

The velocity of reputation risk is much faster than ever before. Therefore, financial institutions need to ensure that their risk management programs are compliant and that they have built resiliency. Reputational risk can arise from any type of situation relating to mismanagement of the bank's affairs or non-observance of the codes of conduct under corporate governance. For instance, it may result from or create credit, liquidity, market, and legal risk.

Bank management must have appropriate policies in place to identify sources of reputational risk when entering new markets, products, or lines of activities. Like any other business institution, a good reputation provides several advantages to the bank:

- Resilience in the event of crisis;
- Strong customer base and business relationships;
- Strong market position and increased shareholder value;
- Lower cost of funding; strong capital position;
- Lower risk of litigation, fines, and penalties;
- Loyalty of shareholders and clients; and
- Ability to attract and retain top-notch employees.

Basel Committee has consistently emphasized that a strong reputation risk management program can help management respond effectively and efficiently to a crisis. A bank must develop methodologies to measure the effect of reputational risk in terms of other risk types, namely credit, liquidity, market, and other risks that they may be exposed to in order to avoid reputational damages and in order to maintain market confidence.[12]

[12] BIS—Basel Committee on Banking Supervision (2009): Enhancements to the Basel II Framework, p. 25.

CHAPTER 12

Banking Regulation Principles

12.1 General

Banking regulation can at best defined as the formulation and issuance by authorized agencies of specific rules or regulations, under governing law, for the conduct and structure of banking. US banking regulation addresses privacy, disclosure, fraud prevention, anti-money laundering, anti-terrorism, anti-usury lending, and the promotion of lending to lower-income populations.

12.2 The Five Elements of Banking Regulation

12.2.1 Safety and Soundness

Safety and soundness regulation is conducted prospectively, that is, banks can be examined prior to any indication of excess risk or any evidence of wrongdoing.[1] Safety and soundness refer to a broad range of issues that relate to the health of a financial institution. Safety and soundness encompass risk management, capital requirements, the diversification of a bank's portfolio, provisions for liquidity, allowances for loan and lease losses, concentrations of transactions with a single counterparty or in

[1] Edward V. Murphy (2015): Who Regulates Whom and How? An Overview of US Financial Regulatory Policy for Banking and Securities Markets, Congressional Research Service, p. 16.

F. I. Lessambo, *The U.S. Banking System*,
https://doi.org/10.1007/978-3-030-34792-5_12

a single region, exposure to potentially expensive litigation, adequate training and expertise of management and staff, adequate procedures for internal controls, and many other issues. Safety and soundness regulation relates to economic policy issues because it can affect the credit cycle and conflicts of interest. Lenders are required to keep capital in reserve against the possibility of a drop in value of loan portfolios or other risky assets. Federal financial regulators take into account compensating assets, risk-based capital requirements, and other prudential standards when examining the balance sheets of covered lenders.[2] The primary focus is an examination of the banks' assets and liabilities, but the exam also commonly includes a review of its adherence to regulations and standards, its compliance with various laws, and an examination of its electronic data processing systems. The examiner uses the CAMELS rating system to help measure the safety and soundness of a bank. Each letter stands for one of the six components of a bank's condition: capital adequacy, asset quality, management, earnings, liquidity, and sensitivity to market risk. When performing an examination to determine a bank's CAMELS rating, instead of reviewing every detail, the examiner evaluates the overall health of the bank and the ability of the bank to manage risk.[3] A bank that successfully manages risk has clear and concise written policies. It also has internal controls, such as separation of duties.[4] The Comptroller of the Currency conducts examinations for national banks, while the Federal Deposit Insurance Corporation (FDIC) or the state banking department conducts those, for state-chartered banks. For bank holding companies, the US Federal Reserve Board conducts examinations. The Federal Reserve examinations take into account that each bank differs markedly in its services and products and that a bank's own management is held responsible for monitoring the institution's exposure to risks.[5] By studying the bank's risk-management procedures and internal controls, Reserve Bank examiners assess whether a bank lends money wisely and can manage the level of loans it makes to customers.

[2]Edward V. Murphy (2015): Who Regulates Whom and How? An Overview of US Financial Regulatory Policy for Banking and Securities Markets, Congressional Research Service, p. 17.

[3]www.federalreserveeducation.gov.

[4]For example, a bank's management will assign one person to make loans and another person to collect loan payments.

[5]Federal Reserve Bank of St. Louis: Making Sense of the Federal Reserve—Safety and Soundness.

Table 12.1 CAMELS

CAMELS rating	*Description*	*Generic bank example rating*
Capital adequacy	Does the bank have enough money loan income, and investments to cover its deposits and business costs?	2
Asset quality	Is the bank making loans that are likely to be paid back? Are the bank's investments likely to be profitable?	3
Management	Does the bank's management make sound decisions?	2
Earnings	Is the bank making a reasonable profit?	4
Liquidity	Does the bank have enough money on hand or is its money tied up in assets?	3
Sensitivity	How sensitive is the bank to market risk? For example, if most of the bank's loans are home mortgages, what will happen to the bank if the housing market shrinks?	3

Source Federal Reserve

Examiners also review a bank's performance in complying with its own internal policies, as well as with federal and state laws and regulations. Bank examiners use a CAMELS rating to describe a bank's soundness. Examiners rank the bank in the following six categories. Banks are issued points from 1 to 5, where 1 is the highest rating and 5 is the lowest (Table 12.1).

12.2.2 Capital Requirements

Capital regulation relates to economic policy problems because it can affect the credit cycle. One way higher bank capital affects the credit cycle is its potential to make the banking system more resilient during downturns. Unexpected loan losses are less likely to cause a bank to fail if it holds more capital. In the aggregate, higher capital requirements will tend to make the banking system more resilient because distressed banks may drain other banks of their liquid reserves while general liquidity is declining.[6] On the other hand, banks are part of a broader financial system; therefore, it may be possible that higher capital requirements for banks might not make the system as a whole safer if the cost of capital causes more financial activity to migrate to securities markets or shadow banking. Financial regulators require the institutions they supervise to maintain specified minimum levels of capital defined in various ways—to increase the resilience of firms to shocks and to minimize losses to investors, customers, and taxpayers when failures occur. The actual capital held by banks should not be confused with statutory minimums. Banks may choose to hold excess capital if bank management believes that economic conditions may deteriorate. A guiding principle of the Basel standards is that capital requirements should be risk-based. The riskier an asset, the more capital a bank should hold against possible losses. Risk-based regulations can be more prudent than simple leverage ratios because two firms with identical amounts of debt may have very different probabilities of failure if their assets are different.[7]

12.2.3 *Asset Management*

Regulation of asset management activities relates to economic policy issues because the asset management services of banks can have broader effects. Banks are not the only firms that offer asset management services. Bank regulators do not make rules for the entire asset management industry; rather, they issue guidance to the firms with particular charters, and they provide examinations to insure that chartered banks have procedures in place that are consistent with sound asset management principles.

12.2.4 *Consumer Protection Compliance*

Banks are required to provide customers clear and accurate information about services, such as savings accounts, loans, and credit cards. For example, a bank's brochure for a savings account should include

[6]Edward V. Murphy (2015): Who Regulates Whom and How? An Overview of US Financial Regulatory Policy for Banking and Securities Markets, Congressional Research Service, p. 18.

[7]Edward V. Murphy (2015): Who Regulates Whom and How? An Overview of US Financial Regulatory Policy for Banking and Securities Markets, Congressional Research Service, p. 19.

information on any minimum balance required, monthly service fee, and the average percentage yield. In addition, the Truth in Lending Act requires banks to disclose the finance charge and the annual percentage rate so that a consumer can compare the prices of credit from different sources. It also limits liability on lost or stolen credit cards. These laws ensure that consumers and banks make decisions based on the same information.[8]

The Dodd–Frank Act gathered much of this authority and personnel into a new Consumer Financial Protection Bureau (CFPB), but bank regulators still supervise many consumer activities of their chartered firms. One reason is that poor customer relations can be a threat to the safety and soundness of the institution, in part because it is usually bad for business. Bank regulators can facilitate consumer compliance by offering an ombudsman to assist in resolving complaints. Ombudsman offices are usually separate from those of the safety and soundness examiners. Such offices may help insure that consumers receive a fair and expeditious resolution of their concerns with a firm that is regulated by that agency. This may help reduce the time and expense of more formal complaint resolution options where consumers might otherwise seek redress (such as courts). Some rulemaking activity for consumer compliance is shared between the CFPB and the bank regulators.

12.2.5 Community Reinvestment

The Community Reinvestment Act (CRA) requires depository institutions to help meet the credit needs of the communities in which they operate, including low- and moderate-income (LMI) neighborhoods, consistent with safe and sound banking operations. Depository institutions take seriously their CRA commitment, which has several implications. For instance, an institution's CRA record is taken into account in considering applications for deposit facilities, including mergers and acquisitions. Likewise, maintaining a satisfactory or better CRA rating also results in less frequent CRA examinations at the institution. The evaluation methods are:

[8] www.federalreserveeducation.gov.

Table 12.2 Five evaluation methods

Five evaluation methods	
Small Bank Evaluation	• For institutions with less than $290 million in total assets • Evaluation, which includes five performance criteria: 1. Loan-to-deposit ratio responsive to credit needs 2. Percentage of loans/lending-related activity in an institution's assessment area 3. Geographic distribution of loans, including LMI areas 4. Record of lending/lending-related activity to: borrowers of different income levels and/or businesses and farms of different sizes 5. Response to CRA-related complaints
Intermediate Small Bank Evaluation	• For institutions with assets between $290 million and $1.16 billion (Regardless of holding company affiliation) • Evaluated under a two-part test which includes: – The Small Bank Lending Evaluation and – The Community Development Test, which considers the number and amount of community development: Loans and Investments of Services
For institutions with more than $1.16 billion in total asset	• For institutions with more than $1.16 billion in total asset • Have a 3-part evaluation: – Lending Test – Investment Test – Service Test
Community Development Test	• For wholesale or limited purpose institutions • In order to receive CRA credit, a bank's activities must have one of the following as its primary purpose: – Affordable housing – services targeted to low- and moderate-income individuals – Activities that promote economic development – Activities that revitalize or stabilize LMI geographies
Strategic Plan	• At option of bank, with regulatory approval • All institutions, no matter their size or business strategy, may take advantage of the strategic plan option, which allows an institution to develop a plan for meeting its CRA responsibilities, subject to approval by its supervisory agency

- Designed to respond to basic differences in institutions' structures and operations;
- Intended to establish performance-based CRA examinations that are (i) complete and accurate and (ii) mitigate the compliance burden for institutions, to the maximum extent possible (Table 12.2).

Further, each institution must hold a Public File, which contains specific information regarding its CRA performance. For example, the Public File must include a copy of your most recent Public Evaluation, as well as the disclosure reports regarding your CRA and HMDA data. Also, each institution must post a notice in its lobby of the availability of the Public File and providing consumers with contacts at the bank and the FDIC (and the Federal Reserve if the bank is affiliated with a holding company) in order to provide comments regarding the bank's CRA performance. Finally, at least one bank director must be responsible to ensure that a system for responding to consumer complaints is in place at the institution.

CHAPTER 13

Banks' Capital Adequacy

13.1 General

Successful development and greater well-being of each particular country in today's global and highly interconnected environment highly depend on a combination of various political, economic, social, technological, and legal factors. With a rapid expansion of financial markets and growing complexity of banking industry, the ability of financial institutions, in particular banks, to serve its customers and assist in capital formation, as such, has become a backbone of long-term economic development. Widespread deregulation and increased diversification of banking activities allowed major banks to access the markets of abundant opportunities, while greatly increasing the risk level they face.

In 1988, Belgium, Canada, France, Germany, Italy, Japan, Luxembourg, Netherlands, Spain, Sweden, and Switzerland (known as G-10 counties) further joined by the UK and the United States formed a Basel I Accord, requiring financial institutions with international presence to hold capital of 8% compared to its risk-weighted assets, in the joint attempt to ensure the proper management of such institutions.

However, further economic developments quickly revealed the inability of Basel I to address latest economic trends; its failure to offer any solutions to booming derivative market and inability to take into consideration the challenges facing developing world lead to the introduction of Basel II Accord, aimed, compared to its predecessor, to address both and operational risks. Though it also offered financial institutions

F. I. Lessambo, *The U.S. Banking System*,
https://doi.org/10.1007/978-3-030-34792-5_13

some particular guidelines to determine the amount that needs to be put under the capital, it failed to protect American and international economies from the global financial crisis of 2007–2010. In 2008 alone, twenty-five American banks have become insolvent while in 2009 another seventy-seven backs were added to this number.[1] As a result of the crisis, the United States has lost more than 6 million jobs, witnessing a steady decline in overall consumer purchasing power at the same time.

To overcome the shortcomings of Basel II and prevent the world from occurrence of another financial crisis on that level, the Basel Committee on Baking Supervision (the leading power behind the move toward establishment of global capital adequacy requirements) introduced Basel 2.5 and Basel III consecutive reforms. Basel III, in particular, aimed toward establishment of more sound and stable banking sector by creating international standards framework for liquidity, and offering more efficient risk management and risk assessment techniques. Would those latest modifications be effective enough to prevent global banks from taking an excessive risk, and further protect countries and its consumers from the devastating effects of the next global financial crisis is the next crucial question next Basel III needs to address.

13.2 Capital Adequacy Role

The primary function of capital is to support the bank's operations, act as a cushion to absorb unanticipated losses and declines in asset values that could otherwise cause a bank to fail, and provide protection to uninsured depositors and debt holders in the event of liquidation. Capital regulation is particularly important because deposit insurance and other elements of the federal safety net provide banks with an incentive to increase their leverage beyond what the market—in the absence of depositor protection—would permit.

13.3 The Basel I

Basel I, also known as the 1988 Basel Accord, is the first accord of the Basel series and was created following the establishment of the Basel Committee on Bank Supervision (BCBS) in 1974, in response to a

[1] S. Joshi (2013): Importance of Basel Accords in Banking Industry. ASM's International E-Journal of Ongoing Research in Management and IT.

series of financial setbacks throughout Europe following the collapse of Bretton Woods and its system of managed exchange rates. Among the market's disarray, the catalyst for the group's formation was the bankruptcy and ensuing liquidation a small German bank, Bankhaus Herstatt, in 1973. Herstatt's insolvency left its expenditures on foreign exchange deals unpaid, prompted other banks in Europe to freeze all outgoing payments, and caused the market to come to an immediate halt. The incident was testament to the importance of maintaining consistent and sufficient capital, and BCBS was tasked with constructing a comprehensive solution to prevent similar tragedies from occurring in the future.[2] Basel I was revolutionary in that it aimed to develop one risk-adjusted capital model to be applied to all major banking countries, and significantly increased capital adequacy ratios for banks globally.[3]

The goal of BCBS, which functions essentially as an international forum, was to "enhance financial stability by improving supervisory know-how and the quality of banking supervision worldwide."[4] BCBS sets the standard for minimum capital requirements of financial institutions in an effort to reduce credit risk, and banks that operate globally are required to maintain a minimum 8% of capital based on a percentage of their respective risk-weighted assets. The 8% capital-to-risk weighted assets minimum ratio was ordered to be in place by all members by the end of 1992.[5]

Basel I's primary focus was the minimization of credit risk in banks and other financial institutions, and was enforced by the Group of Ten (G-10) nations. Its fundamental purpose was to "promote the soundness and stability of the international banking system and provide an equitable basis for international competition among banks" (Federal Reserve Bulletin, 2003). The creation of the bank asset classification system was a result of Basel I and organized a bank's assets into four different risk categories. The level of risk associated with the asset or debtor determines within which category an asset will fall. The first category, 0%, is considered risk-free. It is comprised of the most secure assets, including cash, gold, other commodities, and Treasury debt instruments. Subsequently,

[2] *The Economist* (April, 2001): The Long, Dark Shadow of Herstatt.

[3] Bank for International Settlement (2015): A Brief History on the Basel Committee. Retrieved December 5, 2016, from http://www.bis.org/bcbs/history.pdf.

[4] Idem.

[5] Idem.

the 20% risk category is made up of debt issued by the Organization for Economic Cooperation and Development (OECD), securities issued by US public agencies, and claims of municipalities. Residential mortgages make up the 50% risk category, and all remaining claims fall within the highest (riskiest) 100% category. Such assets include corporate bonds, debt of developing or underdeveloped nations, claims on non-OECD banks, equities, real estate, and plants and equipment. To determine a bank's minimum capital requirement, total risk-weighted assets are multiplied by the agreed-upon 8%. Whether or not the capital ratio meets, exceeds, or falls below, this minimum percentage determines the overall strength of a financial institution.[6]

In addition to the measures set forth to build a stronger capital adequacy framework within banks, Basel I was successful in gaining worldwide adoption of its policies. It established a benchmark for assessment of participating banks, and its relatively uncomplicated structure was put in place by the majority of institutions by the extended 1993 deadline. Basel I set a higher disciplinary standard for banks in managing their capital and "increased competitive equality among internationally active banks" (Basel I, n.d.). The accord is widely believed to have successfully promoted financial stability and foster healthy competition within the global financial market. Furthermore, despite its level of detail in provisions, it allowed for a degree of flexibility by members in implementing regulations within their respective countries.[7]

Basel I set the stage for best practices in banks on an international level, with respect to capital adequacy. Despite the success of the original accord, areas of improvement were exposed in addition to a number of loopholes within the regulations. Banks took advantage of and exploited these loopholes through regulatory capital arbitrage, a practice used by firms to capitalize from such loopholes to avoid compliance with regulatory standards. A major problem was the fact that, while capital adequacy depends heavily on credit risk, other risks (market, operational, etc.) were neglected. Amendments such as the Market Risk Amendment of 1996, which allowed banks to use value-at-risk models when making internal risk calculations, were one such example of intermediary legislation created to improve Basel I before the establishment of Basel II.

[6]Federal Reserve Bulletin (2003, September): Capital Standards for Banks: The Evolving Basel Accord.

[7]Idem.

The amendment was a response to the "exclusion of market risk from the capital requirements (which) induced banks to shift their risk exposure from priced credit risk to unpriced market risk."[8] Risk mitigation techniques were also noticeably absent from the Basel Accord. Basel I's downfalls prompted the establishment of new and improved regulations to supplement and build upon its existing provisions. In 2001, the creation of Basel II would address the unintended consequences produced by the regulations of Basel I.

13.4 Basel II

The Basel II framework requires, among other things, that banks set up a robust system to validate the accuracy and consistency of their rating systems. Released in April 2003, Basel II added three minimal pillars as a requirement of Basel I under the credit risk. These three requirements include the credit risk, operational capital approached, and the supervisory review approach. Each approach is sensitive to the industry and the economy's profile; therefore, it is vital to reinforce the risk management and make it stronger. All of these approaches need to be in compliance with the capital threshold in order for it succeed. Under Basel II, the first pillar would address how risky loans and investments would be measured as held by the bank. Banks could search for the region that the central bank is located in so that they can help the industry determine or classify the asset. Because this pillar is greatly sensitive to risk, securitization will help the process. This is due to the fact that a financial process of illiquid assets can become liquid only if two conditions are met. These conditions are (1) the conversion of the illiquid asset must be within a year or less and (2) it must be at the fair market value. Every bank should be able to evaluate each asset in the ascending order of credit risk.

In addition, Basel II will also determine how banks should approach the operational risk. This requires banks to hold capital against operational risks for the following three years. The basic indicator approach under operations is basically that banks should hold only the positive gross income for fixed percentage calculations.

For example, if a company on the first year had a gross income of \$10 billons, second year −\$5, and on the third year \$15, banks should

[8] L. Allen (2003, December): The Basel Capital Accords and International Mortgage Markets: A Survey of the Literature.

be able to only use the positive gross income. Therefore, the company will be estimated for the two years that they conducted a positive gross income, as well as the calculation of the average of these two years.

Moving forward, the standardized approach under Basel II explains the 8 categories or lines on the banking sector. Every line or category will be treated differently, because depending on the services provided by the bank, they might have services provide directly by the bank or on behalf of customers.

Moreover, "US banks are trying to implement new accord which will help them improve or add more rules and or requirements to the existing Basels" (Basel Committee). Surprisingly, to some extent, there are banks that are based on Basel I, which means that those banks would not be exposed to the operational capital approach. This means that nowadays there are countries which are not well capitalized and the capital ratio of those countries exceed 10%. Therefore, the capital regime is sensitive to the risk under Basel II.

- Operational Risks

The Basel II Committee defines operational risk as the risk of loss resulting from inadequate or failed internal processes, people and systems or from external events. However, banks are permitted to adopt their own definitions of operational risk, provided that the minimum elements in the Committee's definition are included. The Basel II definition of operational risk excludes, for example, strategic risk—the risk of a loss arising from a poor strategic business decision.

Basel II prescribes various soundness standards for operational risk management for Banks and similar financial institutions: (i) basic indicator approach, (ii) standardized approach, and (iii) advanced measurement approaches.

(i) Basic Indicator Approach

Banks using the basic indicator approach must hold capital for operational risk equal to the average over the previous three years of a fixed percentage of positive annual gross income. Figures for any year in which annual gross income is negative or zero should be excluded from both the numerator and denominator when calculating the average.

Table 13.1 Standardized approach

Lines	*Activities*
1.	Corporate finance
2.	Trading and sales
3.	Retail banking
4.	Commercial banking
5.	Payment and settlement
6.	Agency services
7.	Asset management
8.	Retail brokerage

Table 13.2 Business lines/Beta factor

Business lines	*Beta factor (%)*
Corporate finance	18
Trading and sales	18
Retail banking	12
Commercial banking	15
Payments and settlements	18
Agency services	15
Asset management	12
Retail brokerage	12

The fixed percentage "alpha" is typically 15% of annual gross income.

(ii) Standardized Approach

Under the standardized approach, banks' activities are divided into eight business lines (Table 13.1).

Within each business line, gross income is a broad indicator that serves as a proxy for the scale of business operations and thus the likely scale of operational risk exposure within each of these business lines. The capital charge for each business line is calculated by multiplying gross income by a factor (denoted beta) assigned to that business line. Beta serves as a proxy for the industry-wide relationship between the operational risk loss experience for a given business line and the aggregate level of gross income for that business line (Table 13.2).

The total capital charge is calculated as the three-year average of the simple summation of the regulatory capital charges across each of the business lines in each year. In any given year, negative capital charges (resulting from negative gross income) in any business line may offset positive capital charges in other business lines without limit.

To qualify for use of the standardized approach, a bank must satisfy its regulator that, at a minimum:

- Its board of directors and senior management, as appropriate, must be actively involved in the oversight of the operational risk management framework;
- It must have an operational risk management system that is conceptually sound and is implemented with integrity; and
- It must have sufficient resources in the use of the approach in the major business lines as well as the control and audit areas.

On March 4, 2016, the Basel Committee on Banking Supervision finally updated its proposal for calculating operational risk capital, introducing the Standardized Measurement Approach ("SMA"). Building upon its 2014 version, the SMA would not only replace the existing standardized approaches, but also the Advanced Measurement Approach. Under the SMA, regulatory capital levels will be determined using a simple formulaic method which facilitates comparability across the industry.

(iii) Advanced Measurement Approaches (AMA)

Advanced measurement approaches (AMA) is one of three possible operational risk methods that can be used under Basel II by a bank or other financial institution. These methods (or approaches) increase in sophistication and risk sensitivity with AMA being the most advanced of the three. Under AMA the banks are allowed to develop their own empirical model to quantify required capital for operational risk. Banks can use this approach only subject to approval from their local regulators. Once a bank has been approved to adopt AMA, it cannot revert to a simpler approach without supervisory approval.

To qualify for use of the AMA a bank must satisfy its supervisor that, at a minimum:

- Its board of directors and senior management, as appropriate, must be actively involved in the oversight of the operational risk management framework;

- It must have an operational risk management system that is conceptually sound and is implemented with integrity; and
- It must have sufficient resources in the use of the approach in the major business lines as well as the control and audit areas.

Under the BCBS Supervisory Guidelines, an AMA framework must include the use of four data elements: (i) internal loss data (ILD), (ii) external data (ED), (iii) scenario analysis (SBA), and (iv) business environment and internal control factors (BEICFs).

13.5 Enhanced Basel II

These enhancements, entered into force by December 30, 2010, were intended to strengthen the framework and respond to lessons learned from the financial crisis.

- Reinforcing Pillar 1

Banks using the internal ratings-based (IRB) approach to securitization will be required to apply higher risk weights to re-securitization exposures. Banks are encouraged to consult with their national supervisors when there is uncertainty about whether a particular structured credit position should be considered a re-securitization exposure. Further, banks should not be allowed to recognize external ratings when those ratings are based on support provided by the same bank. Put differently, (i) a bank is not permitted to use any external credit assessment for risk-weighting purposes where the assessment is at least partly based on unfunded support provided by the bank, (ii) a bank's capital requirement for such exposures held in the trading book can be no less than the amount required under the banking book treatment, and (iii) banks are permitted to recognize overlap in their exposure.[9]

[9] For example, a bank providing a liquidity facility supporting 100% of the ABCP issued by an ABCP program and purchasing 20% of the outstanding ABCP of that program could recognize an overlap of 20% (100% liquidity facility + 20% CP held—100% CP issued = 20%).

- Reinforcing Pillar 2: Supervisory review process

Supervisors must determine whether a bank has in place a sound firm-wide risk management framework that enables it to define its risk appetite and recognize all material risks, including the risks posed by concentrations, securitization, off-balance sheet exposures, valuation practices, and other risk exposures. The bank can achieve such a supervision by:

- Adequately identifying, measuring, monitoring, controlling, and mitigating these risks;
- Clearly communicating the extent and depth of these risks in an easily understandable, but accurate, manner in reports to senior management and the board of directors, as well as in published financial reports;
- Conducting ongoing stress testing to identify potential losses and liquidity needs under adverse circumstances; and
- Setting adequate minimum internal standards for allowances or liabilities for losses, capital, and contingency funding.

- Reinforcing Pillar 3: Market discipline

The Committee aims to encourage market discipline by developing a set of disclosure requirements which will allow market participants to assess key pieces of information on the scope of application, capital, risk exposures, risk assessment processes, and hence the capital adequacy of the institution.

The Pillar 3 revisions include disclosure requirements that are not specifically required to compute capital requirements under Pillar 1. The Basel Committee expects that the enhancement will help market participants to better understand the overall risk profile of an institution and to avoid a recurrence of market uncertainties about the strength of banks' balance sheets related to their securitization activities.

The Committee's revisions in the six areas are as follow:

(i) Securitization exposures in the trading book
(ii) Sponsorship of off-balance sheet vehicles: On-balance sheet securitization exposures must be disclosed separately from off-balance sheet securitization exposures.

(iii) IAA and other ABCP liquidity facilities: require qualitative information on the Internal Assessment Approach (IAA) process such as the structure, purposes, control mechanisms, etc. in line with the general disclosure requirements for the IRB system. It also requires breakdown of some quantitative information on the banking and trading books for each regulatory capital approach.

(iv) Re-securitization exposures: encourage separate disclosure on the valuation of securitization exposures and re-securitization exposures.

(v) Valuation with regard to securitization exposures: introduces qualitative disclosure requirements on how banks value their securitization positions by adding key assumptions for valuing positions.

(vi) Pipeline and warehousing risks with regard to securitization exposures: It adds two disclosure requirements for accounting policies, which will provide the market with information to determine where they can find exposures intended to be securitized in the future, including information about how such exposures are valued. It also adds a requirement to disclose the total amount of outstanding exposures intended to be securitized broken down by exposure type.

(vii) Other: adds a qualitative requirement to explain significant changes to any of the quantitative information since the last reporting period.

13.6 Basel III

Basel III increases the capital thresholds by raising Tier 1 capital requirements to 6% from 4%, introduces buffers and leverage ratio requirements, and added the Common Equity Tier 1 (CET 1) requirement of 4.5%.[10]

Basel III is a comprehensive set of reform measures, developed by the Basel Committee on Banking Supervision, to strengthen the regulation, supervision, and risk management of the banking sector.[11] These measures aim to:

[10] Sebastian Schneider, Gerhard Schrock et al. (2017): Basel IV: What's Next for Banks? McKinsey & Company, Global Risk Practice, p. 6.

[11] Bank for International Settlements (2017).

- improve the banking sector's ability to absorb shocks arising from financial and economic stress, whatever the source
- improve risk management and governance
- strengthen banks' transparency and disclosures.

The 2008–2010 financial crisis revealed some inconsistencies in the definition of capital across jurisdictions and the lack of disclosure that would have enabled the market to fully assess and compare the quality of capital across jurisdictions. Basel III is designed with such a framework in mind.

The rule sets the Basel III minimum regulatory capital requirements for all organizations. It includes a new Common Equity Tier 1 ratio of 4.5% of risk-weighted assets, raises the minimum Tier 1 capital ratio from 4 to 6% of risk-weighted assets and would set a new conservation buffer of 2.5% of risk-weighted assets. Banking organizations with less than $15 billion in assets may continue to count existing trust preferred securities as capital, consistent with the grandfathering set by the Dodd–Frank Act.

Basel III established a capital conservation buffer above the minimum capital requirements. When a bank's CET1 ratio falls into the buffer range, that bank becomes subject to a restriction on the distribution of future earnings.[12]

13.6.1 Components of Capital

Bank's total regulatory capital consists of the sum of the following elements: (i) Tier 1 Capital and (ii) Tier 2. Total Capital (Tier 1 Capital plus Tier 2 Capital) must be at least 8.0% of risk-weighted assets at all time.

- Tier 1 Capital

Tier 1 Capital must be at least 6.0% of risk-weighted assets at all times and is composed of (a) Common Equity Tier 1 and (b) Additional Tier 1. Dividends are removed from Common Equity Tier 1 in accordance with applicable accounting standards. Likewise, goodwill and all other intangibles are deducted in the calculation of Common Equity Tier 1, including any goodwill included in the valuation of significant

[12]BIS—Basel Committee on Banking Supervision (2014): Assessment of Basel III Regulations—United States of America, p. 18.

investments in the capital of banking, financial, and insurance entities that are outside the scope of regulatory consolidation. With the exception of mortgage servicing rights, the full amount is to be deducted net of any associated deferred tax liability which would be extinguished if the intangible assets become impaired or de-recognized under the relevant accounting standards.[13] Also, the following items are de-recognized in the calculation of Tier 1 Capital:

- Cash flow hedge reserve: The amount of the cash flow hedge reserve that relates to the hedging of items that are not fair valued on the balance sheet (including projected cash flows) is de-recognized in the calculation of Common Equity Tier 1. That is, positive amounts should be deducted and negative amounts should be added back.
- Gain on sale related to securitization transactions;
- Cumulative gains and losses due to changes in own credit risk on fair valued financial liabilities;
- Defined benefit pension fund assets and liabilities;
- Investments in own shares (treasury stock);
- Reciprocal cross holdings in the capital of banking, financial, and insurance entities;
- Investments in the capital of banking, financial, and insurance entities that are outside the scope of regulatory consolidation and where the bank does not own more than 10% of the issued common share capital of the entity;
- Significant investments in the capital of banking, financial, and insurance entities that are outside the scope of regulatory consolidation.

Finally, receive limited recognition when calculating Common Equity Tier 1, with recognition capped at 10% of the bank's common equity (after the application of all regulatory adjustments):

- Significant investments in the common shares of unconsolidated financial institutions (banks, insurance, and other financial entities);
- Mortgage servicing rights (MSRs); and
- DTAs that arise from temporary differences.

[13] Banks that report under local GAAP may use the IFRS definition of intangible assets to determine which assets classify as intangible and thus required to be deducted.

1. Common Equity Tier 1

Common Equity Tier 1 consists of the sum of the following elements:

- Common shares issued by the bank that meet the criteria for classification as common shares for regulatory purposes (or the equivalent for non-joint stock companies);
- Stock surplus (share premium) resulting from the issue of instruments included Common Equity Tier 1;
- Retained earnings[14];
- Accumulated other comprehensive income and other disclosed reserves;
- Common shares issued by consolidated subsidiaries of the bank and held by third parties (i.e., minority interest) that meet the criteria for inclusion in Common Equity Tier 1 Capital. See Sect. 13.4 for the relevant criteria; and
- Regulatory adjustments applied in the calculation of Common Equity Tier 1.

2. Additional Tier 1 Capital

Additional Tier 1 Capital consists of the sum of the following elements:

- Instruments issued by the bank that meet the criteria for inclusion in Additional Tier 1 Capital (and are not included in Common Equity Tier 1);
- Stock surplus (share premium) resulting from the issue of instruments included in Additional Tier 1 Capital;
- Instruments issued by consolidated subsidiaries of the bank and held by third parties that meet the criteria for inclusion in Additional Tier 1 Capital and are not included in Common Equity Tier 1; and
- Regulatory adjustments applied in the calculation of Additional Tier 1 Capital.

[14] Retained earnings and other comprehensive income include interim profit or loss.

- Tier 2 Capital

The objective of Tier 2 is to provide loss absorption on a gone-concern basis, and Tier consists of the sum of the following elements:

- Instruments issued by the bank that meet the criteria for inclusion in Tier 2 Capital (and are not included in Tier 1 Capital);
- Stock surplus (share premium) resulting from the issue of instruments included in Tier 2 Capital;
- Instruments issued by consolidated subsidiaries of the bank and held by third parties that meet the criteria for inclusion in Tier 2 Capital and are not included in Tier 1 Capital.
- Certain loan loss provisions as specified; and
- Regulatory adjustments applied in the calculation of Tier 2 Capital.
- In addition to raising the quality and level of the capital base, Basel III requires that all material risks be captured in the capital framework. Failure to capture major on- and off-balance sheet risks, as well as derivative related exposures, was a key factor that amplified the 2008–2010 financial crisis.

13.6.2 Capital Conservation Buffer

A capital conservation buffer of 2.5%, comprised of Common Equity Tier 1, is established above the regulatory minimum capital requirement.[15] The capital conservation buffer is designed to ensure that banks build up capital buffers outside periods of stress which can be drawn down as losses are incurred.

Although the buffer must be capable of being drawn down, banks should not choose in normal times to operate in the buffer range simply to compete with other banks and win market share. That is, anytime a bank withdraws fund from its capital buffer, it must rebuild it through reducing discretionary distributions of earnings. This includes reducing dividend payments, share-backs, and staff bonus payments. Banks may also choose to raise new capital from the private sector as an alternative to conserving internally generated capital. It is not acceptable for banks which have depleted their capital buffers to use future predictions of

[15] The capital conservation buffer will be phased in between January 1, 2016, and year end 2018 becoming fully effective on January 1, 2019.

Calibration of the Capital Framework

Capital requirements and buffers (all numbers in percent)

	Common Equity Tier 1	Tier 1 Capital	Total Capital
Minimum	4.5	6.0	8.0
Conservation buffer	2.5		
Minimum plus conservation buffer	7.0	8.5	10.5
Countercyclical buffer range*	0 – 2.5		

Fig. 13.1 Calibration of the capital framework (*Source* BIS)

recovery as justification for maintaining generous distributions to shareholders, other capital providers, and employees (Fig. 13.1).

13.6.3 Leverage Ratio

Basel III introduces a leverage ratio that is calibrated to act as a credible supplementary measure to the risk-based capital requirements. It is worthy to remind that one of the underlying features of the 2008–2010 financial crisis was the buildup of excessive on- and off-balance sheet leverage in the banking system. In many cases, banks built up excessive leverage while still showing strong risk-based capital ratios. The newly introduced leverage ratio is intended to achieve the following objectives:

- constrain the buildup of leverage in the banking sector, helping avoid de-stabilizing deleveraging processes which can damage the broader financial system and the economy; and
- reinforce the risk-based requirements with a simple, non-risk-based "backstop" measure.

The capital measure for the leverage ratio should be based on the new definition of Tier 1 Capital. Items that are deducted completely from capital do not contribute to leverage and must therefore also be

Phase-in arrangements

(shading indicates transition periods - all dates are as of 1 January)

	2011	2012	2013	2014	2015	2016	2017	2018	As of 1 January 2019
Leverage Ratio	Supervisory monitoring		Parallel run 1 Jan 2013 – 1 Jan 2017 Disclosure starts 1 Jan 2015					Migration to Pillar 1	
Minimum Common Equity Capital Ratio			3.5%	4.0%	4.5%	4.5%	4.5%	4.5%	4.5%
Capital Conservation Buffer						0.625%	1.25%	1.875%	2.50%
Minimum common equity plus capital conservation buffer			3.5%	4.0%	4.5%	5.125%	5.75%	6.375%	7.0%
Phase-in of deductions from CET1 (including amounts exceeding the limit for DTAs, MSRs and financials)				20%	40%	60%	80%	100%	100%
Minimum Tier 1 Capital			4.5%	5.5%	6.0%	6.0%	6.0%	6.0%	6.0%
Minimum Total Capital			8.0%	8.0%	8.0%	8.0%	8.0%	8.0%	8.0%
Minimum Total Capital plus conservation buffer			8.0%	8.0%	8.0%	8.625%	9.25%	9.875%	10.5%
Capital instruments that no longer qualify as non-core Tier 1 capital or Tier 2 capital			Phased out over 10 year horizon beginning 2013						
Liquidity coverage ratio	Observation period begins				Introduce minimum standard				
Net stable funding ratio	Observation period begins							Introduce minimum standard	

Fig. 13.2 Basel 3-Phase-in arrangements (*Source* BIS)

deducted from the measure of exposure. Where a financial entity is included in the accounting consolidation but not in the regulatory consolidation, the investments in the capital of these entities are required to be deducted to the extent that they exceed certain thresholds. To ensure that the capital and exposure are measured consistently for the purposes of the leverage ratio, the assets of such entities included in the accounting consolidation should be excluded from the exposure measure in proportion to the capital that is excluded (Fig. 13.2).

13.6.4 Basel III and Securitization

13.6.4.1 Hierarchy of Methodologies for Securitization Risk-Based Capital
Basel III established a hierarchy within the securitization framework, which consists of (i) Internal Ratings-Base Approach, (ii) External Ratings-Based Approach, and (iii) the Standard Approach. A bank that cannot use either of the three approaches is required to assign a risk weight of 1250% to such exposure. Securitization exposures are treated differently, depending on the nature or type of the underlying exposures and the information available. The risk-weighted asset amount of a

securitization exposure is computed by multiplying the exposure amount by the appropriate risk weight as determined pursuant to the hierarchy framework. Under all three approaches in the hierarchy, the risk weight for STC-complaint securitizations is subject to a floor of 10% for senior tranches and 15% for non-senior tranches.

The revised Basel III securitization framework represents a significant improvement to the Basel II framework with only three approaches. This securitization framework, which will come into effect in January 2018, aimed to address a number of shortcomings in the Basel II securitization framework and to strengthen the capital standards for securitization exposures held in the banking book.[16]

To reduce the identified shortcomings under Basel II, the revised Basel III aims to achieve the following goals[17]:

- Reduce the mechanistic reliance on external ratings,
- Increase risk weights for highly rated securitization exposures,
- Reduce risk weights for low-rated senior securitization exposures,
- Reduce cliff effects, and
- Enhance the framework by using a more granular calibration.

The Basel III operational requirements for traditional securitizations are as follows[18]:

(a) transfer of significant credit risk associated with the underlying exposures to third parties;
(b) transferor does not maintain effective or indirect control;
(c) the exposures are legally isolated from the transferor, through true sale or sub-participation, such that they are beyond the reach of transferor's creditors, even in bankruptcy or receivership;

[16] BIS (2016): Basel III Document Revisions to the Securitization Framework.

[17] Bjorn Bjerke (2017): The international Comparative Legal Guide to Securitization, Chapter 4, p. 24.

[18] Bjorn Bjerke (2017): The international Comparative Legal Guide to Securitization, Chapter 4, p. 28.

(d) the transferee is a special purpose entity (SPE) where the holders of the beneficial interests in that entity have the right to pledge or exchange such interests without restriction;
(e) any clean-up calls must meet specific criteria[19];
(f) the securitization shall not contain provisions that require the originating bank to alter the underlying exposures to enhance credit quality (other than through sale at market prices to third parties), nor to allow the originating bank to increase its retained first-loss position or any credit enhancement provided by it, or increase the yield payable to any party other than the bank in response to a deterioration in the credit quality of the underlying pool; and
(g) no termination options or triggers except eligible clean-up calls, termination for specific changes in tax and regulation or permitted early amortization provisions.

- Under Basel III securitization framework, the Committee has revised the hierarchy to reduce the reliance on external ratings as well as to simplify it and limit the number of approaches.

(i) *Internal Ratings-Based Approach (SEC-IRBA)*

To calculate capital requirements for a securitization exposure to an IRB pool, a bank must use the SEC-IRBA and the following bank-supplied inputs: The IRB capital charge had the underlying exposures not been securitized, the tranche attachment point (A), the tranche detachment point (D), and the supervisory parameter p, as defined below. Where the only difference between exposures to a transaction is related to maturity, A and D will be the same.

(ii) *External Ratings-Based Approach (SEC-ERBA)*

For securitization exposures that are externally rated, or for which an inferred rating is available, risk-weighted assets under the SEC-ERBA

[19]((x) exercise must be at the banks discretion (cannot be mandatory); (y) cannot be structured to provide credit enhancement or for investors to avoid losses; and (z) can only be exercisable when 10% or less of original underlying portfolio or issued securities remains).

will be determined by multiplying securitization exposure amounts by the appropriate risk weights as determined by paragraphs [66–70], provided that the operational criteria are met.

(iii) *Internal Assessment Approach (IAA)*

Subject to supervisory approval, a bank may use its internal assessments of the credit quality of its securitization exposures extended to ABCP programs provided that the bank has at least one approved IRB model (which does not need to be applicable to the securitized exposures) and if the bank's internal assessment process meets the operational requirements set out below. Internal assessments of exposures provided to ABCP programs must be mapped to equivalent external ratings of an ECAI. Those rating equivalents are used to determine the appropriate risk weights under the SEC-ERBA for the exposures.

(iv) *Standardized Approach (SEC-SA)*

To calculate capital requirements for a securitization exposure to an SA pool using the SEC-SA, a bank would use a supervisory formula and the following bank-supplied inputs: The SA capital charge had the underlying exposures not been securitized (KSA); the ratio of delinquent underlying exposures to total underlying exposures in the securitization pool (W); the tranche attachment point (A); and the tranche detachment point (D).

For re-securitization exposures, banks must apply the SEC-SA specified in paragraphs [78–87], with the following adjustments:

- the capital requirement of the underlying securitization exposures is calculated using the securitization framework;
- delinquencies (W) are set to zero for any exposure to a securitization tranche in the underlying pool; and
- the supervisory parameter p is set equal to 1.5, rather than 1 as for securitization exposures.

13.6.4.2 Treatment of Securitizations Exposures Under the Market Risk Framework

As noted earlier, the market risk framework applies only to the Market Risk banks (banks with trading assets in excess of $1 billion, or 10% of total assets). The market risk framework related changes in Basel III (sometimes referred to as Basel 2.5) has been effective since January 1, 2013.

Under Basel I, and also left unchanged in Basel II, market risk RWA rules required calculation of a general risk component (based on internally developed value-at-risk model) and a specific risk add-on (based on either internal models or supervisory add-on factors). Generally, securitization exposures in the trading book, subject to market risk rules, required lower capital than similar exposures in the banking book, which were subject to credit risk rules.

However, Basel III introduces multiple changes aimed at overall increase of market risk capital in the trading book, with a focus on securitizations. In particular, it imposes due diligence requirements, and also, outside of the correlation trading portfolio, increases the specific risk add-on to be equal to the banking book credit RWA charges, i.e., as per SSFA and SFA, as applicable. Also, Basel III strengthens the eligibility for market risk treatment, such that certain trading book portfolios are no longer eligible for market risk treatment. For market risk covered correlation trading portfolio positions, an internally modeled approach is allowed, but with strict qualification criteria. Thus, securitization exposures in the trading book now receive an equal number of governance requirements, and in most cases, higher capital than similar exposures in the banking book.

13.6.4.3 Securitization Exposures Within the Basel III Leverage Ratios

There is already a leverage ratio requirement as part of Basel I, which has also been retained under Basel III, defined as the ratio of Tier 1 Capital to total on-balance sheet assets. Additionally, the Basel III Advanced Approach also includes a supplementary leverage ratio requirement, which is similar to the leverage ratio but also includes a measure for off-balance sheet assets.

Both leverage ratios require total on-balance sheet assets to be measured as per GAAP, or any other accounting framework no less stringent than GAAP. Accordingly, all exposures that are consolidated as per ASC 810 are included. For off-balance sheet commitments, 10% of the notional amount is used only for unconditionally cancellable commitments; otherwise, the full notional amount is used as the off-balance sheet measure. For derivatives, the CEM approach, as defined in the Basel III capital requirements, is used to calculate the exposure amount.

13.6.4.4 Securitization Exposures Within the Basel III Liquidity Ratios
Liquidity ratio requirements comprise of two ratios: the liquidity coverage ratio (LCR) and the net stable funding ratio (NSFR). LCR requires maintaining high-quality liquid assets (HQLA) in excess of total net cash outflows over a 30-day horizon. Calculation of HQLA and total net cash outflows is based on supervisory defined factors for all assets and liabilities of a bank. NFSR is a similar ratio, but over a one-year horizon.

US regulators recently published a proposal on the implementation of LCR. A proposal on NFSR is pending, subject to further calibrations by the Basel Committee on Banking Supervision.

LCR proposes insensitive treatment for securitization exposures. In particular, it treats most types of securitization exposures, including residential mortgage-backed securities, as ineligible for HQLA. Also, credit and liquidity facilities to SPEs and structured transaction outflow amounts attract a 100% outflow amount factor.

The LCR is applicable only to the mandatory Advanced Approach Basel III banks. A modified LCR, based on 21-day horizon, is applicable to BHCs or SLHCs with more than $50 billion in total assets. For all other banks, there is no quantitative liquidity ratio requirement, but qualitative requirements apply. Supervisors published updated guidance around expectations for liquidity risk management that applies to all banks and also enhanced liquidity standards as part of overall enhanced prudential requirements that apply generally to large US and foreign banks (those with assets of more than $50 billion), and covered non-bank companies. The guidance places special emphasis on monitoring of liquidity implications arising out of securitization activities, i.e., reliance on asset securitization activities for funding or loss of liquidity of complex structured investments.

13.7 Conclusion

As history shows, the capital adequacy framework has undergone significant changes in the past couple of years: Rapidly changing economic conditions and interconnectedness of financial institutions significantly increased "the contagious" effect of any financial failure (or crisis) and resulted in a widespread call for the improved back supervision. The latest Basel III framework was designed, accordingly, to address challenges and inefficiencies brought in by the past experiences of Basel I and Basel II. Thus, among other things, it called for more and better quality capital. Another major introduction was its scope: Taking into consideration the micro- and macroeconomic need to assess financial stability, it aimed to evaluate the individual firms' safety and stability, and various risks major institutions and their imbalances present to the global financial stability overall.

As the financial regulators recognized the need to take numerous factors into account and admitted that there could not be any single/right approach, it marked another major shift following Basel I to Basel III transformation. Built on a number of immediate domestic responses, Basel III, accordingly, aimed to recognize the complexity of global financial markets and larger environment. As financial institutions change in their size and structure over the time, so does various buffers (i.e., countercyclical buffer) vary with them depending on market conditions. In other words, leverage ratio, risk-based approach, and stress test—all have their major strengths and weaknesses. Basel III, no doubt, offers more flexibility in using such models on the case by case basis and uses the authority of supervising entities to evaluate institution's performance. What Basel III still needs to assess, however, is the ability of supervising entities and firms themselves to observe and evaluate the performance of those models, and their ability to apply modifications to it when needed.

It also should be mentioned that Basel III has been already criticized for setting high capital standards, which, first, delay recovery and, secondly, has a potential to negatively affect bank's lending practices. While the evidence to address that is mostly is empirical in its nature, data obtained by the BIS and IMF shows positive correlation between bank capitalization and its lending practices. Banks which have been able to develop larger capital buffers find themselves to be less sensitive to various economic shocks, and, as a result, have lower chances of failure when facing drastic shifts in lending behavior.[20] Another question to be answered yet is whether Basel III would succeed in bringing in more transparency or not; as the past experience reveals it, it is often might be a key part.

[20]A. Bailey (2014, July 10): The Capital Adequacy of Banks: Today's Issue and What We Have Learned from the Past. Bank of England.

CHAPTER 14

Comprehensive Capital Analysis and Review (CCAR) and the Dodd–Frank Stress Testing

14.1 Overview

To prevent the failure of financial institutions, the Federal Reserve has established a regulatory framework for the supervision of its largest and most complex financial institutions. As part of these supervisory frameworks, the Federal Reserve annually assesses whether BHCs with $50 billion or more in total consolidated assets have effective capital planning processes and sufficient capital to absorb losses during stressful conditions while meeting obligations to creditors and counterparties while they continue to serve as credit intermediaries. This annual assessment includes two related programs, the Comprehensive Capital Analysis and Review (CCAR) and the Dodd-Frank Act stress testing (DFAST).

The CCAR evaluates a BHC's capital adequacy, capital planning process, and planned capital distributions, such as any common stock repurchases and dividend payments, whereas the Dodd–Frank Act stress testing on the other hand is a forward-looking quantitative evaluation of the impact of stressful and economic financial market conditions on BHC's capital. The Dodd–Frank test also requires that BHCs conduct their own stress tests twice per year and report the result to the Federal Reserve. Stress testing is for large, complex, and non-complex firms. In conducting the supervisory stress tests, the Federal Reserve projects balance sheets, net income, and resulting post-stress capital levels and regulatory capital ratios over a nine-quarter planning

F. I. Lessambo, *The U.S. Banking System*,
https://doi.org/10.1007/978-3-030-34792-5_14

horizon. The projections are based on three macroeconomics scenarios required by the Dodd–Frank act and developed annually by the Federal Reserve.

14.2 The CCAR Process

The CCAR evaluates a BHC's capital adequacy, capital planning process, and planned capital distributions, such as any common stock repurchases and dividend payments. As part of CCAR, the Federal Reserve assesses whether BHCs have sufficient capital to continue operations in the event of any economic and financial market stress and whether they have any forward-looking capital planning processes in place that can account for their unique risks. It is important to know that while BHC's banks create their own capital plan, the Federal Reserve may object to it on quantitative or qualitative grounds. If the Federal Reserve has any objection to a BHC's capital plan, the BHC cannot make any capital distribution unless the Federal Reserve indicates in writing that it does not object to the distribution.

The qualitative assessment considers key aspects of a firm's capital planning process, ranging from the stress testing methods used to inform the forward-looking assessment of that firm's capital adequacy to risk identification, measurement and management, internal controls, and governance supporting the process. Moreover, the qualitative assessment incorporates supervisory evaluations of related issues in the firms' risk identification, measurement and management practices, internal control processes, and overall corporate governance that may be identified through supervisory assessments carried out throughout the year.

The Federal Reserve's quantitative assessment of a BHC's capital plan is based on the supervisory and company-run stress tests that are conducted, in part, under the Board's rules implementing sections 165(i)(1) and (2) of the Dodd–Frank Wall Street Reform and Consumer Protection Act (Dodd–Frank Act stress testing rules). The quantitative assessment of a BHC's capital plan includes a supervisory assessment of the BHC's ability to maintain capital levels above each minimum regulatory capital ratio, after making all capital actions included in its capital plans, under baseline and stressful conditions throughout the nine-quarter planning horizon (Fig. 14.1).

The Board's capital plan rule requires BHCs with consolidated assets of $50 billion or more to submit a capital plan to the Federal

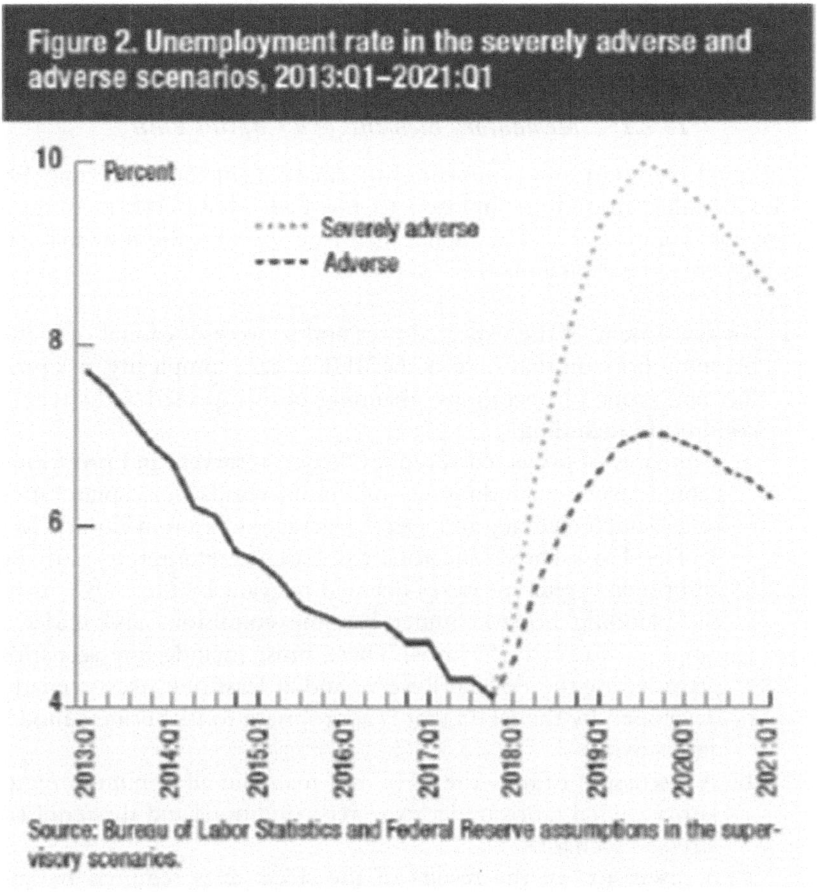

Fig. 14.1 Unemployment in severely adverse and adverse scenarios

Reserve annually. Under the rule, a BHC's capital plan must include a detailed description of the BHC's internal processes for assessing capital adequacy; the board of directors' approved policies governing capital actions; and the BHC's planned capital actions over a nine-quarter planning horizon. Further, a BHC must report to the Federal Reserve the results of stress tests conducted by the BHC under supervisory scenarios provided by the Federal Reserve and under a baseline scenario and a stress scenario designed by the BHC (BHC baseline and BHC stress scenarios). These stress tests assess the sources and uses of capital under baseline and stressed economic and financial market conditions.

14.2.1 Mandatory Elements of a Capital Plan

The capital plan and any supporting information, including certain FR Y-14 schedules, must be submitted to the Federal Reserve through a secure collaboration site. The capital plan rule specifies the four mandatory elements of a capital plan:

1. An assessment of the expected uses and sources of capital over the planning horizon that reflects the BHC's size, complexity, risk profile, and scope of operations, assuming both expected and stressful conditions, including
   a. Estimates of projected revenues, losses, reserves, and pro forma capital levels—including any minimum regulatory capital ratios (e.g., supplementary and Tier 1 leverage, Common Equity Tier 1, Tier 1 risk-based, and total risk-based capital ratios) and any additional capital measures deemed relevant by the BHC—over the planning horizon under baseline conditions and under a range of stressed scenarios. These must include any scenarios provided by the Federal Reserve and at least one stress scenario developed by the BHC that is appropriate to its business model and activities.
   b. A discussion of how the BHC will maintain all minimum regulatory capital ratios under expected conditions and the required stressed scenarios.
   c. A discussion of the results of the stress tests required by law or regulation and an explanation of how the capital plan takes these results into account.
   d. A description of all planned capital actions over the planning horizon.
2. A detailed description of the BHC's processes for assessing capital adequacy.
3. The BHC's capital policy.
4. A discussion of any expected changes to the BHC's business plan that is likely to have a material impact on the BHC's capital adequacy or liquidity.

In addition to these mandatory elements, the Board also requires BHCs to submit supporting information that is necessary to facilitate review of a BHC's capital plan under the Board's capital plan rule and in accordance with the FR Y-14 instruction.

14.3 Stress Test Results Conducted by BHCs

Banks should apply multifactor stress testing scenarios and assess material non-directional risks at least quarterly. Multiple-factor stress tests must, at a minimum, aim to address scenarios in which (i) severe economic or market events have occurred; (ii) broad market liquidity has decreased significantly; and (iii) the market impact of liquidating positions of a large financial intermediary. At a minimum, the results of stress testing for significant exposures must be compared to guidelines that express the bank's risk appetite and elevated for discussion and action when excessive or concentrated risks are present.

The Dodd–Frank Wall Street Reform and Consumer Protection Act requires the Board of Governors of the Federal Reserve System (Board) to conduct an annual supervisory stress test of bank holding companies (BHCs) with $50 billion or greater in total consolidated assets (large BHCs) and to require BHCs and state member banks with total consolidated assets of more than $10 billion to conduct company-run stress tests at least once a year.[1] The Dodd–Frank Act stress tests are one component of the Federal Reserve's analysis during the CCAR, which is an annual exercise to evaluate the capital planning processes and capital adequacy of large BHCs. The stress test aims to make sure that large banks have enough capital on their balance sheets to survive a severe economic downturn akin to the financial crisis. The Board's stress scenarios assume deliberately stringent and conservative hypothetical economic and financial market conditions. The most important metric that the Federal Reserve uses to assess this is the Common Equity Tier 1 Capital ratio (CET1 ratio). That is, banks must maintain a 4.5% CET1 ratio through both stages of the annual tests. Capital is critical to banking organizations, the financial system, and the economy because it acts as a cushion to absorb losses and helps to ensure that losses are borne by shareholders.

[1] Federal Reserve Bank (February 10, 2017): 2017 Supervisory Scenarios for Annual Stress Tests Required Under the Dodd–Frank Act Stress Testing Rules and the Capital Plan Rule, p. 1.

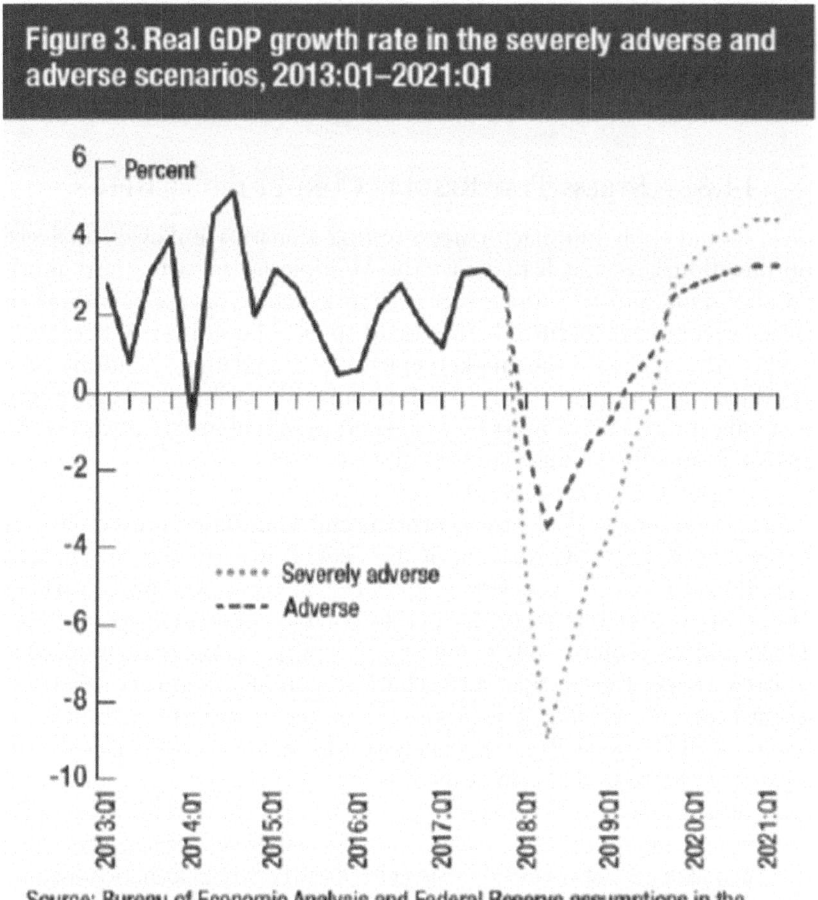

Fig. 14.2 GDP growth in severely adverse and adverse scenarios

The Dodd–Frank Act stress testing (DFAST) uses both (i) the Baseline, Adverse, and Severely Adverse Scenarios and (ii) the Global Market Shock Components for Supervisory Adverse and Severely Adverse Scenarios (Fig. 14.2).

1. The Baseline, Adverse, and Severely Adverse Scenarios;

• Baseline Scenario

The baseline scenario for the United States is a moderate economic expansion through the projection period:

- Real GDP grows on average about 2¼% per year, with a slightly faster pace of growth over the first half of the scenario period.
- The unemployment rate initially declines from around 4¾% at the start of the scenario period to slightly under 4½% in the fourth quarter of 2018. It subsequently rises slightly above that level through the rest of the scenario period.
- CPI inflation moves to a little under 2½% at an annual rate by the end of 2018, before dropping back to about 2¼% and remaining near that level through the end of the scenario period.
- Treasury yields are assumed to rise steadily across the maturity spectrum through the scenario period. Short-term Treasury rates increase from ½% at the beginning of 2017 to about 2¼% by the beginning of 2019, while yields on 10-year Treasury securities rise from 2¼% to a little more than 3¼% over the same period.
- The prime rate increases in line with short-term Treasury rates and mortgage rates rise in line with long-term Treasury yields.
- Spreads between yields on investment-grade corporate bonds and yields on long-term Treasury securities narrow modestly over the scenario period.
- Equity prices rise by an average of about 5% per year and equity market volatility is assumed to remain near its historical average level.
- Nominal house prices rise by an average of 2¾% per year and commercial real estate prices rise by an average of 4¼% per year.
- The baseline scenario features an expansion in international economic activity, albeit one that proceeds at different rates in the four countries or country blocks under consideration. Real GDP growth in developing Asia averages about 6% per year over the scenario period; real GDP growth in both the euro area and the UK averages about 1½% per year; and real GDP growth in Japan averages ¾% per year.

- Adverse Scenario

It is a hypothetical scenario designed to assess the strength of banking organizations and their resilience to adverse economic conditions. This scenario does not represent a forecast of the Federal Reserve.

The adverse scenario is characterized by weakening economic activity across all of the economies included in the scenario. This economic downturn is accompanied by a global aversion to long-term fixed-income assets that, despite lower short rates, brings about a near-term rise in long-term rates and steepening yield curves in the United States and the four countries/country blocks in the scenario. The assumptions are:

- The US economy experiences a moderate recession that begins in the first quarter of 2017.
- Real GDP falls slightly more than 2% from the pre-recession peak in the fourth quarter of 2016 to the recession trough in the first quarter of 2018, while the unemployment rate rises steadily, peaking at about 7¼% in the third quarter of 2018.
- The US recession is accompanied by an initial fall in inflation through the third quarter of 2017, with the rate of increase in consumer prices then rising steadily and reaching 2% by the middle of 2018.
- Short-term interest rates in the United States fall and remain near zero for the rest of the scenario period.
- 10-year Treasury yields gradually rise to a little less than 2¾% by the second half of 2018.
- Spreads between investment-grade corporate bond yields and 10-year Treasury yields widen to about 3¾ percentage points by the end of 2017, while spreads between mortgage rates and 10-year Treasury yields widen to about 2½ percentage points over the same period.
- Equity prices fall approximately 40% through the fourth quarter of 2017, accompanied by a rise in equity market volatility.
- Aggregate house prices and commercial real estate prices experience less sizable but more sustained declines compared to equity prices; house prices fall 12% through the first quarter of 2019 and commercial real estate prices fall 15% through the fourth quarter of 2018.

- Following the recession in the United States, real activity picks up slowly at first and then gains momentum; growth in real US GDP accelerates from an increase of 1% at an annual rate in the second quarter of 2018 to an increase of 3% at an annual rate by the middle of 2019. The unemployment rate declines modestly, from its peak of about 7¼% in the third quarter of 2018 to under 7% by the end of the scenario period. Consumer price inflation remains at roughly 2% from the middle of 2018 through the end of the scenario period. Ten-year Treasury yields show little change after the second half of 2018 and remain around 2¾%.
- The declines in activity in the euro area and the UK are broadly similar and less pronounced than in Japan. Weakness in global demand results in a slowing in inflation in all of the foreign economies under consideration. Japan experiences outright deflation through the first quarter of 2019. Reflecting flight-to-safety capital flows, the US dollar appreciates against the euro, the pound sterling, and the currencies of developing Asia. The dollar depreciates modestly against the yen, also in line with flight-to-safety capital flows.

• Severely Adverse Scenario

Is a hypothetical scenario designed to assess the strength of banking organizations and their resilience to unfavorable economic conditions? This scenario does not represent a forecast of the Federal Reserve. The severely adverse scenario is characterized by a severe global recession that is accompanied by a period of heightened stress in corporate loan markets and commercial real estate markets.

The most severe hypothetical scenario projects $383 billion in loan losses at the 34 participating BHCs during the nine quarters tested. The "severely adverse" scenario features a severe global recession with the US unemployment rate rising by approximately 5.25 percentage points to 10%, accompanied by heightened stress in corporate loan markets and commercial real estate.

The assumptions are as follows:

- The level of US real GDP begins to decline in the first quarter of 2017 and reaches a trough in the second quarter of 2018 that is about 6½% below the pre-recession peak.
- The unemployment rate increases by about 5¼ percentage points, to 10%, by the third quarter of 2018.
- Headline consumer price inflation falls to about 1¼% at an annual rate by the second quarter of 2017 and then rises to about 1¾% at an annual rate by the middle of 2018.
- Short-term Treasury rates fall and remain near zero through the end of the scenario period.
- The 10-year Treasury yield drops to ¾% in the first quarter of 2017, rising gradually thereafter to around 1½% by the first quarter of 2019 and to about 1¾% by the first quarter of 2020.
- Financial conditions in corporate and real estate lending markets are stressed severely.
- The spread between yields on investment-grade corporate bonds and yields on long-term Treasury securities widens to about 5½ percentage points by the end of 2017, an increase of 3½ percentage points relative to the fourth quarter of 2016.
- The spread between mortgage rates and 10-year Treasury yields widens to over 3½ percentage points over the same time period.
- Asset prices drop sharply in this scenario. Equity prices fall by 50% through the end of 2017, accompanied by a surge in equity market volatility, which approaches the levels attained in 2008.
- House prices and commercial real estate prices also experience large declines, with house prices and commercial real estate prices falling by 25 and 35%, respectively, through the first quarter of 2019.
- The international component of this scenario features severe recessions in the euro area, the UK, and Japan and a marked growth slowdown in developing Asia. As a result of the sharp contraction in economic activity, all foreign economies included in the scenario experience a decline in consumer prices. As in this year's adverse scenario, the US dollar appreciates against the euro, the pound sterling, and the currencies of developing Asia but depreciates modestly against the yen because of flight-to-safety capital flows.

2. Global Market Shock Components for Supervisory Adverse and Severely Adverse Scenario

The global market shock is a set of instantaneous, hypothetical shocks to a large set of risk factors. Generally, these shocks involve large and sudden changes in asset prices, interest rates, and spreads, reflecting general market distress and heightened uncertainty. BHCs with significant trading activity are required to include the global market shock as part of their supervisory adverse and severely adverse scenarios.

In addition, certain large and highly interconnected BHCs must apply the same global market shock to their counterparty exposures to project losses under the counterparty default scenario component. The as of date for the global market shock is January 3, 2017.

- 2017 Adverse Scenario

The global market shock component for the adverse scenario simulates an extended low-growth environment and muted market volatility across most asset classes and term structures. Generally, domestic government yields and associated volatility move lower, while swap spreads widen. Due to reduced demand, global commodity prices decline moderately, while mortgage-backed securities (MBS) and domestic credit spreads widen moderately. Select currency markets also experience small flight-to-quality moves. Equity markets experience a mild correction with a measured increase in volatility.

- 2017 Severely Adverse Scenario

The severely adverse scenario's global market shock is designed around three main elements: (i) a sudden sharp increase in general risk premiums and credit risk; (ii) significant market illiquidity; and (iii) the distress of one or more large entities that rapidly sell a variety of assets into an already fragile market.

Liquidity deterioration is most severe in those asset markets that are typically less liquid, such as non-agency securitized products, corporate debt, and private equity and is less pronounced in those markets that are typically more liquid, such as foreign exchange, publicly traded equity, and US Treasury markets. Markets facing a significant deterioration in liquidity experience conditions that are generally comparable to the peak-to-trough changes in asset valuations during the 2007–2009 period. The severity of deterioration reflects the market conditions that could occur in the event of a significant pullback in market liquidity in which market participants are less able to engage in market transactions that could offset or moderate the price dislocations. Worsening liquidity also leads prices of related assets that would ordinarily be expected to move together to diverge markedly. In particular, the valuation of certain cash market securities and their derivative counterparts fail to move together because the normal market mechanics that would ordinarily result in small pricing differentials are impeded by a lack of market liquidity. Notably, option-adjusted spreads on agency MBS increase significantly.

Declines in aggregate US commercial and residential real estate prices should be assumed to be concentrated in regions and property types that have experienced rapid price gains over the past several years. In particular, given that prices of multifamily properties have risen rapidly in recent years, they should be assumed to decline by more than the CRE index. Declines in prices of US housing and commercial real estate should also be assumed to be representative of risks to house prices and commercial real estate prices in foreign regions and economies, particularly where real estate prices have been growing at a fast pace. Spreads on commercial mortgage-backed securities (CMBS) widen to attain the same peaks reached in the 2007–2009 recession.

The global market shock is a set of instantaneous, hypothetical shocks to a large set of risk factors. Generally, these shocks involve large and sudden changes in asset prices, interest rates, and spreads, reflecting general market distress and heightened uncertainty. BHCs with significant trading activity will be required to include the global market shock as part of their supervisory adverse and severely adverse scenarios. In addition, as discussed below, certain large and highly interconnected BHCs must apply the same global market shock to their counterparty exposures to project losses under the counterparty default scenario component. The as of date for the global market shock is January 3, 2017.

14.3.1 Analytical Framework

The Federal Reserve estimated the effect of the supervisory scenarios on the regulatory capital ratios of the 34 BHCs participating in the 2017 DFAST by projecting the balance sheet, risk-weighted assets (RWA), net income, and resulting capital for each BHC over a nine-quarter planning horizon, which begins in the first quarter of 2017 and ends in the first quarter of 2019. The projected net income, adjusted for the effect of taxes, is combined with capital action assumptions to project changes in equity capital. The approach must follow US generally accepted accounting principles (GAAP) and regulatory revised capital framework. Projected net income for the 34 BHCs is generated from projections of revenue, expenses, and various types of losses and provisions that flow into pre-tax net income.[2]

14.3.2 Model Methodology

The Federal Reserve's projections of revenue, expenses, and various types of losses and provisions that flow into pre-tax net income are based on data provided by the 34 BHCs participating in DFAST 2017 and on models developed or selected by Federal Reserve staff and evaluated by an independent team of Federal Reserve model reviewers. The models are intended to capture how the balance sheet, RWAs, and net income of each BHC would be affected by the macroeconomic and financial conditions described in the supervisory scenarios, given the characteristics of the BHCs' loans and securities portfolios; trading, private equity, and counterparty exposures from derivatives and SFTs; business activities; and other relevant factors. Models were developed using multiple data sources, including pooled historical data from financial institutions. The Federal Reserve deviated from the industry-wide modeling approach when the historical data used to estimate the model were not sufficiently granular to capture the impact of firm-specific risk factors, and BHC-specific indicator variables (fixed effects) representing the firm's average longer-term history were more predictive of the firm's future performance than industry variables. In the first approach, the models estimate expected losses under the macroeconomic scenario.

These models generally involve projections of the probability of default, loss given default, and exposure at default for each loan or segment of loans in the portfolio, given conditions in the scenario. In the second approach, the models capture the historical behavior of net charge-offs relative to changes in macroeconomic and financial market variables. Accrual

[2] Federal Reserve, 2017.

loan losses are projected using detailed loan information, including borrower characteristics, collateral characteristics, characteristics of the loans or credit facilities, amounts outstanding and yet to be drawn down (for credit lines), payment history, and current payment status. Data are collected on individual loans or credit facilities for wholesale loan, domestic retail credit card, and residential mortgage portfolios.[3]

For other domestic and international retail loans, the data are collected based on segments of the portfolio. Losses on retail loans for which a BHC chose the fair-value option accounting treatment and loans carried at the lower of cost or market value (i.e., loans held for sale and held for investment) are estimated over the nine quarters of the planning horizon using a duration-based approach. Losses on wholesale loans held for sale or measured under the fair-value option are estimated by revaluing each loan or commitment each quarter of the planning horizon[4] (Federal Reserve, 2017).

14.3.3 Change in Model (Dodd–Frank Act Stress Testing 2017)

Each year, the Federal Reserve has refined both the substance and process of the Dodd–Frank Act stress testing, including its development and enhancement of independent supervisory models. The supervisory stress test models may be revised to reflect advances in modeling techniques, enhancements in response to model validation findings, the incorporation of richer and more detailed data, and identification of more stable models or models with improved performance, particularly under stressful economic conditions. Overall changes in PPNR projections and CRE loan losses are attributable to several other factors, including portfolio composition changes, changes in the macroeconomic scenario, and changes in the historical data used to estimate the models.

For DFAST 2017, the Federal Reserve used an enhanced operational risk model to capture losses from both of these components and discontinued the use of the mortgage repurchase model used in prior years. Mortgage repurchase risk has declined in recent years due to improved underwriting standards and settlements relating to representations and warranties for pre-crisis vintages. Further, new data from recent

[3]Federal Reserve, 2017.

[4]Federal Reserve, 2017.

mortgage repurchase settlements have allowed the operational risk model to better incorporate mortgage repurchase risk, reducing the need to have a separate mortgage repurchase model.

For DFAST 2017, the Federal Reserve used an enhanced regression-based model that forecasts total losses at the industry level and then distributes those losses to each firm based on its asset size. The use of the industry model allows the Federal Reserve to account for operational risk losses more consistently across BHCs. In addition, this approach simplifies the methodology and increases the sensitivity of projected losses to economic conditions.

14.3.4 Model Risk Management

The Federal Reserve places great emphasis on the credibility of its supervisory stress testing process, which is supported by a rigorous program of supervisory model risk management. The Federal Reserve's supervisory model risk management program includes effective oversight of model development to ensure adherence to consistent development principles, rigorous and independent model validation. External parties have reviewed several aspects of the Federal Reserve's supervisory stress testing program, including its model risk management framework.

Federal Reserve staff draws on economic research as well as industry practice in modeling the effects of borrower, instrument, collateral characteristics, and macroeconomic factors on revenues, expenses, and losses. Three groups are, collectively, responsible for managing and validating the Federal Reserve's supervisory stress testing models: the Model Oversight Group (MOG), the System Model Validation Unit, and the Supervisory Stress Test Model Governance Committee. The MOG strives to produce supervisory stress test results that reflect likely outcomes under the supervisory scenarios and ensures that model design across the system of supervisory stress testing models result in projections that are from an independent supervisory perspective and stable such that changes in model projections over time reflect underlying risk factors, scenarios, and model enhancements rather than transitory factors.[5]

[5] Federal Reserve, 2017.

14.3.5 *Data Inputs*

Most of the data used in the Federal Reserve stress rest projections are collected through the capital assessments and stress testing, which include a set of annual, quarterly, or monthly schedules. These reports collect detailed data on pre-provision net revenue (PPNR), loans, securities, trading and counterparty risk, losses related to operational risk events, and business plan changes. The portfolio is deemed to be "material" if the size of the portfolio exceeds either 5% of the BHC's Tier 1 Capital or $5 billion for large institution supervision coordinating Committee (LISCC) and large and complex firms. Each BHC has the option to either submit or not submit the relevant data schedule for a given portfolio that does not meet the materiality threshold. The most important metric that the Federal Reserve employs to determine this is the Common Equity Tier 1 (CET1). This reflects how much high quality, highly liquid capital a bank has relative to its risk-weighted measure of assets, as a proxy for leverage. In the 2017 round of stress testing, 27 out of 34 BHC fairly passed in stress test for year 2017 these includes: Ally Financial; American Express; Bank of America; Bank of New York; Mellon; BB&T; BMO Financial; Capital One; CITI Group; CIT Group; Citizens Financial; Comerica; Discover Financial; Fifth Third Bancorp; Goldman Sachs; Huntington Bancshares; JP Morgan Chase; Keycorp; M&T Bank; Morgan Stanley; Northern Trust; PNC Financial; Regions Financial; State Street; SunTrust Banks; U.S. Bancorp; Wells Fargo; and Zions Bancorp.[6]

14.3.6 *Supervisory Stress Test Results*

The Federal Reserve's projections of RWAs, losses, revenues, expenses, and capital positions for the 34 BHCs participating in DFAST 2017 under the severely adverse and adverse scenarios, results are presented in aggregate for the 34 BHCs as well as for individual BHCs. The aggregate results provide a sense of the stringency of the adverse and severely adverse scenario projections and the sensitivities of losses, revenues, and capital at these BHCs as a group to the stressed economic and financial market conditions contained in those scenarios. Year-over-year changes

[6] J. Maxfield (2017): 2017 Bank Stress Test Results, https://www.fool.com/investing/2017/07/06/2017-bank-stress-test-results.aspx.

in supervisory stress test results reflect changes in BHC starting capital positions, scenarios used for supervisory stress test, portfolio composition, and risk characteristics.

The Federal Reserve projects that the 34 BHCs as a group would experience significant losses on positions and loans under the severely adverse scenario. In this scenario, losses are projected to be $493 billion for the 34 BHCs over the nine quarters of the planning horizon. These losses include $383 billion in accrual loan portfolio losses; 5 billion in realized securities losses; and 18 billion in additional losses from items such as loans booked under the fair-value option.[7] Under the most severe scenario, the 34 banks would suffer $383 billion in loan losses, down from $526 billion in losses recorded by 33 banks in 2016. Notably, projected losses included $100 billion from credit card loans for the banks, at an equal level with Commercial and Industrial Loans losses, for the first time. Therefore, both these categories constitute around 52% of the total projected loan losses worth $383 billion.

In aggregate, Common Equity Tier 1 (CET1) Capital ratio would decline from an actual 12.5% in the fourth quarter of 2016 to a post-stress level of 9.2% at the end of 2017 (Board of Governors of the Federal Reserve System, 2017, C). Most of the other banks that participated in the 2017 stress test emerged with larger margins for error. At the conclusion of the CCAR, the average CET1 ratio among these 27 banks was 6.3%.

That represents a meaningful drop from the average 11.2% CET1 ratio at the start of the tests, but the end result is still comfortably above the 4.5% regulatory minimum. These performances are good news for investors in bank stocks (Fig. 14.3).[8]

The Federal Reserve has recently (2019) made of move to make its stress testing more transparent, providing financial firms more information as to how their portfolios would perform under potential economic shocks. The 2019 tests will include factoring a jump to 10% unemployment from the current four rate percent. More, the 2019 test elevates stress in corporate loan and commercial real estate markets in the most severe scenario.

[7] Federal Reserve, 2017.

[8] J. Maxfield (2017): 2017 Bank Stress Test Results, https://www.fool.com/investing/2017/07/06/2017-bank-stress-test-results.aspx.

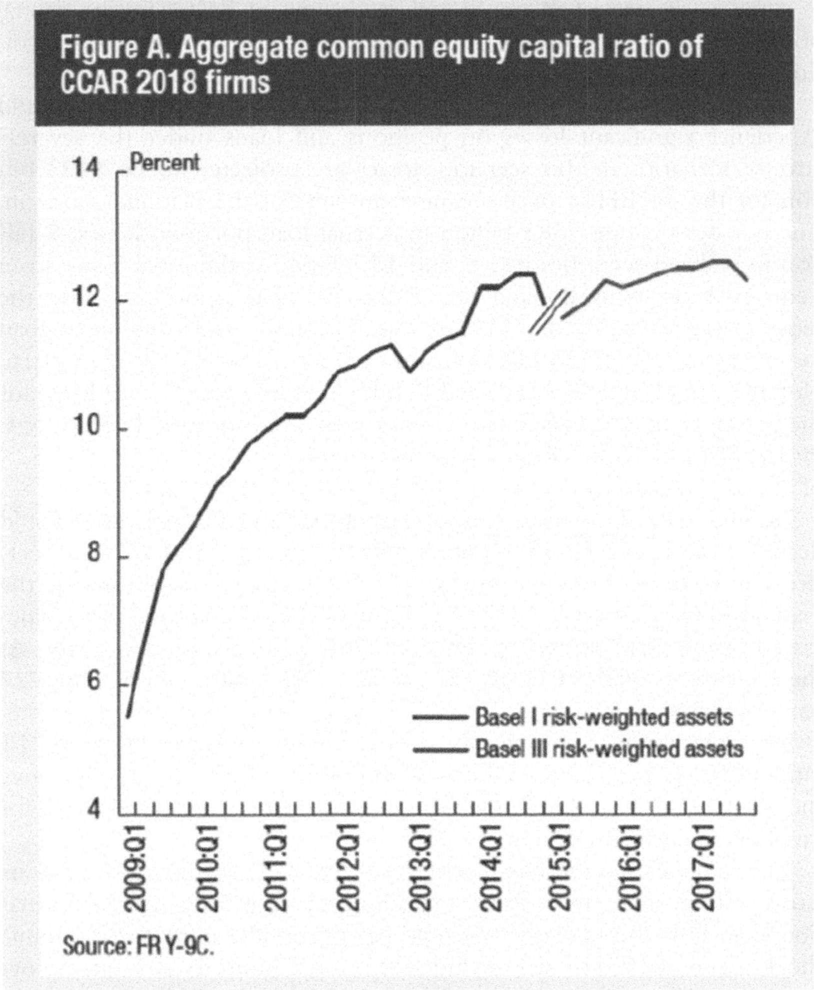

Fig. 14.3 Aggregate common equity capital ratio/CCAR 2018

14.3.7 Supervisory Post-Stress Capital Analysis

The Federal Reserve's supervisory post-stress capital analysis is based on the estimates of losses, revenues, balances, RWA, and capital from the Federal Reserve's supervisory stress test conducted under the

Table 14.1 Bank holding companies

	Bank holding company
1	Ally Financial Inc.
2	American Express Company
3	BankWest Corporation
4	Bank of America Corporation
5	The Bank of New York Mellon Corporation
6	BB&T Corporation
7	BBVA Compass Bancshares, Inc.
8	BMO Financial Corp.
9	Capital One Financial Corporation
10	CIT Group Inc.
11	Citigroup Inc.
12	Citizens Financial Group, Inc. 7.7
13	Comerica Incorporated 9.4
14	Deutsche Bank Trust Corporation 60.2
15	Discover Financial Services 10.4
16	Fifth Third Bancorp 8.0
17	The Goldman Sachs Group, Inc. 8.4
18	HSBC North America Holdings Inc. 12.9
19	Huntington Bancshares Incorporated 7.0
20	JPMorgan Chase & Co. 9.1
21	KeyCorp 6.8
22	M&T Bank Corporation 7.9
23	Morgan Stanley 9.4
24	MUFG Americas Holdings Corporation 12.5
25	Northern Trust Corporation 10.9
26	The PNC Financial Services Group, Inc. 8.0
27	Regions Financial Corporation 8.2
28	Santander Holdings United States, Inc. 12.4
29	State Street Corporation 7.4
30	SunTrust Banks, Inc. 7.1
31	TD Group US Holdings LLC 11.3
32	U.S. Bancorp 7.6
33	Wells Fargo & Company 8.6
34	Zions Bancorporation 8.5

Dodd–Frank Act. The supervisory projections are conducted under three hypothetical macroeconomic and financial market scenarios developed by the Federal Reserve:

- The supervisory baseline,
- Supervisory adverse, and
- Supervisory severely adverse scenarios (Table 14.1).

14.4 Stress Test in the European Union

14.4.1 Objective and Approach

The EU stress test has been established to offer to all market players, among which banks, supervisors, and other market participants sharing the same analytical structure, to regularly confront and evaluate whether EU banks and EU banking system are able to absorb shocks and to challenge the European banks in terms of capital position. The implementation of the banking stress tests is constructed on a common methodology and a set of templates, which can capture both opening data and results. The banks belonging to the European Union are evaluated based on a macroeconomic criterion and a hostile scenario, which is based on the figures of the end of the previous year with an application of the latter ones over a period of three years.

In order to achieve the best results and pursue a course of action that is in accordance with the law, the participating banks must respect severe rules, at the moment of forecasting the effect of the scenarios on banks projected profit and loss and capital position, the banks are expected to follow the common methodology. For example, observing IFRS 9, banks need to clarify expectations on the projection of credit risk losses and to arrange a limit on estimated net interest income.[9] To clarify an IFRS 9 is an International Financial Reporting Standard (IFRS) promoted by the international accounting standards board (IASB), which refers to the accounting for financial instruments (IFRS, 2017).

14.4.2 Methodology and Templates

As mentioned above, the objective of the banking stress test in the European Union is to assess the impact of risk factors on the solvency of the European banks. The request for the banks is to implement a stress test relying on a shared set of risks. The latter set of risks consists of three principal risks, which includes operational risk, which also includes the conduct risk, the credit risk that additionally embraces securitizations, and lastly market risk and counterparty credit risk (CCR).

[9]F.R. Congiu (2017): EBA Issues 2018 EU-Wide Stress Test Methodology for Discussion. EBA European Banking Authority.

The draft methodology is seen as a pattern, which allows banks to discuss in an informal way and dispatch inputs taking into account in the settlement of the documents. Every three years, in the implementation of the draft methodology, changes are made taking into account the approach and the lesson learnt from the previous years. In fact, for 2018, changes are also produced because of the variation of the IFRS 9 which replaced the previous rules of the IAS 39: Financial Instruments: Recognition and Measurement (IFRS, 2017).[10]

14.4.3 Results

The coordination of the European stress test is assigned to the European Bank Authority (EBA), which collaborates with the European Central Bank (ECB), the European Commission (EC), and the European Systemic Risk Board (ESRB), and all the qualified authorities from the pertinent national jurisdictions. Therefore, the EBA is in charge to publish the results of each stress test. Regarding the last results, for instance, the EBA promulgated on date July 29, 2016, the results of 2016-wide stress test considering 51 banks from the 51 EU and EEA countries which comprise around 70% of banking assets within the European Union. Moreover, the EBA offers the balance sheet of the European banks following the procedures for an extreme transparency, providing 16,000 data points per bank, which is a very important data for achieving the maximum discipline within the European market.[11]

Recently, the EU banking sector reported an increase of its capital from an initial position for the stress test of 13.2% CET1 ratio at the end of the year 2015. At this point, it is deemed necessary to highlight the meaning of CET1 for the EBA. CET1 is the acronym of Common Equity Tier 1, which is one of the capital instruments belonging to the regulatory technical standards.[12] The CET1 of 13.2% is a data that

[10]F.R. Congiu (2017): EBA Issues 2018 EU-Wide Stress Test Methodology for Discussion. EBA European Banking Authority.

European Banking Authority (2016): EBA Publishes 2016 EU-Wide Stress Test Results.

[11]European Banking Authority (2015): EBA Updates List of Common Equity Tier 1 (CET1) Capital Instruments.

[12]European Banking Authority (2015): EBA Updates List of Common Equity Tier 1 (CET1) Capital Instruments.

reports 200 bps of increase compared to 2014 and 400 bps related to the results of 2011. The BPS is the Value of Basis Point, which refers to a common unit of measure for interest rates and other percentages in finance.

Additional data testify that the supposed scenario carries to a stressed impact of 380 bps based on CET1 capital ratio, conducting it at 9.4% at the end of the year 2018. According to this adverse scenario, the aggregate leverage ratio falls from 5.2 to 4.2% and the CET1 from 12.6 to 9.2%. It is possible to conclude, following the set of risks mentioned above that the impact for the stress test of 2016 is determined by the credit risk losses of €–360 bn, operational risk of €–105 bn, and market risk of €–98 bn (EBN, 2016). In particular, the results have denoted that European banks were in a healthier position than the last exercise in 2014.

Indeed, the stress test has tested the strength of the European banks based on the standard scenario and the adverse scenario. Unlike the stress test in 2014, this time there was no minimum-security threshold established for the banks under review (set at 5.5% at the previous test). The ranking list of the top 10 European banks based on the CET1 ratio calculated for an adverse scenario in 2018 is as below:

- German NRW.Bank with 35.40%,
- Two Sweden banks, Swedbank with 22.26% and Svenska Handelsbanken with 18.55%.
- N.V. Bank Nederlandse showing 17.62% of CET1 ratio,
- Skandinaviska Enskilda Banken (Sweden): 16.60%,
- Finland and its bank Op-Pohjola Osk come after with 14.90%,
- Dnb Bank Group (Norway): 14.30%,
- Nykredit Realkredit (Denmark): 14.19%,
- Nordea Bank (Sweden): 14.09%,
- Danske Bank (Denmark): 14.02%.

The banks of northern Europe dominate in the list; in fact, four of them are Swedes. German MRW bank reports the highest CET1 in case of an adverse scenario. The Italians banks are absent, but the closest institution to the top ten is Intesa Sanpaolo, which is ranked 18th within the 51 banks, reporting a CET1 ratio of 10.24% in case of unfavorable scenario for 2018. However, it has been highlighted the weakness of specific banks, mainly Italian banks. The worst in the list is Monte dei Paschi, which is the third larger Italian lender. Monte dei Paschi capital ratio of −2.4% is the only negative one in the test. This means that if the worst-case scenario happened, the latter bank would have been bankrupt. Monte dei Paschi has not been the only one; in fact, UniCredit another Italian bank is among the worst in the group, which presented a capital ratio of 7.1%.[13]

Furthermore, the stress test underlined the poor performers in the rest of the European Union. Of this list belongs Allied Irish Bank with a capital ratio of only 4.3% in the adverse scenario. Raiffeisen of Austria reported a CET1 of 6.1% and the two big German banks, Commerzbank (7.42%) and Deutsche Bank (7.80%). Following the trend, the Spanish Banco popular reported 7.01%, Barclays (UK) with 7.03%, and the French Societe Generale with 8.03%.[14]

14.4.4 Criticism

Even though the European Banking System proves in the latest stress test that there has been an improvement on the conditions of the banks' system in the European Union, there are a lot of criticisms among the market's players. In fact, according to Larry Elliott (2016), scholar of economic issues and editors at the Guardian, stress tests are not as useful as the institutions like to exhibit. Due to the fact that they do not show the actual condition of lenders across the continent and stress tests do not provide an accurate understanding of how the 51 banks would resist another crisis. Furthermore, from the results of 2016 stress test, Elliott (2016) stated that the EBS does not consider the fall of 8% on share price of UniCredit, the biggest among the Italian banks. The 3% drop in bank shares across the continent is information, which indicates that investors think in a way that is not the same as the EBS.

Gaps from the latest stress test are determined by a few other lacks. One of them is the absence of banks as Greece and Portugal which are the two of the most troubled Eurozone countries. Moreover, the test did not assess the mostly likely problem, such as the continued period after the Brexit of negative interest rates that would damage in the future the

[13]A. Atte (2016): Stress Test BCE 2016: Classifica Banche: Ecco le 10 migliori e le 10 peggiori in Europa.

[14]*The Economist* (2016): European Banks Still Stressed Out, and Stress Test Results Do Little to Dampen Worries About Italy's Lenders.

Table 14.2 EU tested banks

	Country	*Bank*
1	Austria	Erste Group Bank AG
2		Raiffeisen-Landesbanken-Holding GmbH
3	Belgium	Belfius Banque SA
4		KBC Group NV
5	Denmark	Danske Bank
6		Jyske Bank
7		Nykredit Realkredit
8	Finland	OP Osuuskunta
9	France	Groupe Crédit Mutuel
10		La Banque Postale
11		BNP Paribas
12		Groupe Crédit Agricole
13		Groupe BPCE
14		Société Générale S.A.
15	Germany	Deutsche Bank AG
16		Commerzbank AG
17		Landesbank Baden-Württemberg
18		Bayerische Landesbank
19		Norddeutsche Landesbank Girozentrale
20		Landesbank Hessen-Thüringen Girozentrale
21		NRW.BANK
22		Volkswagen Financial Services AG
23		DekaBank Deutsche Girozentrale
24	Hungary	OTP Bank Nyrt.
25	Ireland	Allied Irish Banks plc
26		The Governor and Company of the Bank of Ireland
27	Italy	Intesa Sanpaolo S.p.A.
28		UniCredit S.p.A.
29		Banca Monte dei Paschi di Siena S.p.A.
30		Banco Popolare—Società Cooperativa
31		Unione Di Banche Italiane Società Per Azioni
32	Netherlands	ING Groep N.V.
33		Coöperatieve Centrale Raiffeisen-Boerenleenbank B.A.
34		ABN AMRO Group N.V.
35		N.V. Bank Nederlandse Gemeenten
36	Norway	DNB Bank Group
37	Poland	Powszechna Kasa Oszczędności Bank Polski SA
38	Spain	Banco Santander S.A.
39		Banco Bilbao Vizcaya Argentaria S.A.
40		Criteria Caixa, S.A.U.
41		BFA Tenedora de Acciones S.A.U.
42		Banco Popular Español S.A.
43		Banco de Sabadell S.A.

(continued)

Table 14.2 (continued)

	Country	*Bank*
44	Sweden	Nordea Bank—group
45		Svenska Handelsbanken—group
46		Skandinaviska Enskilda Banken—group
47		Swedbank—group
48	UK	HSBC Holdings
49		Barclays Plc
50		The Royal Bank of Scotland Group Public Limited Company
51		Lloyds Banking Group Plc

profitability of the banks in Europe. Last but not least, Elliott criticizes the failure of the stress test of information about pass or fail of individual banks. He also assumes that the EBS wanted to give a touch of credibility to the test isolating Monte dei Paschi di Siena, another Italian bank which would see canceled all its capital under a state of recession and the rise of interest rates.[15]

In addition to the aforementioned, some of the market participants have even asked for changes of stress tests. They require that the exam should not be public but remain a simple input for supervisory activity. Responsibility should also be entrusted to the competent authorities (e.g., the National Central Bank and ECBs), while the EBA should only be in a position to harmonize the rules. Furthermore, there is some inherent limitation of the banking stress test that is linked to the methodology; the main concern is related to the use of static balance sheets. Therefore, they are not considered to be the banks' adjustment maneuvers. Moreover, as Ignazio Visco the Governor of BankItalia said, the tests generally show a more produced impact when the economy comes out of a long and severe recession. Many also fear a more severe EBA approach to commercial banks that make loans and have government bonds and, instead, less stringent than those which hold illiquid and derivative securities (Table 14.2).

[15] L. Elliott (2016): The EBA's Stress Tests Reveal Their Own Lack of Credibility, in *The Guardian*.

14.5 Comparison Between US and European Union Stress Tests

The general aim of bank stress testing is to ascertain whether or not a bank would be able to withstand a severe yet plausible scenario over a certain time horizon. A stress test is thus a hypothetical and forward-looking exercise. Upon examination of the approach taken by the European Union and the United States, it is evident that there are some fundamental similarities and differences between the approaches taken to conduct banking stress testing. The purpose of the stress tests in the United States and the European Union was similar; they both emphasize the aim to withstand future economic instabilities and troubles and the ability to survive was accomplished by assessing the capital level of financial institutions. According to the Committee of European Banking Supervisors (2010), the EU-wide supervisory stress testing exercise aimed at assessing the overall resilience of the financial sector in Europe and banks' ability to absorb future shocks. On the other hand, Ryu[16] stated that from the US perspective, supervisory stress tests are one of the key inputs into the CCAR which is a major supervisory program that provides independent, forward-looking assessment of capital adequacy among the largest US banks. Salomé (n.d.) outlined that while the objectives of these stress tests are broadly similar, the extent to which each scenario is comparable remains unclear. There is no hard and fast rule as to who should oversee and/or conduct the banking stress test in many nations. The overriding requirement is that the institution(s) conducting the test are considered credible. In some cases, issues such as expertise, sufficiency of resources, and political economic considerations play an important role in determining who should conduct the stress test. In the United States, the oversight and execution of the stress test relied on collaboration across supervisory agencies, which included the Federal Reserve (FED), the Federal Deposit Insurance Corporation (FDIC), and the Office of the Comptroller of the Currency (OCC); supervisors of individual banks are consulted, but they not involved in the actual stress test analyses.[17] In contrast, the EU-wide stress tests are

[16] L.H. Ryu (2013): Federal Reserve's Philosophy for Supervisory Stress Test. The Board of Governors or the Federal Reserve System, p. 2.

[17] Board of Governors of the Federal Reserve System, 2016 A.

conducted by national supervisory authorities; the tests are overseen and coordinated by the EBA, which does not have direct interaction with the banks prior to or during the exercise. The EBA (2014) stated that the EBA collaborates with the EC and the ECB or ESRB. However, Ong and Pazarbasioglu[18] postulated that the EBA has argued that it needed more legal powers over the exercise to ensure the reliability of the input data and hence the results. Goldstein[19] among several others stated that the 2014 EU-wide bank stress test lacked credibility as such the EU made some concessions related to transparency and disclosure to enhance the credulity of its 2016 stress test results. The Federal Reserve places great emphasis on the credibility of its supervisory stress testing process, which is supported by a rigorous program of supervisory model risk management. The Federal Reserve's supervisory model risk management program includes effective oversight of model development to ensure adherence to consistent development principles; rigorous and independent model validation; a strong supervisory model governance structure; and annual communication of the state of model risk in the overall program to the Board of Governors. To improve the credibility of the stress test, several aspects of the Federal Reserve's supervisory stress testing program, including its model risk management framework, are reviewed by external parties. Despite the criticism of the EU's banking stress test, its provisions for testing are similar to that of the United States. Both nations analyzed banks in light of hypothetical economic scenarios in order to determine their ability to survive a downturn in the market. The Federal Reserve utilizes three supervisory scenarios: baseline, adverse, and severely adverse. However, for the 2017 round of testing the stress test included severely adverse scenarios, adverse scenario, and a global market shock and counterparty default components. These scenarios were developed using the approach described in the Board's Policy Statement on the Scenario Design Framework for Stress Testing (Board of Governors of the Federal Reserve System, 2016 A). The adverse and severely adverse scenarios are not forecasts, but rather, hypothetical scenarios designed to assess the strength of banking organizations and their resilience to an unfavorable economic environment.

[18]L.L. Ong and C. Pazarbasioglu (2013): Credibility and Crisis Stress Testing, International Monetary Fund Working Paper WP/13/178.

[19]M. Goldstein (2014): The 2014 EU-Wide Bank Stress Test Lacks Credibility. Retrieved from http://voxeu.org/article/credibility-aqr-and-bank-stress-test.

The supervisory scenarios include trajectories for 28 variables, which include 16 variables that capture economic activity, asset prices, and interest rates in the US economy and financial markets and three variables (real gross domestic product [GDP] growth, inflation, and the US/foreign currency exchange rate). The EBA employs two sets of economic assumptions: benchmark, based on interim forecasts of the economy by the European Union Commission, and adverse, based on ECB estimates with a separate sovereign risk shock. The adverse scenario, designed by the ESRB, reflects the four systemic risks that are currently assessed as representing the most material threats to the stability of the EU banking sector: (i) an abrupt reversal of compressed global risk premia, amplified by low secondary market liquidity; (ii) weak profitability prospects for banks and insurers in a low nominal growth environment, amid incomplete balance sheet adjustments; (iii) rising of debt sustainability concerns in the public and non-financial private sectors, amid low nominal growth; and (iv) prospective stress in a rapidly growing shadow banking sector, amplified by spillover and liquidity risk.[20] Furthermore, the EU-wide stress test is primarily focused on the assessment of the impact of risk drivers on the solvency of banks. Thus, banks are required to stress credit risk, including securitizations; market risk and CCR; and operational risk, including conduct risk. The application of the market risk methodology is based on a common set of stressed market parameters, calibrated from the macroeconomic scenario as well as from historical experience, including haircuts for sovereign exposures. The credit risk methodology includes a prescribed increase in risk exposure amount for securitization exposures as well as prescribed shocks to credit risk losses for sovereign exposures.

In addition to the aforementioned, both the United States and European Union test the majority of their respective banking assets. In the United States, the Dodd–Frank Wall Street Reform and Consumer Protection Act (Dodd–Frank Act) requires the Federal Reserve to conduct an annual stress test of BHCs with $50 billion or more in total consolidated assets, and any nonbank financial company that the FSOC has determined shall be supervised by the Board (Board of Governors of the Federal Reserve System, 2016 B). While the EU-wide test exercise is carried out on a sample of banks covering broadly 70% of the national

[20] European Banking Authority (2015). EBA Updates List of Common Equity Tier 1 (CET1) Capital Instruments.

banking sector in the Eurozone, each EU member state and Norway, is expressed in terms of total consolidated assets as of end of 2014. Since the EU-wide stress test is run at the highest level of consolidation, lower representativeness is accepted for countries with a wide presence of subsidiaries of non-domestic EU banks. To be included, in the sample banks have to have a minimum of Euros (EUR) 30 billion in assets.[21] The 2017 US stress test included 34 of the largest BHCs. The 2016 EU-wide stress test on the other hand included of 51 banks from 15 EU and the European Economic Area (EEA) countries (37 from euro area countries and 14 from Denmark, Hungary, Norway, Poland, Sweden, and the UK) covering around 70% of banking assets in each jurisdiction and across the EU. However, the flexibility for country authorities to choose which banks to include in the stress tests was perceived to have reduced the legitimacy of the EU-wide stress test.[22]

There is some flexibility to the stress testing approach taken by nations. According to Jobst,[23] a bottom-up (BU) test, cross-validated by a top-down (TD) exercise, would be the superior approach. They further theorized that if only a TD stress test is undertaken, it should be conducted on a bank-by-bank rather than on an aggregated basis. The approach taken to stress testing by the US Federal Reserve is fundamentally different from the approach taken by EBA. The EBA approach to the exercise is that of a constrained bottom-up stress test. Banks are required to project the impact of the defined scenarios but are subject to strict constraints as well as to a thorough review by competent authorities.

The US Federal Reserve approach to stress testing consisted of a BU and TD mix.[24] This involves the Federal Reserve making projections of revenue, expenses, and various types of losses and provisions that flow into pre-tax net income are based on data provided by

[21] Idem.

[22] Z. Witton (2011). Europe Misses Again on Bank Stress Test. Moody's Analytics Regional Financial Review.

[23] A.A. Jobst, L.L. Ong, and C. Schmieder (2013): An IMF Framework for Macroprudential Bank Solvency Stress Testing: Application to S-25 and Other G-20 Country FSAPs. IMF Working Paper No. 13/68, International Monetary Fund, Washington.

[24] L.L. Ong and C. Pazarbasioglu (2013): Credibility and Crisis Stress Testing. International Monetary Fund Working Paper WP/13/178.

the BHC participating in stress test. The models are intended to capture how the balance sheet, RWA, and net income of each BHC would be affected by the macroeconomic and financial conditions described in the supervisory scenarios, given the characteristics of the BHCs' loans and securities portfolios; trading, private equity, and counterparty exposures from derivatives and securities financing transactions (SFT); business activities; and other relevant factors.[25] Upon further examination of the differences, it is apparent that the United States, by not having to coordinate with various governments, had a much easier time performing stress testing than the European Union. One major difference that can be easily identified between the US and the EU-wide stress test is the fact that the FED releases three scenarios, baseline, adverse, and severely adverse, while the EBA releases only two scenarios, baseline and adverse. Furthermore, the Federal Reserve requires that the BHCs provide an internal baseline scenario and, at least, one internal stressed scenario. These additional internal scenarios are not included in the scope of the EU-wide stress tests. As such, the FED approach is more complete and inclusive than that of the European Union. In addition to the aforementioned, the US and European scenarios are materialized by a series of aggregated macroeconomic indicators such as the gross domestic product, short-term interest rates, unemployment rate, inflation rate, and residential and commercial property prices. The Federal Reserve publishes the projections for 28 indicators with a clear economic narrative and a comparison with previous year's scenario. In contrast, the EBA does not provide explicitly the projected values for all the indicators, and each scenario is derived from three broad systemic risks that threatens the EU financial stability. The systematic risk includes credit risk, market risk, and operational risk as the EU-wide stress test primary focus is on the assessment of the impact of risk drivers on the solvency of banks (EBA).

Finally, the last major difference lies in the future of stress testing. The United States has enacted comprehensive legislation requiring stress testing of banks by regulators as well as self-testing. In the wake of the financial crisis, Congress enacted the Dodd–Frank Act, which, among other provisions, requires the Federal Reserve to conduct an annual stress test of BHCs as well as nonbank financial companies.

[25] Board of Governors of the Federal Reserve System, 2016 B.

The Dodd–Frank Act also requires each BHC to conduct its own stress tests and report its results to the Federal Reserve, twice a year (Board of Governors of the Federal Reserve System, 2016 B). On the other hand, there is no slated periodic stress test of banks throughout Europe, which is a cause for concern given the volatile nature of the financial market. However, the European regulator has proposed to create a mandate to coordinate stress tests on a regular basis.[26] The fact that the United States has a legislative mandate requiring banks to conduct stress testing has helped to restore confidence throughout the financial system. If investors are knowledge of the fact that the country's largest banking institutions have a sufficient capital cushion against larger than expected future losses, they will be more than willing to invest in US banks. Europe Union has scheduled its 2017–2018 stress test which indicates significant strides to assure that testing will be conducted regularly in the future. According to North,[27] the stress test for 2017–2018 will be tougher, given that it will include a new accounting rule known as the IFRS No. 9, which requires that banks set aside provisions on all loans in advance of default. Furthermore, the EU supervisors' are also expected to make efforts to harmonize rules to enhance stress testing. Many investors will be interested in the 2017–2018 results of the EU-wide stress test result to ascertain the effects of the Brexit.

14.6 Conclusion

The analysis of both the US and European Union banking stress test reveals that there is some inherent limitation in the approach taken to stress testing in both the United States and EU. Both regions have made some concessions to prevent the failure of its financial institutions by employing frequent stress testing. However, it can be concluded that the United States had an easier time conducting stress tests of its financial institutions to address concerns when compared to the European Union stress tests that did not sufficiently address the issues plaguing the European Union. However, both the US and European Union stress testing were response to financial crisis that threatened the global

[26] European Banking Authority (2014): EU-Wide Stress Test Frequently Asked Questions.

[27] M. North (2017): EU's 2018 Bank Stress Test Will Be Tougher, but Has Limitations.

economy. Therefore, the United States has a specific regulatory legislative framework in place to enable future stress testing while the EU has no such policies. This is a cause for concern since the test results aid policy makers in making future decision that is important to the region's future financial stability. As such, the Europe Union plans to implement new regulation for its stress testing in the future. The EBA will be entrusted with more regulatory power which is expected to hopefully ease the difficulty in coordinating a multi-nation testing of financial institutions.

PART IV

Financial Statements and Statement Analysis

CHAPTER 15

Commercial Banks' Financial Statements

15.1 General

Although the general structure of financial statements for banks is not that much different from a regular company, the nature of banking operations means that there are significant differences in the subclassification of accounts. Financial statements for banks present a different analytical problem than manufacturing and service companies. As a result, analysis of a bank's financial statements requires a distinct approach that recognizes a bank's somewhat unique risks.[1] Banks use much more leverage than other businesses and earn a spread between the interest income they generate on their assets (loans) and their cost of funds (customer deposits).

15.2 Bank Annual Financial Statements

The annual statements of a commercial bank are composed of: (i) the balance sheet, (ii) the statement of income, (iii) the statement of cash flows, and (iv) the statement of change in shareholder equity.

[1] Jeffery W. Johnson (2013): Understanding Bank Financial Statements, p. 1.

F. I. Lessambo, *The U.S. Banking System*,
https://doi.org/10.1007/978-3-030-34792-5_15

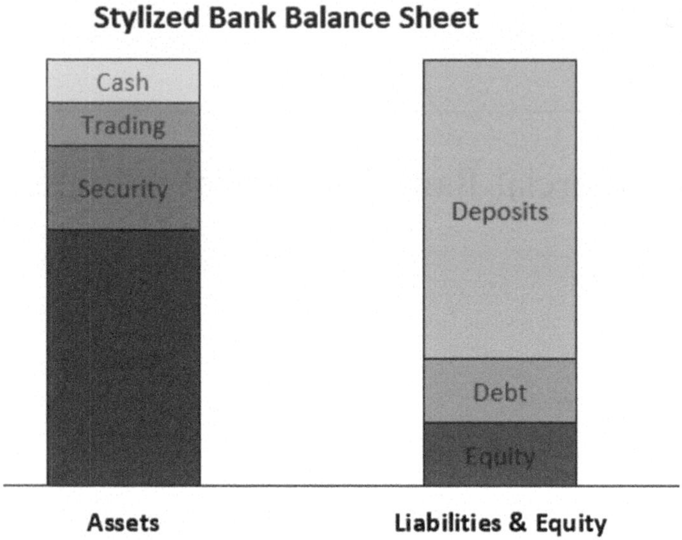

Fig. 15.1 Stylized bank balance sheet

15.2.1 The Balance Sheet

The balance sheet of a commercial bank is composed of assets, liabilities, and owners' equity (Fig. 15.1).

(A) Assets

Assets earn revenue for the banks which include: cash, securities, loans, and property and equipment that allows it to operate. The quality, type, and diversification of on- and off-balance sheet items must be considered when reviewing the adequacy of an institution's capital.

- Cash and Cash Equivalent

A bank holds to cash on demand, whether it is a depositor withdrawing money or writing a check, or a bank customer drawing on a credit line. A bank also needs funds to pay bills, but while bills are predictable in both amount and timing, cash withdrawals by customers are not. Hence, a bank must maintain a certain level of cash compared to its liabilities to maintain solvency. A bank must hold some cash as reserves, which is the amount of money held in a bank's account at the Federal Reserve (FED). The Federal Reserve determines the legal reserves, which is the minimum amount of cash that banks must hold in their accounts to ensure the safety of banks and also allows the FED to effect monetary policy by adjusting the reserve level. Often, banks will keep excess reserves for greater safety. Another source of cash is cash in the process of collection. When a bank receives a check, it must present the check to the bank on which it is drawn for payment, and, previously, this has taken several days. Nowadays, checks are being processed electronically and many transfers of funds are being conducted electronically instead of using checks. So this category of cash is diminishing significantly and will probably disappear when all financial transactions finally become electronic. Cash equivalents are another short-term asset. They are so called because they are nearly equivalent to cash. They represent short-term investments than can either be used as cash or can be quickly converted to cash without loss of value, such as demand deposits, T-bills, and commercial paper. A primary characteristic of financial instruments that are classified as cash equivalents is that they have a short-term maturity of 3 months or less, so interest rate risk is minimal, and they are the most highly rated securities or issued by a government that can print its own money, such as the T-bills issued by the US government, so there is little credit risk.

- Investment Securities

The primary securities that banks own are US Treasuries and municipal bonds. These bonds can be sold quickly in the secondary market when a bank needs more cash, so they are often referred to as secondary reserves. The recent credit crisis has also underscored the fact that banks held many asset-backed securities as well. US banks are not permitted to own stocks, because of the risk, but, ironically, they can hold much riskier securities called derivatives. The most commonly found investments are:

- Treasury bills, notes, and bonds are direct obligations of the US Treasury. Bills are sold at a discount where all interest is price appreciation, while notes and bonds typically carry a fixed term and rate, and coupon interest is paid semiannually.

- Federal Agency securities are obligations of federal agencies such as the Federal Home Loan Bank. They normally carry yields that are slightly above the yield on a comparable maturity Treasury security because they are backed by government entities and not the government directly. Note that government-guaranteed mortgage-backed securities are included under this label. Actual yields earned on mortgage-backed securities often differ sharply from expected yields due to prepayments.
- Municipal securities are obligations of state and local governments and their political subdivisions. They come in many forms. "Bank-qualified" municipals consist of small issue securities ($10 million a year per issuer) issued for essential public purposes. Banks must take a TEFRA disallowance cost in calculating the tax-equivalent yield associated with these municipals.
- Other securities consist primarily of corporate and foreign bonds and various types of mortgage-backed securities.

For reporting purposes, banks are required to designate securities either as held-to-maturity, available-for-sale, or held in a trading account. Regulators require different accounting for each class of securities consistent with the perceived intent behind their purchase. Securities designated as held-to-maturity are valued on the balance sheet at historical, amortized cost. There is no financial statement impact with unrealized gains or losses when interest rates change. Securities designated as available-for-sale are reported at current market values, with unrealized gains and losses included as a component of capital. Thus, when interest rates rise (fall), any decrease (increase) in the value of the securities is balanced by a corresponding unrealized loss (gain) in equity. Trading account securities are reported at market values on the balance sheet with unrealized gains and losses recorded in the income statement. The objective is to provide better information to regulators, analysts, and investors regarding the market value of securities when banks expect to sell them prior to final maturity.

- Loans and Leases

Loans represent the primary earning asset at most banks. Banks serve the needs of their community, and extending loans to businesses and individuals allows a community bank to grow. Loans are typically grouped into categories based on the type of borrower and use of proceeds.

- Commercial and Industrial Loans (C&I) consist of loans to businesses. They appear in many forms but are used primarily to finance working capital needs and new plant and equipment expenditures. They may also be short-term commitments to securities dealers or temporary loans to finance one firm's purchase of another.
- Real estate loans consist of property loans secured by first mortgages or interim construction loans secured by real property.
- Consumer loans are granted to individuals for a wide variety of purposes. They may be installment loans for the purchase of cars, boats, and durable goods or credit card loans.
- Agricultural loans represent credit extended to farmers or agribusinesses.
- International loans are essentially business loans made to foreign enterprises. Foreign governments often guarantee them. Most community banks do not make international loans.

Loans typically earn the highest yields before expenses. They also exhibit the highest risk and default rates and cost more than securities to administer. A loan loss reserve is maintained by the bank to cover future expected loan losses. This account is presented on the balance sheet as a contra asset account to total loans.

Several key profitability ratios use a bank's earning assets, which equals loans plus investment securities and other interest-earning assets.

- Other assets

Other assets are of relatively small magnitudes, representing such items as bank premises and equipment, interest receivables, and other real estate owned. They are essentially nonearning because they generate no interest income.

(B) Liabilities

Bank funding sources are classified by the type of deposit, debt claim, and equity component. The characteristics of each liability vary according to maturity, interest paid, whether the holder can write checks against outstanding balances, and whether they are FDIC-insured. Prior to the early 1980s, regulations limited the maximum interest rates that banks could pay on most deposits. Since 1986, interest rate restrictions have been largely removed on all deposit accounts including demand deposits. Banks now compete for deposits by paying market rates on virtually all liabilities.

- Transaction Accounts

Transaction accounts are accounts on which depositors can withdraw or transfer funds by writing checks, debit cards, mobile banking, drafts, payment orders of withdrawal, or telephone. The various accounts include demand deposits, NOW accounts (Interest-bearing checking accounts), automatic transfers from savings (ATS), and money market deposit accounts (MMDAs).

(a) Demand deposits enable the holder to write checks against the outstanding balance. By regulation, they have an original maturity of less than seven days. Businesses now own most demand deposits, and the majority of these deposit accounts are not interest bearing.
(b) NOW accounts are interest-bearing transaction accounts where the issuing bank can pay any rate desired. Banks often require that customers maintain some minimum balance before interest applies and may limit the number of free checks, but terms vary among institutions. These accounts are available to both personal and businesses.
(c) ATS accounts are combined savings and checking accounts where depositors can transfer funds from an interest-bearing savings account to a demand deposit. These accounts were initially introduced to circumvent restrictions against interest-on-checking accounts. They have thus declined in importance over time because NOW accounts offer the same service. They still appear, however, as sweep accounts whereby a bank can pay interest to a depositor, such as a municipality, for all balances held in excess of some contractual minimum amount.
(d) MMDAs originated in December 1982 to allow banks to compete with money market mutual funds' share accounts and

have both savings and limited check writing features. Holders earn market rates of interest that typically exceed rates on transaction accounts because banks do not have to hold reserves against MMDAs. A customer can make up to six transfers per month from the account, of which three can be by check or debit and three by telephone.

Transaction accounts are attractive funding sources because the depositors are generally not very rate sensitive. Thus, when interest rates change, customers are less likely to move their balances. For this reason, these accounts are referred to as relationship accounts in which the customer's primary rationale for keeping the account is convenient and personal service. These stable or "core" deposits improve a bank's liquidity by reducing the potential for large-scale deposit losses.

- Time and Savings Deposits

These deposits usually comprise most of the interest-bearing liabilities at banks.

- Regular savings are small denomination accounts with no fixed maturity and limited check writing capabilities.
- Time deposits pay higher interest rates, but the funds have a fixed maturity date and cannot be withdrawn until this date. There are two general categories of time deposits distinguished by whether the denomination is greater or less than \$100,000–250,000. The features of small time deposits, or those under \$100,000, are set by each bank in terms of maturity, interest rate, and amount of deposit. Most banks market standardized deposits, so customers are not confused. Large denomination (greater than or equal to \$100,000) deposits are negotiable instruments that can be traded in a well-established secondary market after issue. Labeled jumbo CDs, these are treated as "hot" money by regulatory agencies due to an adage that owners may move for just a slight higher rate at another bank.

Holders of time deposits are typically much more rate sensitive than owners of transaction accounts. Banks must continually change the rates they pay in line with market conditions in order to retain the bulk of these deposits. If they pay a rate on CDs slightly above market, they can usually attract significant new deposits even from outside their immediate trade area. Thus, large time deposits are not viewed as stable core deposits, but are instead labeled non-core (volatile) liabilities or "hot" money.

- Other Interest-Bearing Liabilities

Banks also rely on other funding sources that can be acquired quickly. Large money center and super-regional banks rely heavily on these funding sources, while community banks typically use them less frequently.

- Federal funds purchased represent overnight obligations where one bank borrows clearing balances, such as reserves held at a Federal Reserve Bank, from other institutions. Federal funds are primarily traded between banks to meet reserve deficiencies or offset reserve losses due to unanticipated loan demand and deposit outflows.
- Repurchase agreements (repos) represent the sale of securities under an agreement to repurchase them later at a predetermined price. The maturity is negotiated, but ranges from overnight to several weeks. This source of funds is similar to federal funds purchased, except that the borrowing is collateralized by the security sold. Thus, the rate on a repo is usually lower than the rate on a comparable unsecured federal funds transaction.
- Eurodollar liabilities are similar to the jumbo CDs described earlier, except that the dollar-denominated deposits are issued by a bank or bank subsidiary located outside the United States. Eurodollars are typically issued in $1 million multiples, and the holders are extremely rate sensitive. Most community banks do not deal in Eurodollars.

All of these liabilities are commonly referred to as "purchased" liabilities because banks buy the funds by paying a competitive market interest rate. They are not core deposits, but rather are also volatile liabilities. The discount window is an instrument of monetary policy (usually controlled by central banks) that allows eligible institutions to borrow money from the central bank, usually on a short-term basis, to meet temporary shortages of liquidity caused by internal or external disruptions.

The term originated with the practice of sending a bank representative to a reserve bank teller window when a bank needed to borrow money. The interest rate charged on such loans by a central bank is called the discount rate, base rate, or repo rate and is separate and distinct from the prime rate. It is also not the same thing as the federal funds rate and its equivalents in other currencies, which determine the rate at which banks lend money to each other. In recent years, the discount rate has been approximately a percentage point above the federal funds rate. Because of this, it is a relatively unimportant factor in the control of the money supply and is only taken advantage of at large volume during emergencies.

- Subordinated Debt and Equity

Subordinated notes and debentures represent long-term securities that may meet regulatory requirements as Tier 2 bank capital. Unlike the first $250,000 of transaction accounts and time and savings deposits, the debt is not FDIC-insured. Claims of the bondholders are also subordinated to the claims of depositors, which means that in the event a bank fails, depositors are paid before bondholders.

- Contingent Liabilities

Contingent liabilities reflect potential claims on bank assets. Any actual or direct liability that is contingent upon a future event or circumstance may be considered a contingent liability. Contingent liabilities are divided into two general categories. Category I contingent liabilities result in a concomitant increase in bank assets if the contingencies convert to actual liabilities. These contingencies usually result from off-balance sheet lending activities such as loan commitments and letters of credit. For example, when a bank funds an existing loan commitment or honors a draft drawn on a letter of credit, it generally originates a loan for the amount of liability incurred.

Category II contingent liabilities include those in which a claim on assets arises without an equivalent increase in assets. For example, pending litigation in which the bank is defendant or claims arising from trust operations could reduce an institution's cash or other assets. Such contingencies should be evaluated for credit risk and, if appropriate, listed for Special Mention or subjected to adverse classification. If a Category

I contingent liability is classified Loss, it would be included in the Other Adjustments to and Deductions from Common Equity Tier 1 Capital category on the Capital Calculations page if an allowance has not been established for the classified exposure. Common types and characteristics of contingent liabilities encountered in bank examinations include:

- Litigation

A bank facing lawsuit must address the essential points upon which the suit is based, the total dollar amount of the plaintiff's claim, the basis of the bank's defense, the status of any negotiations toward a compromise settlement, and the opinion of bank management or counsel relative to the probability of a successful defense.

- Trust Liabilities

Contingent liabilities may develop within the trust department due to actions or inactions of the bank acting in its fiduciary capacity.

(C) Shareholders' Equity

Stockholders' equity represents the ownership interest in a bank. Equity components consist of common and preferred stock outstanding at par value; surplus refers to stock proceeds in excess of par value received when the bank issued the stock; and retained earnings represent cumulative net income since the firm started operation minus cash dividends paid to stockholders. If a bank designates any securities as available-for-sale, it will also report unrealized gains or losses, net of tax on those instruments as equity.

Consolidated balance sheets

December 31, (in millions, except share data)		2016		2015
Assets				
Cash and due from banks	$	23,873	$	20,490
Deposits with banks		365,762		340,015
Federal funds sold and securities purchased under resale agreements (included **$21,506** and $23,141 at fair value)		229,967		212,575
Securities borrowed (included **$0** and $395 at fair value)		96,409		98,721
Trading assets (included assets pledged of **$115,847** and $115,284)		372,130		343,839
Securities (included **$238,891** and $241,754 at fair value and assets pledged of **$16,115** and $14,883)		289,059		290,827
Loans (included **$2,230** and $2,861 at fair value)		894,765		837,299
Allowance for loan losses		(13,776)		(13,555)
Loans, net of allowance for loan losses		880,989		823,744
Accrued interest and accounts receivable		52,330		46,605
Premises and equipment		14,131		14,362
Goodwill		47,288		47,325
Mortgage servicing rights		6,096		6,608
Other intangible assets		862		1,015
Other assets (included **$7,557** and $7,604 at fair value and assets pledged of **$1,603** and $1,286)		112,076		105,572
Total assets[(a)]	$	2,490,972	$	2,351,698
Liabilities				
Deposits (included **$13,912** and $12,516 at fair value)	$	1,375,179	$	1,279,715
Federal funds purchased and securities loaned or sold under repurchase agreements (included **$687** and $3,526 at fair value)		165,666		152,678
Commercial paper		11,738		15,562
Other borrowed funds (included **$9,105** and $9,911 at fair value)		22,705		21,105
Trading liabilities		136,659		126,897
Accounts payable and other liabilities (included **$9,120** and $4,401 at fair value)		190,543		177,638
Beneficial interests issued by consolidated VIEs (included **$120** and $787 at fair value)		39,047		41,879
Long-term debt (included **$37,686** and $33,065 at fair value)		295,245		288,651
Total liabilities[(a)]		2,236,782		2,104,125
Commitments and contingencies (see Notes 29, 30 and 31)				
Stockholders' equity				
Preferred stock ($1 par value; authorized 200,000,000 shares: issued **2,606,750** shares)		26,068		26,068
Common stock ($1 par value; authorized 9,000,000,000 shares; issued **4,104,933,895** shares)		4,105		4,105
Additional paid-in capital		91,627		92,500
Retained earnings		162,440		146,420
Accumulated other comprehensive income		(1,175)		192
Shares held in restricted stock units ("RSU") trust, at cost (**472,953** shares)		(21)		(21)
Treasury stock, at cost (**543,744,003** and 441,459,392 shares)		(28,854)		(21,691)
Total stockholders' equity		254,190		247,573
Total liabilities and stockholders' equity	$	2,490,972	$	2,351,698

(a) The following table presents information on assets and liabilities related to VIEs that are consolidated by the Firm at December 31, 2016 and 2015. The difference between total VIE assets and liabilities represents the Firm's interests in those entities, which were eliminated in consolidation.

December 31, (in millions)		2016		2015
Assets				
Trading assets	$	3,185	$	3,736
Loans		75,614		75,104
All other assets		3,321		2,765
Total assets	$	82,120	$	81,605
Liabilities				
Beneficial interests issued by consolidated VIEs	$	39,047	$	41,879
All other liabilities		490		809
Total liabilities	$	39,537	$	42,688

The assets of the consolidated VIEs are used to settle the liabilities of those entities. The holders of the beneficial interests do not have recourse to the general credit of JPMorgan Chase. At December 31, 2016 and 2015, the Firm provided limited program-wide credit enhancement of $2.4 billion and $2.0 billion, respectively, related to its Firm-administered multi-seller conduits, which are eliminated in consolidation. For further discussion, see Note 16.

The Notes to Consolidated Financial Statements are an integral part of these statements.

15.2.2 *The Statement of Income*

A bank's income statement reflects the fact that most assets and liabilities are financial. Revenue consists primarily of interest income and interest payments on liabilities represent the primary expense. The statement format thus starts with interest income then subtracts interest expense. The next step is to subtract provision for loan losses, which represents management's recognition that some revenues will be lost due to bad loans. The format continues by adding noninterest income then subtracting noninterest expense and taxes to produce net income. The main income statement components are:

- Interest Income

Interest income equals the sum of interest earned on earning assets. A statement normally itemizes the source of interest by type of asset. All interest is fully taxable except municipal interest, which may be exempt from federal income taxes. This tax-exempt interest can be converted to a taxable equivalent amount by dividing by one minus the bank's tax rate. Note that interest on loans contributes the most to interest income because loans are the bank's dominant asset and pay the highest gross yields. In general, interest income increases when the level of interest rates increases and/or when a bank can book more earning assets. It decreases when loan balances decline and/or when rates fall.

- Interest Expense

Interest expense equals the sum of interest paid on transaction accounts, time and savings deposits, other purchased liabilities, and subordinated debt. Interest expense is fully tax deductible except for the portion associated with the purchase of municipal bonds after 1982. The session on investments describes this partial deductibility and its impact.

- Net Interest Income

Net interest income equals interest income minus interest expense and plays a crucial role in determining how profitable a bank is in any period. Variations in net interest income are also used to measure how successful a bank has been in managing its interest rate risk.

- Provision for Loan Losses

Provision for loan losses represents a deduction from income for transfers to a bank's loan loss reserve. It is a noncash expense that indicates management's estimate of potential revenue losses from problem loans. Increases in provisions thus lower reported net income. Banks that understate potential losses effectively overstate net income and eventually have to raise provisions in recognition that past income has been overstated. The income statement reports net interest income after provision to account for estimated loan losses.

- Noninterest Income

Noninterest income consists primarily of service charges, fees and commissions, merchant service fees, and gains (or losses) from securities sales. Large banks that operate securities and foreign exchange desks also report trading account profits. Fees arise from loan commitments, standby letters of credit, and trust department services. Since the early 1980s, most banks have concentrated on increasing noninterest income as an alternative source of earnings, and service charges and fees have generally increased. These alternative sources primarily include revenues derived from mortgage banking, credit card, insurance, and electronic or treasury banking operations. Other noninterest income is typically small unless a bank effects some extraordinary transaction. A bank holding company that sells a mortgage banking or data processing subsidiary might similarly report a large gain. These extraordinary or nonrecurring transactions increase earnings on a one-time basis and thus are normally excluded from profit analyses and comparisons.

- Noninterest (Overhead) Expense

Noninterest or overhead expense is composed primarily of personnel, occupancy, equipment, and other expenses. These expenses consist of salaries and fringe benefits paid employees, rent, depreciation, and maintenance on equipment and premises, and other operating expenses including utilities and FDIC insurance premiums. At most banks, noninterest income falls far below noninterest expense. A bank's burden is the difference, measured as noninterest expense minus noninterest income. Improving a bank's burden by raising fees and controlling unit-operating costs has been a major source of bank profits since interest rate deregulation.

A bank's income before taxes thus equals net interest income minus provision for loan losses, minus burden. Net income is then obtained by subtracting taxes. We can clarify these relationships with the following definitions:

Consolidated statements of income

Year ended December 31, (in millions, except per share data)	2016	2015	2014
Revenue			
Investment banking fees	$ 6,448	$ 6,751	$ 6,542
Principal transactions	11,566	10,408	10,531
Lending- and deposit-related fees	5,774	5,694	5,801
Asset management, administration and commissions	14,591	15,509	15,931
Securities gains	141	202	77
Mortgage fees and related income	2,491	2,513	3,563
Card income	4,779	5,924	6,020
Other income	3,795	3,032	3,013
Noninterest revenue	49,585	50,033	51,478
Interest income	55,901	50,973	51,531
Interest expense	9,818	7,463	7,897
Net interest income	46,083	43,510	43,634
Total net revenue	95,668	93,543	95,112
Provision for credit losses	5,361	3,827	3,139
Noninterest expense			
Compensation expense	29,979	29,750	30,160
Occupancy expense	3,638	3,768	3,909
Technology, communications and equipment expense	6,846	6,193	5,804
Professional and outside services	6,655	7,002	7,705
Marketing	2,897	2,708	2,550
Other expense	5,756	9,593	11,146
Total noninterest expense	55,771	59,014	61,274
Income before income tax expense	34,536	30,702	30,699
Income tax expense	9,803	6,260	8,954
Net income	$ 24,733	$ 24,442	$ 21,745
Net income applicable to common stockholders	$ 22,583	$ 22,406	$ 20,077
Net income per common share data			
Basic earnings per share	$ 6.24	$ 6.05	$ 5.33
Diluted earnings per share	6.19	6.00	5.29
Weighted-average basic shares	3,618.5	3,700.4	3,763.5
Weighted-average diluted shares	3,649.8	3,732.8	3,797.5
Cash dividends declared per common share	$ 1.88	$ 1.72	$ 1.58

The Notes to Consolidated Financial Statements are an integral part of these statements.

Consolidated statements of comprehensive income

Year ended December 31, (in millions)	2016	2015	2014
Net income	**$ 24,733**	$ 24,442	$ 21,745
Other comprehensive income/(loss), after-tax			
Unrealized gains/(losses) on investment securities	**(1,105)**	(2,144)	1,975
Translation adjustments, net of hedges	**(2)**	(15)	(11)
Cash flow hedges	**(56)**	51	44
Defined benefit pension and OPEB plans	**(28)**	111	(1,018)
DVA on fair value option elected liabilities	**(330)**	–	–
Total other comprehensive income/(loss), after-tax	**(1,521)**	(1,997)	990
Comprehensive income	**$ 23,212**	$ 22,445	$ 22,735

The Notes to Consolidated Financial Statements are an integral part of these statements.

15.2.3 The Statement of Cash Flows

Consolidated statements of cash flows

Year ended December 31, (in millions)	2016	2015	2014
Operating activities			
Net income	**$ 24,733**	$ 24,442	$ 21,745
Adjustments to reconcile net income to net cash provided by/(used in) operating activities:			
Provision for credit losses	**5,361**	3,827	3,139
Depreciation and amortization	**5,478**	4,940	4,759
Deferred tax expense	**4,651**	1,333	4,362
Other	**1,799**	1,785	2,113
Originations and purchases of loans held-for-sale	**(61,107)**	(48,109)	(67,525)
Proceeds from sales, securitizations and paydowns of loans held-for-sale	**60,196**	49,363	71,407
Net change in:			
Trading assets	**(20,007)**	62,212	(24,814)
Securities borrowed	**2,313**	12,165	1,020
Accrued interest and accounts receivable	**(5,815)**	22,664	(3,637)
Other assets	**(4,517)**	(3,701)	(9,166)
Trading liabilities	**5,198**	(28,972)	26,818
Accounts payable and other liabilities	**3,740**	(23,361)	6,058
Other operating adjustments	**(1,827)**	(5,122)	314
Net cash provided by operating activities	**20,196**	73,466	36,593
Investing activities			
Net change in:			
Deposits with banks	**(25,747)**	144,462	(168,426)
Federal funds sold and securities purchased under resale agreements	**(17,468)**	3,190	30,848
Held-to-maturity securities:			
Proceeds from paydowns and maturities	**6,218**	6,099	4,169
Purchases	**(143)**	(6,204)	(10,345)
Available-for-sale securities:			
Proceeds from paydowns and maturities	**65,950**	76,448	90,664
Proceeds from sales	**48,592**	40,444	38,411
Purchases	**(123,959)**	(70,804)	(121,504)
Proceeds from sales and securitizations of loans held-for-investment	**15,429**	18,604	20,115
Other changes in loans, net	**(80,996)**	(108,962)	(51,749)
All other investing activities, net	**(2,825)**	3,703	2,181
Net cash provided by/(used in) investing activities	**(114,949)**	106,980	(165,636)

Financing activities			
Net change in:			
Deposits	**97,336**	(88,678)	89,346
Federal funds purchased and securities loaned or sold under repurchase agreements	**13,007**	(39,415)	10,905
Commercial paper and other borrowed funds	**(2,461)**	(57,828)	9,242
Beneficial interests issued by consolidated VIEs	**(5,707)**	(5,632)	(834)
Proceeds from long-term borrowings	**83,070**	79,611	78,515
Payments of long-term borrowings	**(68,949)**	(67,247)	(65,275)
Proceeds from issuance of preferred stock	**–**	5,893	8,847
Treasury stock and warrants repurchased	**(9,082)**	(5,616)	(4,760)
Dividends paid	**(8,476)**	(7,873)	(6,990)
All other financing activities, net	**(467)**	(726)	(768)
Net cash provided by/(used in) financing activities	**98,271**	(187,511)	118,228
Effect of exchange rate changes on cash and due from banks	**(135)**	(276)	(1,125)
Net increase/(decrease) in cash and due from banks	**3,383**	(7,341)	(11,940)
Cash and due from banks at the beginning of the period	**20,490**	27,831	39,771
Cash and due from banks at the end of the period	**$ 23,873**	$ 20,490	$ 27,831
Cash interest paid	**$ 9,508**	$ 7,220	$ 8,194
Cash income taxes paid, net	**2,405**	9,423	1,392

The Notes to Consolidated Financial Statements are an integral part of these statements.

15.2.4 *The Statement of Changes in Shareholders' Equity*

Consolidated statements of changes in stockholders' equity

Year ended December 31, (in millions, except per share data)	2016	2015	2014
Preferred stock			
Balance at January 1	**$ 26,068**	$ 20,063	$ 11,158
Issuance of preferred stock	**–**	6,005	8,905
Balance at December 31	**26,068**	26,068	20,063
Common stock			
Balance at January 1 and December 31	**4,105**	4,105	4,105
Additional paid-in capital			
Balance at January 1	**92,500**	93,270	93,828
Shares issued and commitments to issue common stock for employee stock-based compensation awards, and related tax effects	**(334)**	(436)	(508)
Other	**(539)**	(334)	(50)
Balance at December 31	**91,627**	92,500	93,270
Retained earnings			
Balance at January 1	**146,420**	129,977	115,435
Cumulative effect of change in accounting principle	**(154)**	–	–
Net income	**24,733**	24,442	21,745
Dividends declared:			
Preferred stock	**(1,647)**	(1,515)	(1,125)
Common stock (**$1.88**, $1.72 and $1.58 per share for 2016, 2015 and 2014, respectively)	**(6,912)**	(6,484)	(6,078)
Balance at December 31	**162,440**	146,420	129,977
Accumulated other comprehensive income			
Balance at January 1	**192**	2,189	1,199
Cumulative effect of change in accounting principle	**154**	–	–
Other comprehensive income/(loss)	**(1,521)**	(1,997)	990
Balance at December 31	**(1,175)**	192	2,189
Shares held in RSU Trust, at cost			
Balance at January 1 and December 31	**(21)**	(21)	(21)
Treasury stock, at cost			
Balance at January 1	**(21,691)**	(17,856)	(14,847)
Purchase of treasury stock	**(9,082)**	(5,616)	(4,760)
Reissuance from treasury stock	**1,919**	1,781	1,751
Balance at December 31	**(28,854)**	(21,691)	(17,856)
Total stockholders' equity	**$ 254,190**	$ 247,573	$ 231,727

The Notes to Consolidated Financial Statements are an integral part of these statements.

CHAPTER 16

Commercial Bank's Financial Ratios Analysis

16.1 General

Bank capital performs several very important functions. It absorbs losses, promotes public confidence, helps restrict excessive asset growth, and provides protection to depositors and the deposit insurance funds.[1] Capital rules in the United States generally follow a framework of rules adopted by the Basel Committee on Banking Supervision (BCBS), an international standard-setting body that deals with various aspects of bank supervision. Basel III capital standards emphasize common equity Tier 1 capital as the predominant form of bank capital. Common equity Tier 1 capital is widely recognized as the most loss-absorbing form of capital, as it is permanent and places shareholders' funds at risk of loss in the event of insolvency. Moreover, Basel III strengthens minimum capital ratio requirements and risk-weighting definitions, increases Prompt Corrective Action (PCA) thresholds, establishes a capital conservation buffer, and provides a mechanism to mandate countercyclical capital buffers.

[1] Risk Management Manual of Examination Policies Federal Deposit Insurance Corporation (4/2015).

F. I. Lessambo, *The U.S. Banking System*,
https://doi.org/10.1007/978-3-030-34792-5_16

16.2 Capital Adequacy Ratio

Capital adequacy ratio (CAR) also known as Capital to Risk-(Weighted) Assets Ratio (CRAR), is the ratio of a bank's capital to its risk. National regulators track a bank's CAR to ensure that it can absorb a reasonable amount of loss and complies with statutory Capital requirements. It is used to protect depositors and promote the stability and efficiency of financial systems around the world. The Committee's latest pronouncement requires banks to maintain the following minimum ratios as of January 1, 2013:

Common Equity Tier 1 ÷ Risk-weighted Exposures	3.5%
Tier 1 Capital ÷ Risk-weighted Exposures	4.5%
Total Capital ÷ Risk-weighted Exposures	8%

$$\text{Formula: Capital Adequacy Ratio} = \frac{\text{Tier 1 Capital} + \text{Tier 2 Capital}}{\text{Risk-weighted Exposures}}$$

Tier 1 Capital = Common Equity Tier 1 + Additional Tier 1
Total Capital = Tier 1 Capital + Tier 2 Capital

Risk-weighted exposures include weighted sum of the bank credit exposures (including those appearing on the bank's balance sheet and those not appearing). The weights are determined in accordance with the Basel Committee guidance for assets of each credit rating slab.

Part 324 of the FDIC rules and regulations establishes three components of regulatory capital:

- Common Equity Tier 1 Capital

Common equity Tier 1 Capital is the most loss-absorbing form of capital. It includes qualifying common stock and related surplus net of treasury stock; retained earnings; certain accumulated other comprehensive income (AOCI) elements if the institution does not make an AOCI opt-out election, plus or minus regulatory deductions or adjustments as appropriate; and qualifying common equity Tier 1 minority interests.

The federal banking agencies expect the majority of common equity Tier 1 Capital to be in the form of common voting shares.[2]

- Additional Tier 1 Capital

Additional Tier 1 Capital includes qualifying noncumulative perpetual preferred stock, bank-issued Small Business Lending Fund, and Troubled Asset Relief Program instruments that previously qualified for Tier 1 Capital, and qualifying Tier 1 minority interests, less certain investments in other unconsolidated financial institutions' instruments that would otherwise qualify as additional Tier 1 Capital.[3]

- Tier 2 capital.

Tier 2 capital is designated as supplementary capital and is composed of items such as revaluation reserves, undisclosed reserves, hybrid instruments, and subordinated term debt. Tier 2 capital includes the allowance for loan and lease losses up to 1.25% of risk-weighted assets, qualifying preferred stock, subordinated debt, and qualifying Tier 2 minority interests, less any deductions in the Tier 2 instruments of an unconsolidated financial institution.

Note that, Tier 1 capital is the sum of common equity Tier 1 Capital and additional tier 1 Capital. Total capital is the sum of Tier 1 Capital and Tier 2 Capital. Common equity Tier 1 Capital, Tier 1 Capital, and total capital serve as the numerators for calculating regulatory capital ratios. An institution's risk-weighted assets, as defined by Part 324, serve as the denominator for these ratios. Average total assets with certain adjustments serve as the denominator for the Tier 1 leverage capital ratio.

[2] Risk Management Manual of Examination Policies Federal Deposit Insurance Corporation (4/2015).

[3] Risk Management Manual of Examination Policies Federal Deposit Insurance Corporation (4/2015).

Example

Calculate CAR, i.e., total capital to risk-weighted exposures ratio for Small Bank Inc. using the following information:

	Exposure	*Risk weight (%)*
Government Treasury held as asset	1,500,000	0
Loans to Corporates	15,000,000	10
Loans to Small Businesses	8,000,000	20
Guarantees and other non-balance sheet exposures	6,000,000	10

The bank's Tier 1 Capital and Tier 2 Capital are \$200,000 and \$300,000, respectively.

Solution

Banks' total capital = 200,000 + 300,000 = \$500,000

Risk-weighted exposures = $\$1.5 \times 0\% + \$15 \times 10\% + \$8 \times 20\% + \$6 \times 10\% = \$3.7$ million

$$\text{Capital Adequacy Ratio} = \frac{\$0.5 \text{ million}}{\$3.7 \text{ million}} = 14\%$$

If the national regulator requires a CAR of 10%, the bank is safe. However, if the required ratio is 15%, the bank might have to face regulatory actions.

Please note that guarantees and other non-balance sheet exposures are included in the calculation of risk-weighted exposures.

16.3 Key Ratios for Examining Capital Adequacy

16.3.1 Equity Capital Ratio

The Tier 1 Capital ratio is the ratio of a bank's core Tier 1 Capital—that is, its equity capital and disclosed reserves—to its total risk-weighted assets. Risk-weighted assets are constructed by assigning different weights to assets with different levels of risk and summing the totals.

16.3.2 Tier 1 Leverage Ratio

The Tier 1 leverage ratio is the relationship between a banking organization's core capital and its total assets. The Tier 1 leverage ratio is calculated by dividing Tier 1 Capital by a bank's average total consolidated assets and certain off-balance sheet exposures.

16.3.3 Tier 1 Risk-Based Capital Ratio

Tier-1 risk-based capital is the ratio of a bank's "core capital" to its risk-weighted assets. The Tier 1 risk-based Capital ratio measures how much buffer a bank has as a percentage of its riskiness. This ratio because of a particular significance excludes more "exotic" elements from the calculation of capital and so serves as a better approximation of an adequate capital ratio.

16.3.4 Tier 2 Risk-Based Capital Ratio

Tier 2 capital is designated as supplementary capital and is composed of items such as revaluation reserves, undisclosed reserves, hybrid instruments, and subordinated term debt.

16.3.5 Texas Ratio

A bank's Texas ratio is one indicator that helps assess how risky a bank is and provides advance warning of a bank that has made bad investments (without the ability to absorb big losses).

Formula = Divide *nonperforming assets/tangible common equity and loan–loss reserves.*

Nonperforming assets include defaulted loans and real estate that the bank has taken possession of through foreclosure. Those assets are risks that could potentially become expenses for the bank. When calculating tangible equity, be sure to remove *intangible* assets like goodwill—since the bank cannot write a check out of the "goodwill" account to pay creditors.

A bank with a high Texas ratio—especially if the ratio approaches 1 or 100%—is riskier than a bank with a lower Texas ratio.

Example: assume a bank has nonperforming assets of \$90 billion, and tangible common equity *plus* loan-loss reserves of \$100 billion. Divide \$90 billion into \$100 billion for a result of .9 or 90%. This is relatively high, and the bank should be used only with caution (e.g., if the ratio is clearly decreasing, you're staying below FDIC coverage limits, and you know that there's a solid plan in place to further reduce the ratio).

16.4 Key Ratios for Examining Asset Quality

- Loan Loss Reserves/Total Loans

This is a primary measurement for judging capital strength. Traditionally, the amount is a minimum 1.0% but it is not sure if it is adequate unless it is compared to provisions/total loans: percentage of provisions from fiscal income statement as a percentage of the portfolio. In calculating this ratio, intangibles and net unrealized holding gains (losses) on available-for-sale securities are excluded from capital.

16.5 Coverage Ratio

16.5.1 Liquidity Coverage Ratios (LCR)

The objective of the LCR is to promote the short-term resilience of the liquidity risk profile of banks. It does this by ensuring that banks have an adequate stock of unencumbered high-quality liquid assets (HQLA) that can be converted easily and immediately in private markets into cash to meet their liquidity needs for a 30-calendar day liquidity stress scenario.[4] The LCR was introduced on January 1, 2015, but the minimum requirement will be set at 60% and rise in equal annual steps to reach 100% as of January 1, 2019.

The Committee has strengthened its liquidity framework by developing two *minimum* standards for funding liquidity. These standards have been developed to achieve two separate but complementary objectives[5]:

[4]BIS (2013): Basel III: The Liquidity Coverage Ratio and Liquidity Risk Monitoring Tools, p. 2.

[5]BIS (2013): Basel III: The Liquidity Coverage Ratio and Liquidity Risk Monitoring Tools, p. 2.

- The first objective is to promote short-term resilience of a bank's liquidity risk profile by ensuring that it has sufficient HQLA to survive a significant stress scenario lasting for one month.
- The second objective is to promote resilience over a longer time horizon by creating additional incentives for banks to fund their activities with more stable sources of funding on an ongoing basis (the net stable funding ratio [NSFR]).

The LCR has two components:

(a) Value of the stock of HQLA in stressed conditions and
(b) Total net cash outflows

In order to qualify as "HQLA," assets should be liquid in markets during a time of stress and, ideally, be central bank eligible. The following sets out the characteristics that such asset should generally possess and the operational requirements that they should generally possess and the operational requirements that they should satisfy.

The fundamental characteristics of HQLA include: (i) low-risk, (ii) ease and certainty of valuation, (iii) low correlation with risky assets, (iv) listed on recognized exchange, (v) active and sizable market, (vi) low volatility, and (vii) flight to quality. Additionally, a bank should periodically monetize a representative proportion of the assets in the stock through repo or outright sale, in order to test its access to the market, the effectiveness of its processes for monetization, the availability of the assets, and to minimize the risk of negative signaling during a period of actual stress. While the LCR is expected to be met and reported in a single currency, banks are expected to be able to meet their liquidity needs in each currency and maintain HQLA consistent with the distribution of their liquidity needs by currency.[6] More, the stock of HQLA should be well diversified within the asset classes themselves (except for sovereign debt of the bank's home jurisdiction or from the jurisdiction in which the bank operates; central bank reserves; central bank debt securities; and cash). There are two categories of assets that can be included in the stock. Assets to be included in each category are those that the

[6]BIS (2013): Basel III: The Liquidity Coverage Ratio and Liquidity Risk Monitoring Tools, p. 3.

bank is holding on the first day of the stress period, irrespective of their residual maturity. "Level 1" assets can be included without limit, while "Level 2" assets can only comprise up to 40% of the stock.[7]

1. Level 1 assets are limited to:
   (a) coins and banknotes;
   (b) central bank reserves;
   (c) marketable securities representing claims on or guaranteed by sovereigns, central banks, PSEs, the Bank for International Settlements, the International Monetary Fund, the European Central Bank and European Community, or multilateral development banks and satisfying all of the following conditions:
   - assigned a 0% risk weight under the Basel II Standardized Approach for credit;
   - traded in large, deep, and active repo or cash markets characterized by a low level of concentration;
   - have a proven record as a reliable source of liquidity in the markets (repo or sale) even during stressed market conditions; and
   - not an obligation of a financial institution or any of its
   (d) where the sovereign has a non-0% risk weight, sovereign or central bank debt securities issued in domestic currencies by the sovereign or central bank in the country in which the liquidity risk is being taken or in the bank's home country; and
   (e) where the sovereign has a non-0% risk weight, domestic sovereign or central bank debt securities issued in foreign currencies are eligible up to the amount of the bank's stressed net cash outflows in that specific foreign currency stemming from the bank's operations in the jurisdiction where the bank's liquidity risk is being taken.
2. Level 2

Level 2 assets (comprising Level 2A assets and any Level 2B assets permitted by the supervisor) can be included in the stock of HQLA, subject to the requirement that they comprise no more than 40% of the overall

[7]BIS (2013): Basel III: The Liquidity Coverage Ratio and Liquidity Risk Monitoring Tools, p. 3.

stock after haircuts have been applied. Level 2A assets are limited to the following:

(a) Marketable securities representing claims on or guaranteed by sovereigns, central banks, PSEs or multilateral development banks that satisfy all of the following

- assigned a 20% risk weight under the Basel II Standardized Approach for credit risk;
- traded in large, deep, and active repo or cash markets characterized by a low level of concentration;
- have a proven record as a reliable source of liquidity in the markets (repo or sale) even during stressed market conditions (i.e., maximum decline of price not exceeding 10% or increase in haircut not exceeding 10 percentage points over a 30-day period during a relevant period of significant liquidity stress); and
- not an obligation of a financial institution or any of its affiliated

(b) Corporate debt securities (including commercial covered bonds) that satisfy all of the following conditions include:

- in the case of corporate debt securities: not issued by a financial institution or any of its affiliated entities;
- in the case of covered bonds: not issued by the bank itself or any of its affiliated entities; either (i) have a long-term credit rating from a recognized external credit assessment institution (ECAI) of at least or in the absence of a long-term rating, a short-term rating equivalent in quality to the long-term rating; or (ii) do not have a credit assessment by a recognized ECAI but are internally rated as having a probability of default (PD) corresponding to a credit rating of at least AA−; traded in large, deep, and active repo or cash markets characterized by a low level of concentration; and have a proven record as a reliable source of liquidity in the markets (repo or sale) even during stressed market conditions: i.e., maximum decline of price or increase in haircut over a 30-day period during a relevant period of significant liquidity stress not exceeding 10%.

Level 2B assets are limited to the following:

(a) Residential mortgage-backed securities (RMBS) that satisfy all of the following conditions may be included in Level 2B, subject to a 25% haircut:

- not issued by, and the underlying assets have not been originated by the bank itself or any of its affiliated entities;
- have a long-term credit rating from a recognized ECAI of AA or higher, or in the absence of a long-term rating, a short-term rating equivalent in quality to a long-term rating;
- traded in large, deep, and active repo or cash markets characterized by a low level of concentration;
- have a proven record as a reliable source of liquidity in the markets (repo or sale) even during stressed market conditions, i.e., a maximum decline of price not exceeding 20% or increase in haircut over a 30-day period not exceeding 20 percentage points during a relevant period of significant liquidity stress;
- the underlying asset pool is restricted to residential mortgages and cannot contain structured products;
- the underlying mortgages are "full recourse" loans (i.e., in the case of foreclosure, the mortgage owner remains liable for any shortfall in sales proceeds from the property) and have a maximum loan-to-value ratio (LTV) of 80% on average at issuance; and
- the securitizations are subject to "risk retention" regulations which require issuers to retain an interest in the assets they securitize.

(b) Corporate debt securities (including commercial paper) that satisfy all of the following conditions may be included in Level 2B, subject to a 50% haircut:

- not issued by a financial institution or any of its affiliated entities;
- either (i) have a long-term credit rating from a recognized ECAI between A+ and BBB− or in the absence of a long-term rating, a short-term rating equivalent in quality to the long-term rating; or (ii) do not have a credit assessment by a recognized ECAI and are internally rated as having a PD corresponding to a credit rating of between A+ and BBB−;
- traded in large, deep, and active repo or cash markets characterized by a low level of concentration; and
- have a proven record as a reliable source of liquidity in the markets (repo or sale) even during stressed market conditions, i.e., a maximum decline of price not exceeding 20% or increase in haircut over a 30-day period not exceeding 20 percentage points during a relevant period of significant liquidity stress.

(c) Common equity shares that satisfy all of the following conditions may be included in Level 2B, subject to a 50% haircut:

- not issued by a financial institution or any of its affiliated entities;
- exchange traded and centrally cleared;
- a constituent of the major stock index in the home jurisdiction or where the liquidity risk is taken, as decided by the supervisor in the jurisdiction where the index is located;
- denominated in the domestic currency of a bank's home jurisdiction or in the currency of the jurisdiction where a bank's liquidity risk is taken;
- traded in large, deep, and active repo or cash markets characterized by a low level of concentration; and
- have a proven record as a reliable source of liquidity in the markets (repo or sale) even during stressed market conditions, i.e., a maximum decline of share price not exceeding 40% or increase in haircut not exceeding 40 percentage points over a 30-day period during a relevant period of significant liquidity.

16.5.2 Loan Loss Reserves/Non-performing or Non-current Loans and Leases

Non-performing or non-current loans consist of loans that are 90 days or more overdue and still accruing and nonaccrual loans. The ratio, also known as the coverage ratio, should be in excess of 1.5x

16.5.3 Overdue Loans to Total Loan Ratio

Formula: Total Loans 30–89 Days Past Due/Total Loans

It indicates that either credit underwriting standards are inappropriate or collection procedures are inadequate.

16.5.4 90-Day Overdue Loans to Total Loans Ratio

Formula: Total Loans 90-Day Past Due/Total Loans

It indicates that the loan portfolio may be experiencing some deterioration through either poor underwriting and/or collections.

16.6 Earnings (Profitability)

Earnings determine the ability of a bank to increase capital (through retained earnings), absorb loan losses, support the future growth of assets, and provide a return to investors. The largest source of income for a bank is net interest revenue (interest income from lending activity less interest paid on deposits and debt). The second most important source is from investing activity. A substantial source of income also comes from foreign exchange and precious metal trading, and commissions/transaction fees, and trust operations.

16.6.1 Net Interest Margin

Formula: Net Interest Income (annualized)/Average Interest-Earning Assets

This is net interest income expressed as a percentage of average earning assets. Net interest income is derived by subtracting interest expense from interest income. Indicates how well management employed the earning asset base (the denominator focuses strictly on assets that generate income). May come under pressure from offering preferential rates to customer base, a low level of growth in savings and the higher percentage of more expensive wholesale funds available. The lower the net interest margin, approximately 3.0% or lower, generally it is reflective of a bank with a large volume of non-earning or low-yielding assets. Conversely, are high or increasing margins the result of a favorable interest rate environment, or are they the result of the bank moving out of safe but low-yielding, low-return securities into higher-risk, higher yielding, and less liquid loans or investment securities?

16.6.2 The Loan-to-Assets Ratio

The loan-to-assets ratio is another industry-specific metric that can help investors obtain a complete analysis of a bank's operations. Banks that have a relatively higher loan-to-assets ratio derive more of their income from loans and investments, while banks with lower levels of loans-to-assets ratios derive a relatively larger portion of their total incomes from more-diversified, noninterest-earning sources, such as asset management or trading. Banks with lower loan-to-assets ratios may fare better when interest rates are low or credit is tight. They may also fare better during economic downturns.

16.6.3 The Return on Assets Ratio

The return on assets (ROAs) ratio is frequently applied to banks because cash flow analysis is more difficult to accurately construct. The ratio is considered an important profitability ratio, indicating the per-dollar profit a company earns on its assets. Since bank assets largely consist of money the bank loans, the per-dollar return is an important metric of bank management. The ROAs ratio is a company's net, after-tax income divided by its total assets. An important point to note is since banks are highly leveraged, even a relatively low ROAs of 1 to 2% may represent substantial revenues and profit for a bank. Bank managers and bank analysts generally evaluate overall bank profitability in terms of return on equity (ROE) and return on assets (ROAs). When a bank consistently reports a higher than average ROE and ROA, it is designated as a high-performance bank. In order to earn higher returns, a bank must either take on above-average risk or have a competitive advantage in offering certain products or services.

$$\boxed{\text{ROE} = \text{Net income/Stockholders' equity}}$$

Return on equity equals net income divided by stockholders' equity and thus measures the percentage return on stockholders' investment. The higher the return, the better, as management can pay higher dividends and support greater future growth.

$$\boxed{\text{ROA} = \text{Net income/Total assets}}$$

Return on assets equals net income divided by total assets and thus measures the percentage return per dollar of average assets held during the period. Again, the higher is ROA, the better is the bank's profitability. ROAs vary between banks largely due to differences in net interest income, provisions for loan losses, and burden. ROE is tied to ROA through a bank's equity multiplier (EM), which equals total assets divided by stockholders' equity. EM measures a bank's financial leverage or its amount of liabilities compared with equity. The greater are aggregate liabilities, the greater is financial leverage and EM.

16.6.4 *Operating Profit Margin*

Formula = Operating profits/Net operating revenues

Operating profits (before the loan loss provision and excluding gains or losses from asset sales and amortization expense of intangibles)/net operating revenues (interest income less interest expense plus noninterest income). This ratio measures the percent of net operating revenues consumed by operating expenses, providing the remaining operating profit (the higher the margin, the more efficient the bank).

16.6.5 *Loan-to-Deposit Ratio (LTD)*

The loan-to-deposit ratio (LTD) is a commonly used statistic for assessing a bank's liquidity by dividing the bank's total loans by its total deposits. This number is expressed as a percentage. If the ratio is too high, it means that the bank may not have enough liquidity to cover any unforeseen fund requirements, and conversely, if the ratio is too low, the bank may not be earning as much as it could be. The LTD ratio is the ratio of a bank's total outstanding loans for a period to its total deposit balance over the same period. So an LDR figure of 100% indicates that a bank lends a dollar to customers for every dollar that it brings in as deposits. But this also means that the bank doesn't have significant cash on hand for contingencies. A combination of prudence and regulatory requirements suggests that for a traditional bank, the LDR should be around 80–90%.

16.6.6 *Non-interest Income to Average Assets Ratio*

Non-Interest Income (annualized)/Total Average Assets

Non-interest income is income derived from fee-based banking services such as service charges on deposit accounts, consulting and advisory fees, rental of safe deposit boxes and other fee income, fiduciary, brokerage, and insurance activities. Realized gains on the sale of securities are excluded. It is important that a bank develops non-interest income sources but it should become a major portion of the bank's total revenue unless it really is an annual core business operation.

16.6.7 Average Collection of Interest (Days)

Accrued Interest Receivable/Interest Income × 365a

This is a measurement of the number of days interest on earning assets remains uncollected and indicates that the volume of overdue loans is increasing or repayment terms are being extended to accommodate a borrower's inability to properly service debt.

16.6.8 Overhead Ratio

Total Non-Interest Expenses (annualized)/Total Average Assets

Non-interest expenses (annualized) are the normal operating expenses associated with the daily operation of a bank such as salaries and employee benefits plus occupancy/fixed asset costs plus depreciation and amortization. These costs tend to rise faster than income in a time of inflation or if the institution is expanding by the purchase or construction of new branches. Provisions for loan and lease losses realized losses on securities and income taxes should not be included in non-interest expense.

16.6.9 Efficiency Ratio

Total Non-Interest Expenses/Total Net Interest Income (before provisions) plus Total Non-Interest Income

Efficiency improves as the ratio decreases, which is obtained by increasing net interest income, increasing non-interest revenues and/or reducing operating expenses. Non-interest expenses (expenses other than interest expense and loan loss provisions, such as salaries and employee benefits plus occupancy plus depreciation and amortization) tend to rise faster than income in a time of inflation. This is a measure of productivity of the bank and is targeted at the middle to low 50% range. This may seem like break-even but it is not; what this is saying is that for every dollar the bank is earning it gets to keep 50 cents and it has to spend 50 cents to earn that dollar. The ratio can be as low as the mid-to-low 40% range, which means that for every dollar the bank earns, it gets to keep 60 cents and spends 40 cents, a very efficient bank. Ratios in excess of 75% mean the bank is very expensive to operate.

16.7 Key Ratios for Examining Liquidity

16.7.1 Liquidity and Funding

Funding and Liquidity are related; however, they are separate situations. Funding is what a bank relies upon to grow its business and the asset side of the balance sheet above and beyond what could be accomplished with just equity. Funding is provided by deposits, short-term debt, and longer-term debt. Funding means access to capital. Liquidity is what a bank requires if funding is interrupted and the bank must still be able to meet certain obligations (bank's ability to repay depositors and other creditors without incurring excessive costs). What is the liability structure/composition of the institution's liabilities, including their tenor, interest rate, payment terms, sensitivity to changes in the macroeconomic environment, types of guarantees required on credit facilities, sources of credit available to the institution, and the extent of resource diversification.

A bank's least expensive means of funding loan growth is through deposit accounts. When this is not available, banks must rely on more expensive funding sources such as borrowing funds at wholesale rates or liquidating investment securities portfolios. The best type of deposits is "core" deposits, which are balances that are left at the bank due to convenience (the depositor resides in the area) or through loyalty. Non-core deposits/funding are sources that can be very sensitive to changes in interest rates such as brokered deposits, CDs greater than $100,000, and borrowed money.

16.7.2 Loans (Gross)/Total Deposits

It indicates the percentage of a bank's loans funded through deposits (measures funding by borrowing as opposed to equity), maximum 80–90% (the higher the ratio, the more the institution is relying on borrowed funds). However, it cannot also be too low as loans are considered the highest and best use of bank funds (indicates excess liquidity). Between 70 and 80%, it indicates that the bank still has capacity to write new loans. A high loan-to-deposit ratio indicates that a bank has fewer funds invested in readily marketable assets, which provide a greater margin of liquidity to the bank.

16.7.3 Liquid Assets to Total Deposits

Liquid Assets/Total Deposits

Measures deposits matched to investments and whether they could be converted quickly to cover redemptions.

PART V

Auditing and Bankruptcy

CHAPTER 17

Bank Audit Systems

17.1 General

To ensure that banks comply with the industry standards and jurisdictional regulations, banks and other financial institutions are called to audit, to review their services and procedures. One of their primary duties is to focus on the accuracy, completeness, and legitimacy of the bank's financial activities. The majority of banks and financial institutions find the bank auditing procedure a strenuous experience; nonetheless, it is one of the most important procedures that must be completed periodically. Some of the procedures and services reviewed in the bank audit include:

- Financial transactions
- Bank wires
- Automated clearing house (ACH)
- Bank account monetary flow.

17.2 Internal Audit

Banks should have an internal audit function with sufficient authority, stature, independence, resources, and access to the board of directors.[1] The internal audit function duties consist of developing an independent

[1] Basel Committee on Banking Supervision (2012): The Internal Audit Function in Banks, p. iv.

F. I. Lessambo, *The U.S. Banking System*,
https://doi.org/10.1007/978-3-030-34792-5_17

and informed view of the risks faced by the bank based on its access to the bank records and data, its enquiries, and professional competence. Therefore, the internal audit function must be able to discuss its views, findings, and conclusions directly with the audit Committee and the board of directors.

> An effective internal audit function provides independent assurance to the board of directors and senior management on the quality and effectiveness of a bank's internal control, risk management, and governance systems and processes, thereby helping the board and senior management protect their organization and its reputation.[2]

The Internal audit function is accountable to the board of directors or its audit Committee. It should also promptly inform senior management about its findings. The bank's board of directors has the ultimate responsibility for ensuring that senior management establishes and maintains an adequate, effective, and efficient internal control system. To that end, the board has to support the internal audit function in discharging its duties effectively. To facilitate a consistent approach to internal audit across all the banks within a banking organization, the board of directors of each bank within a banking group or holding company structure should ensure that either[3]:

(i) the bank has its own internal audit function, which should be accountable to the bank's board and should report to the banking group or holding company's head of internal audit; or
(ii) the banking group or holding company's internal audit function performs internal audit activities of sufficient scope at the bank to enable the board to satisfy its fiduciary and legal responsibilities.

[2] Basel Committee on Banking Supervision (2012): The Internal Audit Function in Banks, Principle 1, p. 2.

[3] Basel Committee on Banking Supervision (2012): The Internal Audit Function in Banks, Principle 14, p. 3.

17.2.1 Scope of Activities

The scope of internal audit activities includes the examination and evaluation of the effectiveness of the internal control, risk management and governance systems and processes of the entire bank, including the organization's outsourced activities and its subsidiaries and branches.[4]

The internal audit function should independently evaluate the:

- Effectiveness and efficiency of internal control, risk management, and governance systems in the context of both current and potential future risks;
- Reliability, effectiveness and integrity of management information systems and processes (including relevance, accuracy, completeness, availability, confidentiality and comprehensiveness of data);
- Monitoring of compliance with laws and regulations, including any requirements from supervisors (see the following sub-section for more details); and
- Safeguarding of assets.

The head of internal audit is responsible for establishing an annual internal audit plan that can be part of a multi-year plan. The plan should be based on a robust risk assessment (including input from senior management and the board) and should be updated at least annually (or more frequently to enable an ongoing real-time assessment of where significant risks lie). The board's approval of the audit plan implies that an appropriate budget will be available to support the internal audit function's activities. The budget should be sufficiently flexible to adapt to variations in the internal audit plan in response to changes in the bank's risk profile.[5]

17.2.2 Matters Covered

The scope of the internal audit function's activities should ensure adequate coverage of matters of regulatory interest within the audit plan. The internal audit function of a bank must have the capacity to review

[4] Basel Committee on Banking Supervision (2012): The Internal Audit Function in Banks, p. 7.

[5] Basel Committee on Banking Supervision (2012): The Internal Audit Function in Banks, p. 7.

key risk management functions, regulatory capital adequacy and liquidity control functions, regulatory and internal reporting functions, the regulatory compliance function and the finance function. These include:

(a) Risk management

Therefore, internal audit should include in its scope the following aspects of risk management:

(i) the organization and mandates of the risk management function including market, credit, liquidity, interest rate, operational, and legal risks;
(ii) evaluation of risk appetite, escalation and reporting of issues and decisions taken by the risk management function;
(iii) the adequacy of risk management systems and processes for identifying, measuring, assessing, controlling, responding to, and reporting on all the risks resulting from the bank's activities;
(iv) the integrity of the risk management information systems, including the accuracy, reliability, and completeness of the data used; and
(v) the approval and maintenance of risk models including verification of the consistency, timeliness, independence, and reliability of data sources used in such models.

(b) Capital adequacy and liquidity

Banks are subject to the global regulatory framework for capital and liquidity as approved by the Committee and implemented in national regulation. The scope of internal audit must include all provisions of this regulatory framework and in particular the bank's system for identifying and measuring its regulatory capital and assessing the adequacy of its capital resources in relation to the bank's risk exposures and established minimum ratios. More, the internal audit in a bank must review management's process for stress testing its capital levels, taking into account the frequency of such exercises, their purpose, the reasonableness of scenarios and the underlying assumptions employed, and the reliability of the processes used. Additionally, the bank's systems and processes for measuring and monitoring its liquidity positions in relation to its risk profile, external environment, and minimum regulatory requirements fall within the ambit of the internal audit universe.

(c) Regulatory and internal reporting

A bank internal audit function must regularly evaluate the effectiveness of the process by which the risk and reporting functions interact to produce timely, accurate, reliable, and relevant reports for both internal management and the supervisor. It may also include public disclosures intended to facilitate transparency and market discipline such as the Pillar 3 disclosures and the reporting of regulatory matters in the bank's public reports.

(d) Compliance

Compliance laws, rules, and standards include primary legislation, rules, and standards issued by legislators and supervisors, market conventions, codes of practice promoted by industry associations, and internal codes of conduct applicable to the staff members of the bank. The audit of the compliance function includes an assessment of how effectively it fulfills its responsibilities.

(e) Finance

A bank's finance function is responsible for the integrity and accuracy of financial data and reporting. Key aspects of finance's activities have an impact on the level of a bank's capital resources and therefore associated controls should be robust and consistently applied across similar risks and businesses. As such, it is important that these controls are subject to periodic internal audit review, using resources and expertise to provide an effective evaluation of bank practices.

The bank internal audit team must devote sufficient resources to evaluate the valuation control environment, availability and reliability of information or evidence used in the valuation process and the reliability of estimated fair values. This is achieved through reviewing the independent price verification processes and testing valuations of significant transactions.

17.2.3 *Assessment of the Internal Audit Function*[6]

Bank supervisors should regularly assess whether the internal audit function has sufficient standing and authority within the bank and operates according to sound principles. The supervisory authority must consider the extent to which the board of directors, its audit Committee, and senior management promote a strong internal control environment supported and assessed by a sound internal audit function. The assessment of the internal audit function shall be based on the supervisory expectations. This includes:

- The basic features of the internal audit function;
- The internal audit function's standing and authority within the bank;
- The existence and content of the internal audit charter;
- The scope of the internal audit function's work and its output;
- The corporate governance arrangements that apply to the internal audit function;
- The organization of the function within a group or holding company;
- The professional competence, experience, and expertise within the internal audit function;
- The remuneration structure of the head of the internal audit function and the key internal auditors; and
- Outsourced internal audit activities, if any.

17.2.4 *Bank Audit Committee*

The audit Committee is a specialized Committee within the board of directors. As such, it prepares the work of, and reports to the board of directors in specific areas for which it has designated responsibility. The board of directors assumes final responsibility.[7]

The audit Committee may invite the head of internal audit, the head of compliance, senior management, in particular the chief executive

[6] Basel Committee on Banking Supervision (2012): The Internal Audit Function in Banks, Principle 17, p. 17.

[7] Basel Committee on Banking Supervision (2012): The Internal Audit Function in Banks, Principle 17, p. 27.

officer and other officials deemed relevant for the purpose of fulfilling its responsibilities to attend meetings of the Committee. It is a sound practice that the head of internal audit and members of the audit Committee have a private session, i.e., in the absence of management, to discuss issues of interest. The responsibilities of an audit Committee may be assumed directly by the board of directors in some banks or in some countries. The audit Committee remains liable even for outsourced services. The FDIC imposed a $15 million penalty on the First Bank of Delaware for AML violations due to failures in monitoring third-party payment processors. Discover Bank, Capital One, and American Express were fined for failing to supervise outsourced services to telemarketers, debt collection agencies, and call centers.[8] A bank's audit Committee has a key role in fostering a quality bank audit through the effective exercise of its responsibilities with respect to the external auditor and the statutory audit. The audit Committee approves, or recommends to the board of directors for approval, the appointment, reappointment, dismissal, and compensation of the external auditor. The audit Committee also monitors and assesses the independence of the external auditor. Key aspects of the audit committee's work encompass the assessment of the effectiveness of the external audit process.

- Appointment of the external auditor

The audit Committee should have the primary responsibility for approving, or recommending to the board of directors for approval, the appointment, reappointment, removal, and remuneration of the external auditor. The audit Committee's procedures for approving or recommending the approval of the external auditor should also include a risk assessment of the likelihood of the withdrawal of the external auditor from the audit, and how the bank would respond to that risk. The audit Committee should assess the overall quality of the external auditor, before its first appointment and at least annually thereafter. The audit Committee should consider the quality control standards applicable to the external audit and request that the external auditor report on its own internal quality control procedures, including the audit firm's engagement

[8] Philip J. Weights (2015): Auditing Trends Within the Banking Industry, Ethicalboardroom.

quality control process, and any significant matters of concern arising from these procedures.

The audit Committee should discuss and agree to the terms of the engagement letter issued by the external auditor prior to the approval of the engagement. The audit Committee should maintain an understanding and knowledge of:

- The structure and governance of the audit firm;
- The current nature of the audit environment, including in jurisdictions abroad where the bank operates;
- Significant issues and concerns raised by the relevant audit oversight body regarding the audit firm, and the auditor's actions in addressing these concerns, to understand how these issues/concerns may affect the quality of the audit of the bank;
- The nature of banking regulatory actions and conditions that could have an impact on the external auditor's work on the bank, including any regulatory actions and conditions specific to the bank being audited, and any that the supervisor is imposing on all banks (e.g., through newly implemented regulations and policies); and
- Public lessons learned from any recent external audit failures associated with the bank's auditor, and other audit firms and how the audit firms have dealt with them so that similar audit risks are appropriately identified and limited.

17.3 External Audit

The external auditor of a bank should respond appropriately to the significant risks of material misstatement in the bank's financial statements.

Core Principle 27 of the Basel Committee's Core Principles for Effective Banking Supervision (September 2012) states that:

> [t]he supervisor determines that banks and banking groups maintain adequate and reliable records, prepare financial statements in accordance with accounting policies and practices that are widely accepted internationally and annually publish information that fairly reflects their financial condition and performance and bears an independent external auditor's opinion. The supervisor also determines that banks and parent companies of banking groups have adequate governance and oversight of the external audit function.[9]

[9]BIS—Basel Committee on Banking Supervision (2014): External Audits of Banks, p. 1.

An external auditor conducts the audit of a bank's financial statements to obtain reasonable assurance about whether the financial statements as a whole are free from material misstatement, whether due to fraud or error, thereby enabling the auditor to express an opinion on whether the financial statements are prepared, in all material respects, in accordance with an applicable financial reporting framework, and to report on the financial statements, and communicate as required by internationally accepted auditing standards, in accordance with the auditor's findings. One the external auditor has identified and assessed the risks of material misstatement, whether due to fraud or error, at the financial statement level and the assertion level, the auditor should design and implement appropriate responses to those risks, including testing controls in the current period that the auditor plans to rely performing substantive procedures that are specifically responsive to that risk.[10]

Below are areas where there is often a significant risk of material misstatement:

17.3.1 Loan Loss Provisioning[11]

Loan loss provisions are a standard accounting adjustment made to a bank's loan loss reserves included in the financial statements of banks. The loan loss reserves account is a "contra-asset" account, which reduces the loans by the amount the bank's managers expect to lose when some portion of the loans are not repaid. It is reviewed, periodically, by the bank's manager who decides how much to add to the loan loss reserves account and charges this amount against the bank's current earnings.[12] In 2014, the IASB issued a new standard, IRFS 9, which changed the way banks reported their loan losses. IFRS 9—Financial Instruments—moves from an incurred loss model to an expected loss model, marking a big change for banks, insurance companies, and the users of financial statements. The new standard, effective since 2018, requires banks

[10] IFRS 9 changes the impairment model for how companies recognize losses.

[11] BIS—Basel Committee on Banking Supervision (2014): External Audits of Banks, p. 33.

[12] Eliana Balla, Morgan J. Rose, and Jessie Romero (2012): Loan Loss Reserve Accounting and Bank Behavior, The Federal Reserve Bank of Richmond, Economic Brief 12-03.

to recognize not only credit losses that have already occurred but also losses that are expected in the future. This is designed to help ensure that they are appropriately capitalized for the loans that they have written. Banks applying IFRS 9 would have the burden of calculating impairment loss on two different bases. In the United States, the FASB has not yet embraced the new IFRS. Thus, an analyst comparing an IFRS-reporting bank to a US GAAP-reporting bank would have to address this conflicting approach in his financial analysis.

The Committee expects the external auditor to consider the following factors in identifying and assessing the significant risks of material misstatement in relation to loan loss provisioning and the related allowance for loan losses. This list is not intended to be comprehensive.

(a) The estimation techniques used to compute provisions and how the techniques vary within and among banks (where possible).
(b) Whether an appropriate degree of caution has been exercised by management in judging anticipated cash flows and making other assumptions.
(c) All known and relevant impairment indicators for loan exposures which include previously unexpected adverse developments in the market or economic environment, adverse movements in interest rates, restructurings, inadequate underwriting policies adopted by the bank, overdue payments, failure of the borrower to meet budgeted revenues or net income, covenant breaches and forbearance.
(d) Whether the bank has sought perspectives and data from different functions within the bank, including risk management, credit and internal audit, as well as reliable sources external to the bank, including peer data and regulator perspectives so as to consider all relevant and available information in assessing impairment.
(e) Financial accounting rules for provisioning may differ from the provisioning rules that apply for regulatory reporting or capital purposes. It may therefore be customary for banks to have different processes and systems to generate loan loss provisions for financial accounting purposes and for regulatory purposes. Further, there can be material differences in the application of the same set of financial accounting and regulatory rules by individual banks. Nevertheless, large differences between provisions for financial accounting purposes and for regulatory capital purposes

should be investigated by the auditor to ensure there is not a risk of material misstatement of the loan loss provision reported in the financial statements. In addition, while for regulatory capital purposes under the Basel framework the accounting loan loss provision for internal ratings-based approach portfolios is replaced by the regulatory expected loss provision, the level of the accounting provision may nevertheless have an impact on the level or the composition of regulatory capital, due to the treatment of the tax effect of provisions and the allocation of any excess provision to capital tiers. External auditors are alert to any management bias in this area.

(f) Disclosures should enable users to assess the loan loss provisioning methodology applied by the bank, regarding how it relates to credit risk for that bank, and how it compares with methodologies applied across the banking sector.

17.3.2 Financial Instruments, Including Fair Value Measurements

According to ASC 820-10-20, "Fair value is the price that would be received to sell an asset or paid to transfer a liability in an orderly transaction between market participants at the measurement date." A three-level valuation hierarchy has been established under US GAAP for disclosure of fair value measurements. The valuation hierarchy is based on the transparency of inputs to the valuation of an asset or liability as of the measurement date. The three levels are defined as follows:

- Level 1—inputs to the valuation methodology are quoted prices (unadjusted) for identical assets or liabilities in active markets.
- Level 2—inputs to the valuation methodology include quoted prices for similar assets and liabilities in active markets, and inputs that are observable for the asset or liability, either directly or indirectly, for substantially the full term of the financial instrument.
- Level 3—one or more inputs to the valuation methodology are unobservable and significant to the fair value measurement.

A financial instrument's categorization within the valuation hierarchy is based on the lowest level of input that is significant to the fair value measurement. However, determining whether an instrument is Level 2 or Level 3 can be more challenging. In practice, it can be quite difficult to distinguish between a Level 2 and a Level 3 instrument, a lot of judgment may be required.[13] A bank's portfolio of financial instruments measured at fair value can range from "plain vanilla" financial instruments that are frequently traded in liquid markets with observable market prices, and involve less measurement uncertainty, to those that are customized, complex, and where the valuation is based on significant unobservable inputs requiring a substantial amount of management judgment. Financial instruments measured at fair value also include financial instruments that are subject to an impairment assessment which may be a key area of judgment, even manipulation. Where there are changes in the composition of a bank's portfolio of financial instruments—whether due to changes in customer demand, the bank's approach to managing risk and liquidity, or changes in prudential regulation—the bank will need to evaluate any accounting implications of the changes.[14] Accounting standards for financial instruments contain requirements for recognition; initial and subsequent measurement (including impairment); reclassification from fair value to amortized cost; de-recognition; presentation; and Because these requirements are complex, they may be difficult to interpret and apply, and therefore the external auditor often needs to utilize more complex and wider-ranging audit procedures to obtain sufficient appropriate audit evidence to obtain reasonable assurance that the financial statements are not materially misstated. The accounting classification of an individual financial instrument may be particularly important for achieving a favorable regulatory outcome. Researchers have expressed concerns that fair value measurements described in SFAS 157 give managers more discretion over asset and liability valuation and fair values are more difficult and costly to audit (Benston 2008).

[13]Xu Xiaolu (2013): Fair Value Measurements and Earnings Management: Evidence from the Banking Industry, Syracuse University (Dissertation thesis), p. 9.

[14]BIS—Basel Committee on Banking Supervision (2014): External Audits of Banks, p. 34.

17.3.3 Liabilities Including Contingent Liabilities Arising from Non-compliance with Laws and Regulations, and Contractual Breaches

Non-compliance with, or material breaches of, the prudential framework, conduct requirements, legal requirements or contractual agreements could lead to legal or supervisory actions against a bank, thereby exposing the bank to potential litigation and/or the imposition of substantial penalties. Such events may require recognition of provisions, contingent liabilities and/or qualitative disclosures in the bank's financial statements. Further, any adverse impact on the bank's reputation resulting from this non-compliance could have consequences for the bank's going concern assessment[15] International Accounting Standard (IAS 37)[16] refers to a contingent liability as:

- A possible obligation that arises from past events and whose existence will be confirmed only by the occurrence or non-occurrence of one or more uncertain future events not wholly within the control of the company, or
- A present obligation that is not recognized because the future expenditures is not probable or the obligation cannot be measured with sufficient reliability.

Internationally accepted auditing standards require the external auditor to remain alert to the possibility that other audit procedures applied for the purpose of forming an opinion on the financial statements may bring instances of identified or suspected non-compliance with laws and regulations to the auditor's attention. If the external auditor identifies any such breaches of material by the bank's supervisor, the auditor directly notifies the supervisor immediately (or, where not permitted, indirectly through the bank).

[15] BIS—Basel Committee on Banking Supervision (2014): External Audits of Banks, p. 35.

[16] IAS 37, paragraph 10.

17.3.4 *Disclosures*

A number of factors have contributed to an increased demand from users of financial statements for more relevant and extensive qualitative and quantitative disclosures. This increased demand results from the greater complexity of business transactions, including off-balance sheet transactions and non-recognition of assets and liabilities, and the greater use of fair value and other accounting estimates, with significant uncertainties and changes in measurement attributes. While accounting standards may specify disclosure objectives, the standards may not always prescribe in all circumstances specific disclosures to meet those disclosure objectives. Therefore, the external auditor may need to exercise a substantial amount of judgment in assessing whether disclosures are presented fairly in accordance with the disclosure objectives in the relevant accounting framework. Increased transparency through fairly presented public disclosures enhances market confidence. It is therefore important that the bank provide disclosures that present the bank's financial condition, identify and describe the risks to which the bank is exposed and how they are managed, and are meaningful and responsive to changes in market conditions and perceived risks. In responding to the significant risks of material misstatement in this area of an audit, the external auditor has an important role to play in evaluating whether the bank's disclosures are consistent and meaningful and, when taken as a whole, present the bank's financial condition in a way that is informative and understandable to users of financial statements. The BIS Committee recommends that the external auditor evaluate whether the disclosures included in the financial statements, both quantitative and qualitative, are sufficient and are consistent with his/her understanding of the bank's risk profile, activities, and strategy, in particular with regard to[17]:

(a) The bank's overall objectives and strategies;
(b) The bank's control framework for managing its key business risks;
(c) The uncertainties associated with its key business risks; and
(d) All other related information included in the financial statements.

[17]BIS—Basel Committee on Banking Supervision (2014): External Audits of Banks, p. 36.

For banks in some jurisdictions, certain regulatory ratios may be published with the financial statements and are material to a wide range of users in assessing the performance of banks. In the course of its audit work, the BIS Committee expects the external auditor to be alert to any indications that the regulatory ratios published with or included in the financial statements may not be consistent with the auditor's understanding of the bank's risk profile, activities, and strategy.

17.3.5 Going Concern Assessment

Under internationally accepted auditing standards, the external auditor is responsible for obtaining sufficient appropriate audit evidence about the appropriateness of management's use of the going concern assumption in the preparation of the financial statements and to conclude whether there is a material uncertainty about the entity's ability to continue as a going concern, the external auditor should remain alert throughout the audit for evidence of events or conditions that may cast significant doubt on this ability to continue as a going concern.[18] The work the external auditor performs to assess the going concern status of a bank is different from that likely to be performed for a non-bank entity because of the contractual terms of bank assets and liabilities (maturity mismatch) and the significant exposure to credit risk and the effect that provisioning may have on a bank's profit and loss and capital. In addition, the potential for regulatory intervention, and the impact that the signaling of any uncertainty over the bank's ability to continue as a going concern could have on the short-term viability of the bank, give rise to difficult and sensitive issues related to the reporting and disclosure of the bank's going concern status. Given these and other risks, banks are required to meet liquidity requirements and capital ratios set by the bank supervisory authority. There should be appropriate emphasis on the evaluation of liquidity and solvency of the bank for the period over which the going concern assumption has been assessed[19]:

[18]BIS—Basel Committee on Banking Supervision (2014): External Audits of Banks, p. 36.

[19]BIS—Basel Committee on Banking Supervision (2014): External Audits of Banks, p. 37.

(a) Liquidity factors to assess include the reasonableness and reliability of the cash forecast for at least 12 months after the date of the financial statements, liquidity risk disclosures, regulatory or contractual restrictions on cash, loan covenants, and pension funding.
(b) Solvency given the potential adverse impact of capital adequacy concerns on the confidence in a bank and, as a consequence, on the bank operating as a going concern Committee expects the external auditor to consider the robustness of the bank's system for managing capital in response to the credit, market and other risks to which the bank is exposed addition, the external auditor considers the capital position in relation to the current and any known future capital requirements, definitions of capital components, and challenges in raising capital. This is particularly critical where capital levels are strained, access to capital resources is restricted or where, for example, the bank's annual report or internal capital projections include ambitious projections of improvements in capital levels.

In responding to the significant risks of material misstatement in this area of the external audit, and in assessing management's assertion that a bank is a going concern, the Committee expects the external auditor to consider at least the following factors[20]:

(a) the effectiveness of the bank's own systems and controls for managing liquidity, capital, and market risk;
(b) the prudential information that is reported to supervisors covering the bank's solvency and capital;
(c) any external indicators that reveal liquidity or funding concerns; and
(d) the availability of short-term liquidity support.

Given the above risks and the possible systemic implications, if there are any material uncertainties related to events or conditions that may cast significant doubt over the bank's ability to continue as a going concern, the external auditor should promptly communicate this fact directly (or, where not permitted, indirectly through the bank) to the supervisors.

[20]BIS—Basel Committee on Banking Supervision (2014): External Audits of Banks, p. 37.

17.3.6 Securitizations—SPEs

Securitization is the financial practice of pooling various types of contractual debt such as residential mortgages, commercial mortgages, auto loans, or credit card debt obligations (or other non-debt assets which generate receivables) and selling their related cash flows to third-party investors as securities, which may be described as bonds, pass-through securities, or collateralized debt obligations (CDOs). Investors are repaid from the principal and interest cash flows collected from the underlying debt. The global securitized market is $9.8 trillion in size, with the US securitized market representing 86%.[21] The banking sector is involved in activities such as sponsoring (or originating) structured products/transactions that support maturity, credit, and liquidity transformation risks more often than other industry sectors. The sponsoring bank may be exposed to risks such as reputational risk in the event that the sponsored entity encounters financial or operational difficulties. The Committee expects that these activities would merit special consideration by the external auditor and are of interest to the supervisor for the following reasons[22]:

(a) Accounting concern—Accounting frameworks are often principles-based, which may require significant management judgments and may result in different treatments of each of these complex transactions. In addition, because these are highly structured products, their accounting treatment may vary based on the facts and circumstances of each transaction. In these instances, it is necessary for the auditor to evaluate the judgments made by the sponsoring bank's management and consider whether the accounting treatment is appropriate and the disclosures are sufficient.

(b) Regulatory concern—Because of the complexity of many securitization transactions and the chain of financial intermediation, the sponsoring bank may misstate the real risk transferred or the risk retained on its balance sheet (including reputational risk which

[21] eMBS, KDSVal, Bloomberg, as of 12/30/2016. Sifma as of Q3 2016 and J.P. Morgan International ABS and CB Research, as of Q3 2016.

[22] BIS—Basel Committee on Banking Supervision (2014): External Audits of Banks, p. 38.

might incentivize it to support its securitizations, and conflicts of interest in case of defaults on the securitized assets). Even so, the originator may be able to benefit from an off-balance sheet accounting treatment for the assets underlying these transactions, and may not be required to hold regulatory capital against its securitization exposures unless specifically required by the supervisor or the relevant regulatory rules.

CHAPTER 18

Bank Bankruptcy

18.1 General

Bankruptcy is a legal term for when a person or business cannot repay their outstanding debts. The bankruptcy process begins with a petition filed by the debtor, which is most common, or on behalf of creditors, which is less common. When assets are exceeded by liabilities and the bank cannot meet Federal Reserve banking deposit requirements. Banks typically do not go bankrupt but may be declared insolvent at which point another bank will buy their assets and liabilities and take over the bank and it's branches. Put differently, a bank failure occurs when a bank is unable to meet its obligations to its depositors or other creditors because it has become insolvent or too illiquid to meet its liabilities. … As such, the bank is unable to fulfill the demands of all of its depositors on time. Sufficient supervisory tools are necessary in order to restructure a failing bank and contain widespread instability. The ideal would require establishing a bridge bank to which the assets and liabilities of a failing bank are transferred during the dissolution and liquidation processes.

In addition to Chapter 11 of the Bankruptcy Act, The United States has a number of specialized insolvency regimes, including the Federal Deposit Insurance Act of 1950 ("FDIA") and the Securities Investor Protection Act ("SIPA").

F. I. Lessambo, *The U.S. Banking System*,
https://doi.org/10.1007/978-3-030-34792-5_18

18.2 Historical Background

As the economic depression deepened in the early 1930s, and as farmers had less and less money to spend in town, banks began to fail at alarming rates. ... After the crash during the first 10 months of 1930, 744 banks failed 10 times as many. In all, 9000 banks failed during the decade of the 1930s. The banking crisis that ensued spelled the demise of hundreds of institutions: From 2008 through 2015, more than 500 banks failed, according to Federal Deposit Insurance Corporation (FDIC) data. In contrast, in the 7 years that preceded the recession, 25 banks failed. The stock market crash of 1929 was not the sole cause of the Great Depression, but it did act to accelerate the global economic collapse of which it was also a symptom. By 1933, nearly half of America's banks had failed, and unemployment was approaching 15 million people, or 30 percent of the workforce. The 2008 financial crisis led to the failure of a large number of banks in the United States. The FDIC closed 465 failed banks from 2008 to 2012. In contrast, in the five years prior to 2008, only 10 banks failed (Fig. 18.1).

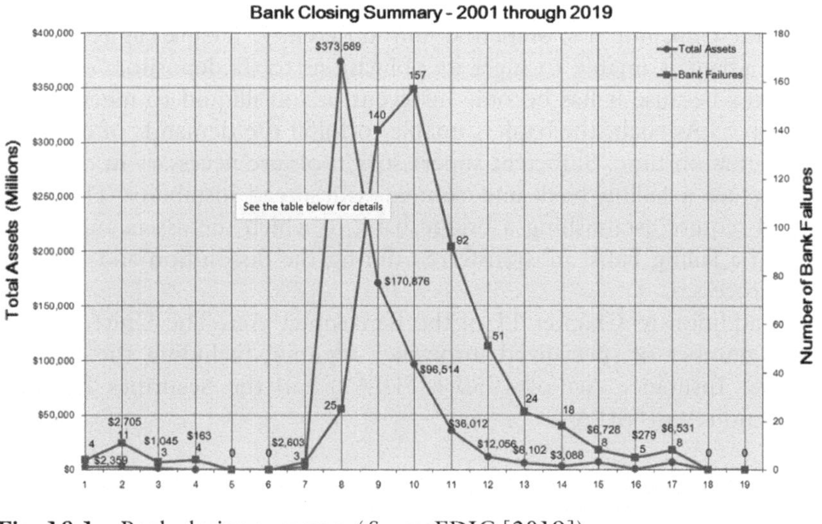

Fig. 18.1 Bank closing summary (*Source* FDIC [2019])

18.3 The United Stated Dual Bankruptcy Proceeding

Country bankruptcy regimes can be classified as either (i) court-led or (ii) administrative regimes. Administrative bank bankruptcy regimes are associated with less court involvement in the resolution process, less likely forbearance, a higher possibility of court appeal, greater availability of supervisory tools, weaker supervisory powers with respect to managers and stronger supervisory powers with respect to shareholders.[1] However, administrative bank bankruptcy regimes are more prone to political pressures from various interested groups. By contrast, court-led bankruptcy procedures are heavy to process, very often with unpredictable outcomes. Court-led bankruptcy regimes differ from one country to another. In most EU countries, Germany, France, banks as commercial corporations are subject to general bankruptcy laws or company laws. Other countries apply Special Resolution Regimes for banks. That is the case for the United States, Canada, Italy, South Korea, Russia, and the UK since 2009.[2]

18.4 Bank Bankruptcy and the FDIC

A bank failure is an extreme event involving the chartering authority or the FDIC to shutting down its operations, re-distributing its assets and liabilities and, if necessary, paying off insured depositors.[3] The FDIC has the authority, under the FDIC Improvement Act of 1991, to close any bank that it considers to be critically undercapitalized, and that does not have a plan to restore capital to an adequate level. In the event of a bank failure, the FDIC acts as a receiver and is in charge of the failure resolution. Jacob Trieber[4] has defined receivership as one of the remedial agencies of a court of equity to preserve a fund or property from spoliation, waste, or removal beyond the jurisdiction of the court pending litigation,

[1] Matej Marinc and Vasja Rant (2014): A Cross-Country Analysis of Bank Bankruptcy Regimes, *Journal of Financial Stability* 13: 134–150.

[2] Jihong Zhang (2016): A Comparative Analysis of Application of Bank Insolvency, *Arizona Journal of International and Comparative Law* 33(1): 304.

[3] Jeffrey Ng, and Sugata Roychowdhury (2009): Loan Loss Reserves, Regulatory Capital, and Bank Failures: Evidence from the 2008–2009 Economic Crisis, p. 8.

[4] Jacob Trieber (1910): The Abuses of Receiverships, *Yale Law Journal* 19(4), Article 4.

so that it may, by final decree, be appropriated according to the rights of the parties.

Federal laws governing the resolution of failed depository institutions were designed to promote the efficient and expedient liquidation of failed institutions. The FDIC, as receiver, is not subject to the direction or supervision of any other agency or department of the United States or of any state in the operation of the receivership. That is, it operates without interference from any executive agencies and to exercise its discretion in determining the most effective resolution of the institution's assets and liabilities.[5]

18.4.1 The FDIC Role as a Receiver

To become the receiver of a failed institution, the FDIC must be appointed by either the failing institution's chartering authority, or itself under Federal Deposit Insurance Company Improvement Act (FDICIA) of 1991. In many ways, the FDIC's powers as a receiver of a failed institution are similar to those of a bankruptcy trustee. That is, as a bankruptcy trustee, a receiver steps into the shoes of an insolvent party but with different rights and responsibilities. As soon as it takes possession of the premises, the FDIC posts notices to explain the action to the public. It then notifies correspondent banks and other appropriate parties of the failed institution.

The primary goals of the resolution process are to provide depositors with timely access to their insured funds and resolve the failing institution in the least costly manner.[6] The FDIC is expected to maximize the return on the assets of the failed institution and to minimize any loss to the insurance fund that may result from closing the institution. As part of its resolution process, the FDIC collects detailed information on the assets and liabilities held by the failing institution. Information regarding the deposits; bank facilities and branches; loan portfolio characteristics; securities; information and technology systems; contracts and leases; subsidiaries; and specialized activities, such as mortgage originations, credit card processing, and international operations, are also collected.[7]

[5]FDIC (2019): Resolutions Handbook, p. 26.

[6]FDIC (2019) Resolutions Handbook, p. 8.

[7]FDIC (2019) Resolutions Handbook, p. 10.

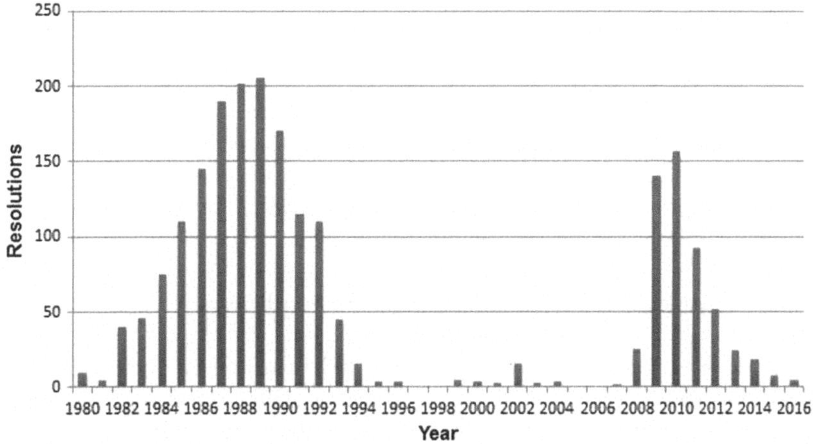

Fig. 18.2 FDIC Resolutions (*Source* FDIC [2019]: Resolutions Handbook)

The FDIC performs a least cost analysis to compare the cost of liquidating the failing financial institution to the cost of bids received from other interested institutions (Fig. 18.2).[8]

Types of resolutions Transactions

Since the passage of the FDICIA, the two common resolution methods are (1) The Purchase and Assumption Transactions (P&A) and (2) the deposit payoffs being two common resolution methods.

1. The Purchase and Assumption Transactions

A P&A is a resolution transaction in which a healthy institution purchases some or all of the assets of a failing institution and assumes some of the liabilities, including all insured deposits. It is the most common method used by the FDIC to resolve a failing institution and is considered the least disruptive to local communities.[9] In general, the FDIC attempts to dispose of as many of the failing institution's assets as possible at the time of closing; however, the results of the winning bid must meet the mandated least cost test requirements. There are various types of P&A transactions:

[8] FDIC (2019) Resolutions Handbook, p. 12.

[9] FDIC (2019) Resolutions Handbook, p. 16.

- Basic P&A

Under the basic P&As, assets that pass to acquirers generally are limited to cash, cash equivalents, and marketable securities. Optional loan pools may be offered. The premises of failed institutions often are offered to acquirers on an optional basis. The liabilities assumed by the acquirer include the portion of the deposit liabilities covered by FDIC insurance and may also include all deposits, if that is the least costly bid.[10]

- Whole Bank P&A P&A with Optional Shared Loss

As an effort to persuade acquirers of failed institutions, the FDIC has developed the whole bank P&A. Bidders are called to bid on all assets of the failed institution on an "as is" discounted basis (with no guarantees). It is often stated that the whole bank P&A provides some benefits to the FDIC: (i) loan customers continue to be served locally by the AI, (ii) the whole bank P&A minimizes the one-time FDIC cash outlay by having the AI purchase all assets, with the FDIC having no further financial obligation to the AI, and (iii) a whole bank transaction reduces the amount of assets held by the FDIC for liquidation.

- P&A with Optional Shared Loss

An optional shared loss P&A is a resolution transaction where the FDIC, as receiver, agrees to share losses on certain types of assets with the AI. This agreement is similar to the whole bank P&A except for the sharing provision on the assets purchased.[11] Shared loss assets are distressed assets of the failing institution that otherwise might not appeal to potential acquirers without some sort of incentive or protection from losses. Under a shared loss option, the FDIC splits defined losses and expenses on certain assets with the acquirer. The shared loss option also reduces the FDIC's immediate cash needs, is operationally simpler, and moves assets quickly into the private sector. Moreover, loss share bidders may be able to submit a value appreciation instrument (VAI) along with their bid. The VAI grants to the FDIC a warrant to purchase a certain interest

[10] FDIC (2019) Resolutions Handbook, p. 17.

[11] FDIC (2019) Resolutions Handbook, p. 18.

in the bidder's stock at a certain price on a certain date. Such a warrant enables the FDIC to participate in any increase in the market value of the bidder's stock that may result from entering into the transaction.[12]

- Bridge Bank P&As

A bridge bank transaction is a P&A in which the FDIC acts temporarily as the AI. The original failed institution is closed by its chartering authority and placed in receivership. A new, temporary national bank chartered by the OCC is created and controlled by the FDIC. This new institution is designed to "bridge" the gap in time between the failure of the original institution and the time it takes the FDIC to evaluate and market the institution to a third party.[13] A bridge bank can be operated for two years, with three one-year extensions, after which time it must be sold or otherwise resolved. Prior to establishing a bridge bank, a cost analysis must show that the franchise value of the bank is greater than the marginal costs of operating the bridge bank, thus being less costly than a payoff. A resolution timetable and strategy are also completed.

2. Deposit Payoffs

A deposit payoff is executed when the FDIC does not receive a least costly bid for a P&A transaction or if no bids are received at all. Under the deposit payoff, no liabilities are assumed, and no assets are purchased by another institution. However, the FDIC must pay depositors of the failed institution the amount of their insured deposits.[14] There are three types of deposit payoff: (i) straight deposit payoff, (ii) insured deposit transfer (IDT), and (iii) deposit insurance national bank (DINB).

- Straight Deposit Payoff

A straight deposit payoff is a resolution method that is used when the liquidation, closing, or winding down of affairs is determined to be the least costly resolution. In a straight deposit payoff, the FDIC determines

[12] FDIC (2019) Resolutions Handbook, p. 18.
[13] FDIC (2019) Resolutions Handbook, p. 19.
[14] FDIC (2019) Resolutions Handbook, p. 19.

the amount of insured deposits and pays that amount directly to each depositor. Once the insured deposits are determined, the FDIC mails a check to each depositor. The FDIC retains all assets and other liabilities, and the receivership bears the responsibility and cost of liquidating all of the assets.[15]

- Insured Deposit Transfer

The IDT is a type of deposit payoff in which the insured and secured deposits of a failed financial institution are transferred to a transferee or agent institution in the community, permitting a direct payoff of the failed institution's depositors by the agent institution. The agent institution pays customers of the failed institution the amount of their insured deposits or, at the customer's request, opens a new account in the agent institution for the customer.[16]

- Deposit Insurance National Bank

A DINB is a bank of limited life and powers that is chartered without any capitalization. To protect depositors, the FDIC may create a DINB to ensure that depositors, particularly those in underserved areas, have continued access to their insured funds, as well as time to open accounts at other insured institutions, when no other bank has agreed to assume the insured deposits. The goal of a DINB is to provide time for account holders to transfer their banking relationships via uninterrupted direct deposits and automated payments from customer accounts to other financial institutions. By using a DINB rather than a payoff, the transferring of accounts to account holders occurs in a less disruptive and more orderly manner for the local community.[17]

Claims against the failed institution are paid from monies recovered by the receiver through its liquidation efforts. Under the National Depositor Preference Amendment and related statutory provisions, claims are paid in the following order of priority:

[15] FDIC (2019) Resolutions Handbook, p. 20.

[16] FDIC (2019) Resolutions Handbook, p. 20.

[17] FDIC (2019) Resolutions Handbook, p. 20.

1. Administrative expenses of the receiver
2. Deposit liability claims (the FDIC claim takes the position of all insured deposits)
3. Other general or senior liabilities of the institution
4. Subordinated obligations
5. Shareholder claims.

18.4.2 Orderly Liquidation of Covered Financial Companies

A failed systemically important financial institution is deemed a covered financial company for purposes of Title II of the Dodd–Frank Act once a systemic determination has been made by the Secretary of the Treasury pursuant to section 203(b) thereof, 12 U.S.C. § 5383(b). Title II of the Dodd–Frank Act defines the framework for orderly resolution proceedings and establishes the powers and duties of the FDIC when acting as receiver for a covered financial company. The FDIC is instructed to liquidate the covered financial company in a manner that maximizes the value of the company's assets, minimizes losses, mitigates risk, and minimizes moral hazard.

1. Title I: Credible Resolution Plan

Title I of the Dodd–Frank Act significantly enhances regulators' ability to conduct advance resolution planning in respect of systemically important financial institutions through a variety of mechanisms, including heightened supervisory authority and the resolution plans, or living wills, required under section 165(d) of Title I of the Dodd–Frank Act. This will enable the FDIC, working in tandem with the Federal Reserve and other regulators, to collect and analyze information for resolution planning purposes in advance of the impending failure of the institution.

An essential part of such plans will be to describe how this process can be accomplished without posing systemic risk to the public and the financial system. If the company does not submit a credible resolution plan, the statute permits increasingly stringent requirements to be imposed that, ultimately, can lead to divestiture of assets or operations identified by the FDIC and the Federal Reserve to facilitate an orderly resolution. The Dodd–Frank Act requires each designated financial company to produce a resolution plan, or living will, that maps its business lines to legal entities and provides integrated analyses of its corporate structure; credit and other exposures; funding, capital, and cash flows; domestic and foreign jurisdictions in which it operates; its supporting information systems and other essential services; and other key components of its business operations, all as part of the plan for its rapid and orderly resolution. The elements contained in a resolution plan will not only help the FDIC and other domestic regulators to better understand a firm's business and how that entity may be resolved, but the plans will also enhance the FDIC's ability to coordinate with foreign regulators in an effort to develop a comprehensive and coordinated resolution strategy for a cross-border firm. Once the structure is developed, the FDIC would seek bids from qualified, interested bidders for the business lines or units that have going-concern value. The FDIC would analyze the bids received and choose the bid or bids that would provide the highest recovery to the receivership. The winning bidder would be informed and would take control of the business lines or units concurrent with the closing of the institution.

2. Title II: Orderly Resolution

The orderly liquidation authority of Title II would be a remedy of last resort, to be used only after the remedies available under Title I—including the increased informational and supervisory powers—are unable to stave off a failure. In particular, it is expected that the mere knowledge of the consequences of a Title II resolution, including the understanding that financial assistance is no longer an option, would encourage a troubled institution to find an acquirer or strategic partner on its own well in advance of failure. The key to an orderly resolution and liquidation of a systemically important financial institution is the ability to plan for its resolution and liquidation, provide liquidity to maintain key assets and operations, and preserve financial stability. More, the Dodd–Frank Act provides the means to preserve systemically important operations and reduce systemic consequences while limiting moral hazard by imposing losses on the stockholders and unsecured creditors of the failed systemically important financial institution rather than on the US taxpayer.

- Appointment
  Under section 203 of the Dodd–Frank Act, at the Secretary of the Treasury's (Secretary) request, or of their own initiative, the Board of Governors of the Federal Reserve System (Federal Reserve) and

the FDIC are to make a written recommendation requesting that the Secretary appoint the FDIC as receiver for a systemically important financial institution that is in default or danger of default. The Secretary is responsible for making a determination as to whether the financial company should be placed into receivership, and that determination is based on, among other things, the Secretary's finding that the financial company is in default or in danger of default; that the failure of the company and its resolution under otherwise applicable State or Federal law would have serious adverse consequences on the financial stability of the United States; and that no viable private sector alternative is available to prevent the default of the financial company. The Dodd–Frank Act provides an expedited judicial review process of the Secretary's determination. Should the board of directors of the covered financial company object to the appointment of the FDIC as receiver, a hearing is held in federal district court, and the court must make a decision on the matter within 24 hours. Upon a successful petition (or should the court fail to act within the time provided), the Secretary is to appoint the FDIC receiver of the covered financial company.

- Special powers under Title II
  The Dodd–Frank Act authorizes the FDIC, as receiver of a covered financial company, to establish a bridge financial company to which assets and liabilities of the covered financial company may be transferred. Fundamental to an orderly liquidation of a covered financial company is the ability to continue key operations, services, and transactions that will maximize the value of the firm's assets and operations and avoid a disorderly collapse in the marketplace. To facilitate this continuity of operations, the receivership can utilize one or more bridge financial companies. The bridge financial company is a newly established, federally chartered entity that is owned by the FDIC and includes those assets, liabilities, and operations of the covered financial company as necessary to achieve the maximum value of the firm. Shareholders, debt holders, and other creditors whose claims were not transferred to the bridge financial company will remain in the receivership and will receive payments on their claims based upon the priority of payments set forth in section 210(b) of the Dodd–Frank Act. Like the bridge banks used in the resolution of large insured depository institutions, the bridge financial company authority permits the FDIC to stabilize the key

operations of the covered financial company by continuing valuable, systemically important operations. While the covered financial company's board of directors and the most senior management responsible for its failure will be replaced, as required by section 204(a)(2) of the Dodd–Frank Act, operations may be continued by the covered financial company's employees under the strategic direction of the FDIC, as receiver, and contractors employed by the FDIC to help oversee those operations. A bridge financial company also provides the receiver with flexibility in preserving the value of the assets of the covered financial company and in effecting an orderly liquidation. The receiver can retain certain assets and liabilities of the covered financial company in the receivership and transfer other assets and liabilities, as well as the viable operations of the covered financial company, to the bridge financial company. The receiver may also transfer certain qualified financial contracts to the bridge financial company, as discussed below. The bridge financial company can operate until the receiver is able to stabilize the systemic functions of the covered financial company, conduct marketing for its assets and find one or more appropriate buyers.
The Dodd–Frank Act expressly permits the FDIC to transfer qualified financial contracts to a solvent financial institution (an acquiring investor) or to a bridge financial company. In such a case, counterparties are prohibited from terminating their contracts and liquidating and netting out their positions on the grounds of an event of insolvency. The receiver's ability to transfer qualified financial contracts to a third party in order for the contracts to continue according to their terms—notwithstanding the debtor company's insolvency—provides market certainty and stability and preserves the value represented by the contracts. As such contracts continue, following such transfer, to be valid and binding obligations of the bridge financial company (before being eventually wound down), the bridge financial company is required to perform the obligations thereunder, including in respect of meeting collateral requirements, hedging, and being liable for gains and losses on the contracts. The Dodd–Frank Act provides that the FDIC may borrow funds from the Department of the Treasury, among other things, to make loans to, or guarantee obligations of, a covered financial company or a bridge financial company to provide liquidity for the operations of the receivership and the bridge financial company. Section 204(d)

of the Dodd–Frank Act provides that the FDIC may make available to the receivership funds for the orderly liquidation of the covered financial company. Funds provided by the FDIC under section 204(d) of the Dodd–Frank Act are to be given a priority as administrative expenses of the receiver or as amounts owed to the United States when used for the orderly resolution of the covered financial company, including, inter alia, to: (i) make loans to or purchase debt of the covered financial company or a covered subsidiary; (ii) purchase (or guarantee) the assets of the covered financial company or a covered subsidiary; (iii) assume or guarantee the obligations of a covered financial company or a covered subsidiary; and (iv) make additional payments or pay additional amounts to certain creditors. Once the new bridge financial company's operations have stabilized as the market recognizes that it has adequate funding and will continue key operations, the FDIC would move as expeditiously as possible to sell operations and assets back into the private sector. Under certain circumstances, the establishment of a bridge financial company may not be necessary, particularly when the FDIC has the ability to pre-plan for the sale of a substantial portion of the firm's assets and liabilities to a third-party purchaser at the time of failure.

18.5 Non-bank Bankruptcy and the Office of the Comptroller of the Currency

Uninsured national trust banks have fundamentally different business models compared to commercial and consumer banks and savings associations and therefore face very different types of risks. These banks do not make loans, nor rely on deposit funding, and consequently have simple liquidity management programs. Their liquidation is managed by the OCC and not by the FDIC. Most of these uninsured national trust banks are subsidiaries or affiliates of a full-service insured national bank or are affiliates of an insured state bank. In the event of liquidation, the Comptroller appoints a receiver for an uninsured bank, generally under the same grounds for appointment of the FDIC as receiver for insured national banks.

Approved or adjudicated claims are paid solely out of the assets of the uninsured national bank in receivership. As receiver, the OCC appoints and oversees receivers for uninsured national banks, thereby facilitating the winding down of bank operations, assets, and accounts while minimizing disruptions to customers and creditors of the institution. Under the "separate capacities" doctrine, which has long been recognized in litigation involving the FDIC, it is well established that the agency, when acting in one capacity, is not liable for claims against the agency acting in its other capacity.

As receiver, the OCC appoints and oversees receivers for uninsured national banks, thereby facilitating the winding down of bank operations, assets, and accounts while minimizing disruptions to customers and creditors of the institution. The receiver liquidates the assets of the uninsured bank, with court approval, and pays the proceeds into an account as directed by the OCC. The categories of claims and the priority thereof for payment are set out in the final rule. The final rule also clarifies certain powers held by the receiver.

18.6 The Dodd–Frank Act

The Financial Stability Oversight Council and Orderly Liquidation Authority monitors the financial stability of major firms whose failure could have a major negative impact on the economy (companies deemed "too big to fail"). It also provides for liquidations or restructurings via the Orderly Liquidation Fund, which provides money to assist with the dismantling of financial companies that have been placed in receivership, and prevents tax dollars from being used to prop up such firms. The council has the authority to break up banks that are considered to be so large as to pose a systemic risk; it can also force them to increase their reserve requirements. Similarly, the new Federal Insurance Office is supposed to identify and monitor insurance companies considered "too big to fail".

18.7 The Bank Living Wills

Section 165(d) of the Dodd–Frank Wall Street Reform and Consumer Protection Act, which became law in 2010, requires banks to set up living wills. The FDIC and Federal Reserve, as key regulators, required the most complex Wall Street firms to file beginning in 2012 "resolution plans," or living wills, which would guide regulators through the process of liquidating a bank without disrupting other parts of the global financial system. Each plan, commonly known as a living will, must describe the company's strategy for rapid and orderly resolution in the event of material financial distress or failure of the company, and include both public and confidential sections. In so doing, the FDIC and the Federal Reserve seek to ensure no bank's failure can create systemic collapses in the overall financial industry. Not all banks are concerned. Bank holding companies with consolidated assets of $50 billion or more are required to submit living wills. The Dodd–Frank Act requires the agencies to take actions upon jointly determining that a firm's living will is deficient, or "not credible." That is, the Federal Reserve and the FDIC issue a joint notice of deficiency. The firm then has 90 days to resubmit a living will that addresses the outlined deficiencies. Thereafter, if the resubmitted living will is still deemed deficient, a two-stage process is initiated:

- First, if a firm does not cure the deficiencies in a timely manner, the Federal Reserve and the FDIC may jointly impose (a) more stringent capital, leverage, or liquidity requirements or (b) restrictions on the company's growth, activities, or operations.
- Second, if the Federal Reserve and the FDIC have jointly imposed any of the requirements or restrictions under the first step above, and the firm has still failed to submit a revised living will that adequately remedies the identified deficiencies within two years, the agencies may jointly order the divestiture of certain assets or operations, subject to the following requirements: (a) the agencies must first consult with the FSOC; and (b) the agencies must jointly determine that divestiture is necessary to facilitate an orderly resolution under the Bankruptcy Code in the event of the company's failure.

The living will details a contingency plan for how the bank will sell off assets or be liquidated in a manner that does not generate chaotic aftershocks elsewhere in the financial system. In 2017, the bank living will was improved by the Financial Institution Living Will Improvement Act of 2017, which amends Title I of the Dodd–Frank Wall Street Reform and Consumer Protection Act to reform the living will process and require bank holding companies to submit to the Board of Governors of the Federal Reserve System and the FDIC resolution plans every two years. Living Will Improvement Act of 2017 also requires the Federal Reserve and FDIC to provide feedback to a bank holding company regarding a submitted resolution plan within six months after its submission. This bill also requires the Federal Reserve and FDIC to publicly disclose the assessment framework used to review the adequacy of resolution plans.

18.8 The International Swaps and Derivatives Association Resolution

The US banking regulators, along with a number of other major global banking organizations, adhere to the International Swaps and Derivatives Association Resolution Stay Protocol (the ISDA Protocol) that was developed and updated in coordination with the FSB. The ISDA Protocol imposes a stay on certain cross-default and early termination rights within standard ISDA derivatives contracts and securities financing transactions between adhering parties in the event that one of them is subject to resolution in its home jurisdiction, including a resolution under OLA in the United States.

- The ISDA US Stay Protocol

The ISDA US Stay Protocol was created to allow market participants to comply with regulations issued by the Board of Governors of the Federal Reserve System, the Federal Deposit Insurance Corporation and the Office of the Comptroller of the Currency (collectively, the US Stay Regulations).[18] The US Stay Regulations impose requirements on the terms of swaps, repos, and other qualified financial contracts (QFCs)[19] of global systemically important banking organizations (G-SIBs). The ISDA US Stay Protocol allows Regulated Entities[20] (or entities subject

[18] ISDA (2018): US Resolution Stay Protocol (ISDA U.S. Stay Protocol).

[19] However, certain QFC are excluded; These include: (i) QFCs that do not expressly contain any default rights or transfer restrictions against an Entity Subject to US Regulations; (ii) Certain retail investment advisory contracts; (iii) Warrants in respect of shares of Entities Subject to US Regulations issued shortly after publication of the US Stay Regulations; (iv) Transactions to which a central counterparty is a party; (v) Transactions to which each party other than the Entity Subject to US Regulations is a "financial market utility"; and (vi) Other QFCs excluded by the FRB, the FDIC and the OCC pursuant to a process set forth in the US Stay Regulations.

[20] Regulated Entities under the US Stay Regulations generally include: (i) with respect to US G-SIBs, all US and non-US subsidiaries (subject to minor exceptions described below); and (ii) with respect to non-US G-SIBs, all US subsidiaries, US branches and US agencies.

to US Regulations and their counterparties) to amend the terms of the covered agreements between them (unless they are excluded or exempted) to:

- Expressly recognize existing limits on the exercise of default rights by counterparties under the Orderly Liquidation Authority provisions of Title II of the Dodd–Frank Wall Street Reform and Consumer Protection Act (OLA) and the Federal Deposit Insurance Act (FDI Act) as well as the powers of the FDIC under OLA and the FDI Act to transfer contracts and
- Limit the ability of counterparties to exercise default rights related, directly or indirectly, to affiliates of Entities Subject to US Regulations (as defined below) entering into insolvency proceedings (including under the US Bankruptcy Code) and permit the transfer of related credit support provided by a covered affiliate in such a resolution scenario.

The most two relevant sections under the ISDA US Protocol are:

- Section 1 of the ISDA US Stay Protocol applies with respect to OLA and the FDI Act, and
- Section 2, which provides for contractual stays on the exercise of default rights triggered by affiliates of Regulated Entity counterparties entering into proceedings under certain insolvency regimes such as the US Bankruptcy Code or receivership under the FDI Act. Section 2 allows a Regulated Entity in insolvency proceedings to transfer credit support with respect to a Protocol Covered Agreement to a transferee. Section 2 overrides any restrictions on such transfer, assuming certain creditor protections are satisfied.

The ISDA Protocol is expected to be adopted more broadly in the future, following the adoption of regulations by banking regulators (including the Federal Reserve Board's proposal on QFCs described above), and expanded to include instances where a US financial holding company becomes subject to proceedings under the US Bankruptcy Code.

- The US Qualified Financial Contracts Rules

To create a framework for directing an orderly resolution of a distressed systemically important financial institution, US federal banking regulators have adopted new rules which require buy-side firms to relinquish certain termination rights that have long been part of bankruptcy "safe harbors" under bankruptcy and insolvency regimes in order to continue trading with large financial institutions. These rules apply to derivatives transactions, repurchase and reverse repurchase transactions and securities lending transactions with large financial institutions. Institutional investors, hedge funds, mutual funds, sovereign wealth funds, and other buy-side market participants who enter into these transactions as of January 1, 2019 would need to bring their covered qualified financial contracts with large covered financial institutions into compliance with the rules. These new rules aim to facilitate an insolvency proceeding of a failing or failed financial institution under the US Bankruptcy Code by prohibiting a covered financial institution[21] from entering into qualified financial contracts that allow a counterparty to exercise default remedies with respect to such financial institution because an affiliate of such financial institution enters into resolution or bankruptcy proceedings.

The QFC Rules require that Covered Entities amend their Covered QFCs with their counterparties to include the following provisions:

- in the event the Covered Entity becomes subject to resolution under a US special resolution regime, the transfer of the QFC from the Covered Entity will be effective to the same extent it would be under the US special resolution regime if the QFC was governed by the laws of the United States or a state of the United States and

[21] A "covered entity" includes US global systemically important banking organization ("GSIB") top-tier bank holding companies, certain subsidiaries of such bank holding companies, and certain US operations of foreign GSIBs. The following US banking institutions have been identified as GSIBs: Bank of America Corporation, the Bank of New York Mellon Corporation, Citigroup, Inc., Goldman Sachs Group, Inc., JPMorgan Chase & Co., Morgan Stanley Inc., State Street Corporation, and Wells Fargo & Company. The following foreign banking institutions have been identified as GSIBs: Agricultural Bank of China, Bank of China, Barclays, BNP Paribas, China Construction Bank, Credit Suisse, Deutsche Bank, Groupe BPCE, Groupe Crédit Agricole, Industrial and Commercial Bank of China Limited, HSBC, ING Bank, Mitsubishi UFJ FG, Mizuho FG, Nordea, Royal Bank of Scotland, Santander, Société Générale, Standard Chartered, Sumitomo Mitsui FG, UBS, and Unicredit Group.

- in the event a covered entity or its affiliate becomes subject to resolution under a US special resolution regime, the counterparty's ability to exercise its default rights under the QFC are limited to the same extent they would be limited under the US special resolution regime, if the QFC were governed by the laws of the United States or any of its states.

The ultimate aim of this provision is to limit the ability of counterparties to declare cross-defaults based on the bankruptcy of affiliates of Covered Entities to the extent that the Covered Entity itself remains solvent. Bank regulators are concerned that the insolvency of one entity in a consolidated group triggers cross-defaults that cause their otherwise solvent affiliates to become insolvent. Bank regulators want the ability and the flexibility to resolve the insolvent entity's affairs while allowing its solvent affiliates to remain in operation.

Glossary

Alpha the amount of return expected from an investment from its inherent value

Annualized rate of return the average annual return over a period of years, taking into consideration the effect of compounding. Annualized rate of return also can be called compound growth rate

Appreciation the increase in value of a financial asset

Asset allocation the process of dividing investments among cash, income, and growth buckets to optimize the balance between risk and reward based on investment needs

Asset class securities with similar features. The most common asset classes are stocks, bonds, and cash equivalents

Asset-based lending is a business loan secured by collateral (assets). The asset-based loan, or line of credit, is secured by inventory, accounts receivable, equipment, and/or other balance-sheet assets

Assuming institution a healthy financial institution that purchases some or all of the assets and assumes some or all of the liabilities of a failed institution in a P&A transaction

Bank holding company a business incorporated under state law, which controls through equity ownership ("holds") one or more banks and, often, other affiliates in financial services as allowed by its regulator, the Federal Reserve. On the federal level, these businesses are regulated through the Bank Holding Company Act

F. I. Lessambo, *The U.S. Banking System*,
https://doi.org/10.1007/978-3-030-34792-5

Bear market is a prolonged period of falling stock prices, usually marked by a decline of 20% or more. The opposite of a bull market

Beta is a measurement of volatility where 1 is neutral; above 1 is more volatile; and less than 1 is less volatile

Blue chip is a high-quality, relatively low-risk investment; the term usually refers to stocks of large, well-established companies that have performed well over a long period. The term blue chip is borrowed from poker, where the blue chips are the most valuable

Borrowing base is an accounting metric used by financial institutions to estimate the available collateral on a borrower's assets in order to evaluate the size of the credit that may be extended. Typically, the calculation of borrowing base is used for revolving loans, and the borrowing base determines the maximum credit line available to the borrower

Bull market any market in which prices are advancing in an upward trend. In general, someone is bullish if they believe the value of a security or market will rise. The opposite of a bear market

Capitalization the market value of a company, calculated by multiplying the number of shares outstanding by the price per share

Chartering authority a state or federal agency that grants charters to new depository institutions. For state-chartered institutions, the chartering authority is usually the state banking department; for national banks and for federal savings institutions, it is the OCC

Commercial bank a deposit-taking institution that can make commercial loans, accept checking accounts, and whose deposits are insured by the Federal Deposit Insurance Corporation. National banks are chartered by the Office of the Comptroller of the Currency and state banks, by the individual states

Credit union a nonprofit financial cooperative of individuals with one or more common bonds (such as employment, labor union membership, or residence in the same neighborhood). Credit unions accept deposits of members' savings and transaction balances in the form of share accounts, pay dividends (interest) on them out of earnings, and primarily provide consumer credit to members

Currency the coin and paper money of the United States or of any other country that is designated as legal tender and that circulates and is customarily used and accepted as a medium of exchange in the country of issuance. Currency includes US silver certificates, US notes, and Federal Reserve notes. Currency also includes official foreign banknotes that are customarily used and accepted as a medium of exchange in a foreign country

Cyber-enabled crime illegal activities carried out or facilitated by electronic systems and devices, such as networks and computers

Cyber-event an attempt to compromise or gain unauthorized electronic access to electronic systems, services, resources, or information

Deposits margins the difference between rates paid on retail deposits and alternative market funding rates such as the federal funds rate

Dow Jones industrial average (Dow) is the most commonly used indicator of stock market performance, based on prices of 30 actively traded blue chip stocks, primarily major industrial companies. The average is the sum of the current market price of 30 major industrial companies' stocks divided by a number that has been adjusted to take into consideration stock splits and changes in stock composition

Dual banking system refers to the fact that banks may be either federal- or state-chartered

Federal funds rate (FED funds rate) the interest rate charged by banks with excess reserves at a Federal Reserve district bank to banks needing overnight loans to meet reserve requirements. The most sensitive indicator of the direction of interest rates, since it is set daily by the market, unlike the prime rate and the discount rate, which are periodically changed by banks and by the Federal Reserve Board

The FFIEC Federal Financial Institutions Examination Council. It comprises the principals of the following, the Board of the Governors of the Federal Reserve System, Federal Deposit Insurance Corporation, National Credit Union Administration, Office of the Comptroller of the Currency (OCC), Bureau of Consumer Financial Protection, and State Liaison Committee

Financial holding company a form of bank holding company authorized by the Gramm–Leach–Bliley Act that may control one or more banks, securities firms, and insurance companies

Fixed-income fund a fund or portfolio where bonds are primarily purchased as investments. There is no fixed maturity date and no repayment guarantee

Fixed-income security a security that pays a set rate of interest on a regular basis

Index an investment index tracks the performance of many investments as a way of measuring the overall performance of a particular investment type or category. The S&P 500 is widely considered the benchmark for large-stock investors. It tracks the performance of 500 large US company stocks

Insured deposit the portion of a deposit in an FDIC-insured commercial bank, savings bank, or savings association that is fully protected by FDIC deposit insurance. Savings, checking, and other deposit accounts, when combined, are generally insured up to $250,000 per depositor in each financial institution insured by the FDIC. Deposits held in different ownership categories, such as single or joint accounts, are separately insured. Also, separate $250,000 coverage is usually provided for retirement accounts, such as individual retirement accounts

Investment bank a financial intermediary, active in the securities business. Investment banking functions include underwriting (marketing newly registered securities to individual or institutional investors), counseling regarding merger and acquisition proposals, brokerage services, advice on corporate financing, and proprietary trading

Large-cap the market capitalization of the stocks of companies with market values greater than $10 billion

Letter of intent may also be issued by a mutual fund shareholder to indicate that he/she would like to invest certain amounts of money at certain specified times. In exchange for signing a letter of intent, the shareholder would often qualify for reduced sales charges. A letter of intent is not a contract and cannot be enforced; it is just a document stating serious intent to carry out certain business activities

Long-term investment strategy a strategy that looks past the day-to-day fluctuations of the stock and bond markets and responds to fundamental changes in the financial markets or the economy

Market risk the possibility that an investment will not achieve its target

Market timing a risky investment strategy that calls for buying and selling securities in anticipation of market conditions

Maturity the date specified in a note or bond on which the debt is due and payable

Maturity distribution the breakdown of a portfolio's assets based on the time frame when the investments will mature

Median market cap the midpoint of market capitalization (market price multiplied by the number of shares outstanding) of the stocks in a portfolio, where half of the stocks have higher market capitalization and half have lower

Mid-cap the market capitalization of the stocks of companies with market values between $3 and $10 billion

Mining is a reward that can be earned when an individual or entity participates in the process of verifying the legitimacy of transactions on the public ledger

Money consists of both currency issued by the government and deposits at banks

Money market mutual fund a short-term investment that seeks to protect principal and generate income by investing in Treasury bills, CDs with maturities less than one year, and other conservative investments

NASDAQ National Association of Securities Dealers Automated Quotations system, which is owned and operated by the National Association of Securities Dealers. NASDAQ is a computerized system that provides brokers and dealers with price quotations for securities traded over-the-counter as well as for many New York Stock Exchange-listed securities

Price-to-book the price per share of a stock divided by its book value (net worth) per share. For a stock portfolio, the ratio is the weighted average price-to-book ratio of the stocks it holds

Price-to-earnings (P/E) ratio a stock's price divided by its earnings per share, which indicates how much investors are paying for a company's earning power

P/E ratio price of a stock divided by its earnings from the latest year

P/E ratio price of a stock divided by its projected earnings for the coming year

Resolution the disposition plan for a failed institution, designed to protect insured depositors and minimize the losses to the insurance fund that are expected from covering insured deposits and disposing of the institution's assets. Resolution methods generally include P&A transactions, insured deposit transfers, and straight deposit payoffs

Risk tolerance the degree to which you can tolerate volatility in your investment values

Sharpe ratio a risk-adjusted measure that measures reward per unit of risk. The higher the Sharpe ratio, the better. The numerator is the difference between the Fund's annualized return and the annualized return of the risk-free instrument (T-Bills)

Small-cap the market capitalization of the stocks of companies with market values less than $3 billion

Standby letter of credit (SLOC) is a guarantee of payment by a bank on behalf of their client. It is a loan of last resort in which the bank fulfills payment obligations by the end of the contract if their client cannot afford

Virtual wallet is similar to an investment account held at a brokerage firm. Funds are transferred into the account and remain in the form of fiat money until invested/converted into crypto-currency

Bibliography

Allen, L. (2003): The Basel Capital Accords and International Mortgage Markets: A Survey of the Literature. *Financial Markets Institutions & Instruments* 13(2): 41–108.
Amadeo, K. (2016): The Great Recession of 2008: Explanation with Dates.
Atte, A. (2016): Stress Test BCE 2016: Classifica Banche: Ecco le 10 migliori e le 10 peggiori in Europa.
Bailey, A. (2014): The Capital Adequacy of Banks: Today's Issue and What We Have Learned from the Past. Bank of England.
Baker, James C. (2002): The Bank for International Settlements.
Balla, Eliana, Rose, Morgan J., and Jessie Romero (2012): Loan Loss Reserve Accounting and Bank Behavior, The Federal Reserve Bank of Richmond, Economic Brief 12-03.
Bank for International Settlements (2017).
Basel Art Trade Anti-Money Laundering Principles (2018).
Basel Committee on Banking Supervision (2011): Principles for the Sound Management of Operational Risk.
Basel Committee on Banking Supervision (2012): The Internal Audit Function in Banks.
Berman, Ana (2019): IMF and World Bank Launch Quasi-Crypto-Currency in Exploration of Blockchain Tech.
Bessis, Joel (2011): *Risk Management in Banking*, Wiley, Chichester.
BIS (2013): Basel III: The Liquidity Coverage Ratio and Liquidity Risk Monitoring Tools.
BIS (2015, October): A Brief History on the Basel Committee.

F. I. Lessambo, *The U.S. Banking System*,
https://doi.org/10.1007/978-3-030-34792-5

BIS (2016): Banking Committee on Banking Supervision—Minimum Capital Requirement for Market Risk.
BIS (2016): Basel III Document Revisions to the Securitization Framework.
BIS—Basel Committee on Banking Supervision (2009): Enhancements to the Basel II Framework.
BIS—Basel Committee on Banking Supervision (2014): Assessment of Basel III Regulations—United States of America.
BIS—Basel Committee on Banking Supervision (2014): External Audits of Banks.
Bjerke, Bjorn (2017): The International Comparative Legal Guide to Securitization, Chapter 4.
Board of Governors of the Federal Reserve System, 2016 A.
Board of Governors of the Federal Reserve System, 2016 B.
Clayton, Jay (2017): Statement on Crypto-Currencies and Initial Coin Offerings.
Committee on Homeland Security and Governmental Affairs (2013): Beyond Silk Road: Potential Risks, Threats, and Promises of Virtual Currencies.
Congiu, F. R. (2017): EBA Issues 2018 EU-Wide Stress Test Methodology for Discussion. EBA European Banking Authority.
El-Hindi, Jamal (2017): Conference of State Bank Supervisors (CSBS) Federal Supervisory Forum.
Elliott, L. (2016): The EBA's Stress Tests Reveal Their Own Lack of Credibility, in *The Guardian*.
eMBS, KDSVal, Bloomberg, as of 12/30/2016. Sifma as of Q3 2016 and J.P. Morgan International ABS & CB Research, as of Q3 2016.
European Banking Authority (2014): EU-Wide Stress Test Frequently Asked Questions.
European Banking Authority (2015): EBA Updates List of Common Equity Tier 1 (CET1) Capital Instruments.
European Banking Authority (2016): EBA Publishes 2016 EU-Wide Stress Test Results.
FDIC (2019): Resolutions Handbook.
Federal Reserve Bank (2017): Supervisory Scenarios for Annual Stress Tests Required Under the Dodd–Frank Act Stress Testing Rules and the Capital Plan Rule.
Federal Reserve Bulletin (2003): Capital Standards for Banks: The Evolving Basel Accord.
FFIEC Bank Secrecy Act Anti-Money Laundering Examination Manual, https://www.ffiec.gov/bsa_aml_infobase/pages_manual/manual_online.htm.
FinCEN (2016): Stopping Terror Finance: A Coordinated Government Effort United States House of Representatives Committee on Financial Services Task Force to Investigate Terrorism Financing.

Ghosh, Amalendu (2012): Managing Risks in Commercial and Retail Banking, Chapter 3.

Goldstein, M. (2014): The 2014 EU-Wide Bank Stress Test Lacks Credibility.

Good, B. A. (1996): The Credit Union Industry: An Overview in Federal Reserve Bank of Cleveland Economic Commentary.

Hieronymi, Otto (2009): *Globalization and the Reform of the International Banking and Monetary System*, Palgrave Macmillan, Basingstoke.

Hughes, Scott D. (2017): Crypto-currency Regulations and Enforcement in the US, *Western State Law Review*, 45 W. St. L. Rev.

IMF (2018): Casting Light on Central Bank Digital Currency.

IMF (2019): FinTech: The Experience so Far.

International Consortium of Investigative Journalists (2018): New Panama Papers Leak Reveals Firm's Chaotic Scramble to Identify Clients, Save Business Amid Global Fallout.

IRS Publication 2014–21, https://www.irs.gov/pub/irs-drop/n-14-21.pdf.

Jenik, Ivo, and Lauer, Kate (2017): Regulatory Sandboxes and Financial Inclusion.

Jobst, A. A., Ong, L. L., and Schmieder, C. (2013): An IMF Framework for Macro-prudential Bank Solvency Stress Testing: Application to S-25 and Other G-20 Country FSAPs. IMF Working Paper No. 13/68, International Monetary Fund, Washington.

Johnson, Jeffery W. (2013): Understanding Bank Financial Statements.

Johnston, Matthew (2019): History of the Banking Industry in the US.

Joshi, S. (2013): Importance of Basel Accords in Banking Industry, ASM's International e-Journal of Ongoing Research in Management and IT.

Kishan, R. P., and Opiela, T. P. (2000): Bank Size, Bank Capital, and the Bank Lending Channel, *Journal of Money, Credit and Banking* 32(1): 121–141.

Loutskina, E., and Strahan, P. (2009): Securitization and the Declining Impact of Bank Finance on Loan Supply: Evidence from Mortgage Originations, *Journal of Finance* 64(2): 861–889.

Marinc, Matej, and Rant, Vasja (2014): A Cross-Country Analysis of Bank Bankruptcy Regimes, *Journal of Financial Stability* 13: 134–150.

Maxfield, J. (2017): Bank Stress Test Results. https://www.fool.com/investing/2017/07/06/2017-bank.

Mitchell, Stacy (2015): Public Banks: Bank of North Dakota, Institute for Local Self Reliance.

Murphy, Edward V. (2015): Who Regulates Whom and How? An Overview of U.S. Financial Regulatory Policy for Banking and Securities Markets, Congressional Research Service.

Myles, Danielle (2018): "Top 1000 World Banks 2018," The Banker, July 2.

Ng, Jeffrey, and Roychowdhury, Sugata (2009): Loan Loss Reserves, Regulatory Capital, and Bank Failures: Evidence from the 2008–2009 Economic Crisis, p. 8.

North, M. (2017): EU's 2018 Bank Stress Test Will Be Tougher, but Has Limitations.

Ong, L. L., and Pazarbasioglu, C. (2013): Credibility and Crisis Stress Testing. International Monetary Fund Working Paper WP/13/178.

Peek, Joe, and Rosengren, Eric S. (2013): The Role of Banks in the Transmission of Monetary. Public Policy Discussion Papers, no. 13-5, Federal Reserve Bank of Boston, MA.

Pollard, Patricia S. (2003) A Look Inside Two Central Banks: The ECB and the Federal Reserve, The Fed of St. Louis.

Rapoport, Abby (2013): The People's Bank. American Prospect.

Risk Management Manual of Examination Policies Federal Deposit Insurance Corporation (4/2015).

Roubini, Nouriel, and Backus, David (1998): Lectures in Macroeconomics, Chapter 12: Monetary Policy and Commercial Banking.

Ryu, L. H. (2013): Federal Reserve's Philosophy for Supervisory Stress Test. The Board of Governors or the Federal Reserve System, p. 2.

Scherer, F. M. (2014): The Banking Industry, Harvard Kennedy School.

Sebastian, Schneider, Schrock, Gerhard, et al. (2017): Basel IV: What's Next for Banks? McKinsey & Company, Global Risk Practice.

Segala, John P. (1979): A Summary of the International Banking Act of 1978, Economic Review.

Solomon, Davidoff S. (2016): Fed Proposes Ban on Merchant Banking, a Practice with Little Risk, NYT.

Stiglitz, Joseph (2010): Free Fall: America Free Markets, and the Sinking of the World Economy, the Gilder Lehrman Institute of American History (2009–2019).

Sumerlin, Marc (2010): The Fed's Dual Mandate Is Not the Problem, WSJ.

Sylla, Richard (2009–2019): The US Banking System: Origin, Development, and Regulation, the Gilder Lehrman Institute of American History.

The Economist (2001): The Long, Dark Shadow of Herstatt.

The Economist (2016): European Banks Still Stressed Out, Stress Test Results Do Little to Dampen Worries About Italy's Lenders.

Timothy, Clark, Dick, Astrid, and others (2007): The Role of Retail Banking in the US Banking Industry-Risk, Return, and Industry Structure, FRBNY Economic Policy Review.

Trieber, Jacob (1910): The Abuses of Receiverships, *Yale Law Journal* 19(4), Article 4.

US Department of the Treasury (2017): A Financial System That Creates Economic Opportunities—Banks and Credit Unions.

US Department of the Treasury (2017): Public-Private Exchange—Risks and Vulnerabilities of Virtual Currency.

US Department of the Treasury—FIN-2013-G001 (2017): Application of FinCEN's Regulations to Persons Administering, Exchanging, or Using Virtual Currencies.

US Department of the Treasury—FIN-2019-G001 (2019): Application of FinCEN's Regulations to Certain Business Models Involving Convertible Virtual Currencies.

US Department of the Treasury—Financial Crimes Enforcement Network (FinCEN) Guidance on the Application of FinCEN's Regulations to Persons Administering, Exchanging, or Using Virtual Currencies-FIN-2013-G001 (March 18, 2013).

US Department of the Treasury—FinCEN Rule "Customer Due Diligence Requirements for Financial Institutions" (May 11, 2016).

US Department of the Treasury—Office of the Comptroller of Currency (2013): A Short History.

Van Fenstermaker, J. (1965): The Development of American Commercial Banking.

Weights, Philip J. (2015): Auditing Trends Within the Banking Industry, Ethical Boardroom.

Witton, Z. (2011): Europe Misses Again on Bank Stress Test. Moody's Analytics Regional Financial Review.

Xiaolu, Xu (2013): Fair Value Measurements and Earnings Management: Evidence from the Banking Industry, Syracuse University.

Zhang, Jihong (2016): A Comparative Analysis of Application of Bank Insolvency, *Arizona Journal of International and Comparative Law* 33: 301.

Index

F. I. Lessambo, *The U.S. Banking System*,
https://doi.org/10.1007/978-3-030-34792-5

The manufacturer's authorised representative in the EU is Springer Nature Customer Service Centre GmbH, Europaplatz 3, 69115 Heidelberg, Germany. If you have any concerns regarding our products, please contact ProductSafety@springernature.com

Printed and bound by CPI Group (UK) Ltd, Croydon, CR0 4YY
30/09/2026
02225656-0015